How Everyday Products Are Made

VOLUME 2: H–Z

How Everyday Products Are Made

VOLUME 2: H–Z

U·X·L

A part of Gale, Cengage Learning

GALE
CENGAGE Learning·

Farmington Hills, Mich • San Francisco • New York • Waterville, Maine
Meriden, Conn • Mason, Ohio • Chicago

GALE
CENGAGE Learning

How Everyday Products Are Made

Thomas Riggs, Editor

Project Editors: Sara Constantakis, Matthew Derda, Kristin B. Mallegg

Imaging and Multimedia: John L. Watkins

Composition: Evi Abou-El-Seoud

Manufacturing: Wendy Blurton

Product Design: Kristine A. Julien

Rights Acquisition and Management: Amanda Kopczynski, Ashley Maynard

Acquisitions Editor: Judy Galens

Cover photographs and interior graphics: Batteries © cigdem/Shutterstock.com; remote © BaLL LunLa/Shutterstock.com; jeans © robert_s/Shutterstock.com; cpu © peuceta/Shutterstock.com; coaster © Christopher Sykes/Shutterstock.com; flip-flops © Jasmin Awad/Shutterstock.com; lava lamp © kwest/Shutterstock.com; headphones © Maksym Bondarchuk/Shutterstock.com; atv © risteski/Shutterstock.com; car © Rawpixel/Shutterstock.com; skateboards © Sergiy1975/Shutterstock.com; cans © nevodka/Shutterstock.com; bandages © Mega Pixel/Shutterstock.com; sunglasses © Nordling/Shutterstock.com; background © Hluboki Dzianis/Shutterstock.com; icons © Macrovector/Shutterstock.com, ©Blan-k/Shutterstock.com

For product information and technology assistance, contact us at
Gale Customer Support, 1-800-877-4253.
For permission to use material from this text or product,
submit all requests online at **www.cengage.com/permissions.**
Further permissions questions can be emailed to
permissionrequest@cengage.com

LIBRARY OF CONGRESS CATALOGING-IN-PUBLICATION DATA

Riggs, Thomas, 1963- author.
How everyday products are made / Thomas Riggs ; Sara Constantakis and Kristin Mallegg, project editors.
   volumes cm
Includes bibliographical references and index.
ISBN 978-0-7876-6547-0 (set : alk. paper) — ISBN 978-0-7876-6548-7 (vol. 1 : alk. paper) — ISBN 978-0-7876-6549-4 (vol. 2 : alk. paper)
  1. Manufacturing processes. 2. Manufactures. I. Title.

TS183.R55 2016
670—dc23   2015035015

Gale
27500 Drake Rd.
Farmington Hills, MI, 48331-3535

ISBN-13: 978-0-7876-6547-0 (set)
ISBN-13: 978-0-7876-6548-7 (vol. 1)
ISBN-13: 978-0-7876-6549-4 (vol. 2)

This title is also available as an e-book.
ISBN-13: 978-1-4144-0986-3
Contact your Gale, a part of Cengage Learning, sales representative for ordering information.

Printed in China
1 2 3 4 5 6 7 20 19 18 17 16

Table of Contents

How Everyday Products Are Made

Reader's Guide

How Everyday Products Are Made explores the manufacture, as well as the history and use, of fifty products that students commonly see or hear about in their daily lives. These everyday products include food items, such as beef jerky and gummy bears; emerging high-tech products, including 3D printers and electric cars; and such firmly established items in popular culture as lava lamps, spray string, and mood rings. In discussing the manufacture of these products, the book has a secondary goal: teaching basic scientific ideas, such as density, kinetic energy, and chemiluminescence, as well as common materials used in manufacturing, such as resins and polymers.

The entries in *How Everyday Products Are Made* are easy to read and understand. Students will often be surprised by how a product, such as a billiard ball, is made. A billiard ball might seem like ordinary hard plastic, but Saluc, the Belgian company that produces the majority of the world's billiard balls, developed a chemical and computerized manufacturing process that takes as long as twenty-three days to complete.

Format

The entries in *How Everyday Products Are Made* are arranged alphabetically across two volumes. In each entry students will learn who invented the product and why, how the product was developed and how it works, what raw materials are used to make the product, and how the product might be used in the future. At the end of the entry is a list of books, periodicals, and websites that offer additional information.

Subheads make it easy for students to scan entries for the information they need. Although the headings in each entry vary somewhat, the subheads in all entries follow the same subject order: critical thinking questions, an introduction, historical and other background information, raw materials, design, the manufacturing process (including byproducts, when appropriate), quality control, the product's outlook in the future, and a further reading section.

Each entry has two sidebars. One sidebar adds to the student's understanding of the topic by exploring the product's role in popular culture; discussing a young inventor, a designer, or an entrepreneur; or offering an activity that allows the student to experiment with concepts discussed in the entry. A "Think about It!" sidebar encourages critical thinking by asking students to connect the product in some way to their own lives. Each entry also includes a list of "Words to Know" and their definitions.

Spread throughout the book are more than 150 color photos and illustrations. At the end of both volumes is a general index, as well as suggested classroom activities related to the topics of the entries. These activities help students understand scientific concepts and manufacturing processes and practice researching, writing, problem solving, and analytical thinking.

Suggestions

We welcome any comments on this work and suggestions for entries to feature in future editions. Please write:

The Editors of *U•X•L How Everyday Products Are Made*
Gale
27500 Drake Rd.
Farmington Hills, MI 48331-3535

Hand Warmer

Personal hand and foot warmers are small devices that use chemical reactions to produce temporary heat for use outdoors or in emergency situations. Several types of hand warmers are available, but the most common is a disposable packet that uses the oxidation of iron powder to create heat. This is sometimes called a self-activating hand warmer because each one produces heat when removed from its protective wrapper and shaken, exposing the iron powder inside to oxygen. Warmers are made in a variety of sizes for hands, toes, and feet and are generally packaged in airtight plastic or foil packets to prevent them from activating on their own. Disposable warmers heat up quickly to about 100 degrees Fahrenheit (38 degrees Celsius) and stay warm for as many as seven hours.

Oxidation-based hand warmers originated in Japan, where several other types of personal warming devices were also invented. Their ease and convenience made them popular throughout the country in the late 1970s, and they were soon exported to other areas. Within ten years of

Hand warmers are used by many people in cold weather, including construction workers and crossing guards.
© STUDIOMODE/ALAMY

their introduction, hundreds of millions of units were being sold each year. By the early twenty-first century, disposable hand warmers were widely and inexpensively available.

Disposable warmers are useful on cold days, when traditional heat sources are unavailable or insufficient. People who work in outdoor jobs, such as construction workers and crossing guards, often place warming packets in their gloves or shoes to fight off the cold. Hand warmers are also helpful in outdoor recreational activities, such as skiing, camping, or watching outdoor sporting events. Because they are pocket-sized, inexpensive, and easily purchased at hardware, sporting goods, or convenience stores, hand and foot warmers have become standard equipment for camping gear and emergency supply kits.

Beating the cold

Before the invention of heated cars and central heating in the home, people who lived in cold climates used a variety of personal heating devices to fight the chill of winter, both indoors and out. Working people often placed heated rocks in their pockets to warm their hands on cold days, while wealthy women sometimes put ceramic bottles filled with hot water in muffs, an article of clothing made of fur or fabric into which they placed their hands for warmth.

The Chinese and Japanese became especially good at keeping their hands and feet warm in cold weather. Winter travelers in China carried small boxes called *shou lu,* which were filled with hot coals. Japanese homes contained small ceramic or metal pots called *te-aburi* that were filled with glowing coals and given to guests to warm the hands and body. *Te-aburi* were often highly decorative and were viewed as household decorations as well as appliances. Personal hand warmers called *kairo* were filled with heated materials and placed in pockets or socks to provide heat to the fingers and toes.

Evolution of the modern hand warmer

In the early 1900s, the Mycoal Company of Japan introduced a commercial hand warmer consisting of a pocket-sized case with a piece of charcoal. When lit, the charcoal produced a lasting heat. The company then developed a more efficient charcoal made from the stems of hemp, a fibrous plant used in fabric and rope making. Hemp charcoal heated up quickly and provided comfortable and long-lasting heat. Mycoal hand and foot warmers became popular among all classes of Japanese society and were particularly useful to soldiers exposed to cold winters during long military campaigns in China and Russia during the 1930s and 1940s.

In 1923 Japanese inventor Niichi Matoba invented the *Hakukin-kairo,* a different type of hand warmer that did not need hot coals to produce heat. Matoba used the scientific principle of oxidation to create a hand warmer that used the chemical reaction between the metal platinum and fumes from benzene, a flammable compound of hydrogen, and carbon. When heated with a match or a lighter, platinum causes benzene to break down into carbon dioxide and water, releasing heat in the process. The *Hakukin-kairo,* a refillable metal container with a platinum strip and benzene, soon joined the charcoal warmer as one of the most popular hand warmers in Japan.

The disposable revolution

During the 1970s hemp became less common in Japan as textiles and rope were increasingly made of synthetic materials. Inventors looked for new materials for manufacturing hand warmers. One lucky industrial accident pointed the way to a new technology. The Lotte Company, a Japanese candy manufacturer, was experimenting with the use of packets of iron powder to keep its products dry and fresh. The experiment failed, however, because the iron became hot when exposed to air and water. Lotte executives saw possibilities in this chemical reaction, and they began to manufacture hand warmers that used this newly discovered oxidation process.

Iron oxidation hand warmers could only be used once, but because of their low cost and the availability of their components, they were produced cheaply. They quickly became popular throughout Japan. In the early 1980s, they were exported to the United States, where they were used widely among hunters, campers, and others who worked or played outdoors in cold weather. A number of U.S. manufacturers began to sell their own brands of disposable iron oxidation hand warmers, including Heat Factory, Grabbers, and HotHands.

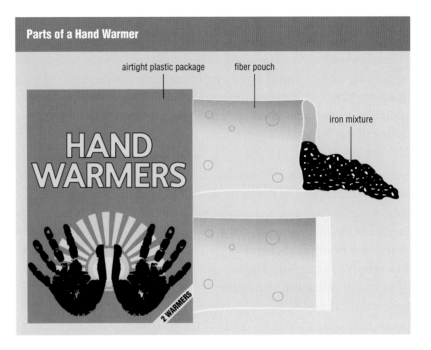

Parts of a Hand Warmer

airtight plastic package

fiber pouch

iron mixture

HAND WARMERS

2 WARMERS

Airtight plastic packages prevent the iron mixture inside each hand warmer from oxidizing before use.
ILLUSTRATION BY LUMINA DATAMATICS LTD. © 2015 CENGAGE LEARNING

Raw materials

The basic parts of a disposable hand warmer are iron powder and water, which work together when they are exposed to air to produce heat. A small amount of vermiculite, a lightweight, absorbent compound of magnesium, aluminum, iron, and silicon, is added because of its ability to hold water. Most modern hand warmers use salt to speed and intensify heat production. Activated carbon, which has been treated through a high-heat chemical process to become highly absorbent, is often included to help hold water until the warmer is activated. Activated carbon also helps to reduce any bad smells that may be released when the iron is oxidized. Compressed fibers of cellulose, a plant material, or plastic such as polyethylene or polystyrene are used to make the packet that holds the active materials.

Design

Iron powder hand warmers are generally designed in the shape of small envelopes made of porous fabric, which has a seam running down the middle of one side and is sealed at each end into a closed packet. The fabric used is very permeable to air, meaning air passes through it easily but does not allow the fine powder to leak out. The most common size is the pocket hand warmer, which is approximately 3.5 inches (9 centimeters) long, 2 inches (5 centimeters) wide, and 0.125 to 0.25 inch (3 to 5 millimeters) thick. The envelope is sealed in an airtight foil or plastic package, which is printed with the brand name, product information, and instructions.

Manufacturers also produce specially shaped warmers for toes and inside shoes, as well as larger pads to warm other body parts. Some body warmers come with a sticky backing to help keep them in place. The Grabber brand includes "Mega" and "Ultra" warmers that are larger and provide heat for a longer period of time than typical warmers.

Safety

Users should take care when using any personal warming device. Cold hands and feet may be the result of a medical condition, such as diabetes or an injury to the nerves. People with these conditions may have less sensitivity to pain and could burn themselves by overusing hand warmers. No type of personal hand warmer should be placed directly on sensitive skin.

The manufacturing process

Hand warmers are produced through a fairly simple process of mixing ingredients and directing them into fabric tubes that are then sealed into individual packets. Most manufacturers purchase the fabric for their hand warmers from textile producers who make it according to industry specifications. Other materials are available from chemical supply houses.

1 The fabric used to enclose the hand warmers is made by compacting fibers of cellulose or plastic into a dense (very close or crowded together), nonwoven sheet of material. This sheet is covered with a layer of breathable resin to connect the fibers and keep the powdery materials from leaking out.

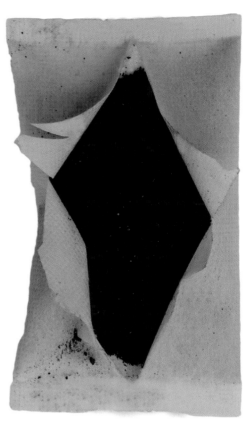

Hand warmers are filled with iron powder and other elements, which produce heat when exposed to air. For safety reasons, never open a disposable hand warmer. © THOMAS RIGGS & COMPANY

Think about It!

American author Laura Ingalls Wilder (1867–1957), who wrote about nineteenth-century pioneer life in Wisconsin in her many novels, describes a mother placing hot baked potatoes in her children's pockets for warmth on a sleigh ride. Unlike disposable hand warmers, potatoes are biodegradable, making them a "green" way to stay warm on a cold day. Would you rather use a disposable hand warmer or a potato? Why?

2 The fabric is then punched with tiny holes to help oxygen enter the packet once it is activated. The number of holes is determined by the type of warmer being manufactured: hand warmers generally have holes spaced approximately 0.125 inch (3 millimeters) apart, while foot warmers, which are used in the enclosed space of a shoe, have more closely spaced holes.

3 The powdered hand warmer ingredients (iron, salt, carbon, vermiculite, and water) are placed into a large mixing machine, where they are blended thoroughly. They are then placed in airtight plastic bags where they cure, or age, for about seven days. The bags are "burped" several times during this period to remove any remaining air.

4 After the mixture is cured, it is fed into a machine with a number of chutes. Wide rolls of fabric above the machine feed sheets of fabric down to the chutes, where they are cut into strips. Each strip is mechanically wrapped around a chute, formed into a tube with a side seam, and sealed at the bottom.

5 As the hand warmer mixture is fed into the fabric tube, the tube is sealed, producing a finished packet.

6 Conveyor belts move the completed hand warmers to a packaging machine where they are enclosed in airtight plastic or foil. Before they are sealed, the packages pass over a vacuum pad to remove extra air.

When air mixes with the iron mixture inside the bag, a chemical reaction occurs. Heat is given off as a byproduct of that reaction. ILLUSTRATION BY LUMINA DATAMATICS LTD. © 2015 CENGAGE LEARNING

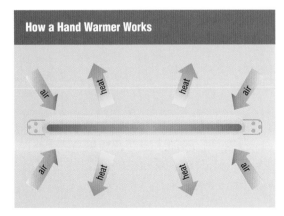

How a Hand Warmer Works

Quality control

Much of the quality control in hand warmer production is built into the manufacturing machinery. The machines that funnel the powdered ingredients into the fabric packets are calibrated, or adjusted, to recognize and throw away improperly filled or sealed bags. Sample tests are carried out during the manufacturing process by removing a few heat warmers from each batch. These are tested for temperature and length of heat by placing them in a temperature sensor

WORDS TO KNOW

Absorbent: Capable of taking in and holding liquid.

Benzene: A flammable compound of hydrogen and carbon.

Biodegradable: Able to be broken down naturally with the help of living things.

Calibrate: To adjust.

Cellulose: A substance from the cell walls of plants that is used to make many products.

Export (verb): To send to another country to sell.

Oxidation: Interaction between oxygen molecules and other substances that results in the loss of electrons.

Permeable: Capable of being passed through, especially liquid or gas.

Porous: Having small holes, or pores, that allow liquid or gas to pass through.

Resin: A substance obtained from tree gum or sap or created synthetically that is commonly used in the manufacture of plastics and varnishes.

that reproduces the conditions inside a user's pocket. Other samples are dropped into a pressurized water tank to test the seal on their packaging.

More hot ideas

Hand warmers continue to be popular products for those looking for inexpensive and convenient ways to stay warm in chilly conditions. As a growing number of people discover the advantages of disposable hand warmers, manufacturers are developing new uses for them, from warming sleeping bags and tea cups to heating sore muscles. Some companies, such as Heat Factory, have created lines of warming apparel, including mittens, hats, and face masks with pouches to hold a standard disposable hand warmer.

Although most of the ingredients of disposable hand warmers are biodegradable, the fabric that encloses them may contain nonbiodegradable ingredients. Manufacturers are working to produce a completely biodegradable product. Inventors have also developed reusable hand warmers that may be more friendly to the environment than those that can only be used one time. Some of these are rechargeable or battery-powered electronic devices, and some use other types of chemical reactions that can produce heat repeatedly. Most of the designs are more expensive to make and buy than disposable versions, and they tend to be less compact.

Try This!

Handmade hand warmers

You can make your own hand warmer using a few common materials.

You will need:

- safety goggles
- rubber gloves
- calcium chloride crystals (commonly found in products used to melt ice on sidewalks and roadways)
- 1 zipper-seal food storage bag, sandwich or pint size
- 1 zipper-seal food storage bag, snack or cup size
- room-temperature water

1. Put on gloves and goggles.
2. Place 1/2 cup of the calcium chloride crystals into the larger zipper bag.
3. Place 1/2 cup of water into the smaller zipper bag and seal tightly.
4. Carefully dry the outside of the water bag and place it inside the bag containing the chloride crystals. Tightly seal the larger bag. You may place this in a second zipper bag to make sure there are no leaks.
5. To activate your hand warmer, squeeze the small bag until it opens and releases water into the crystals. Within a few minutes, you will feel the temperature inside the bag begin to rise. It will reach approximately 140 degrees Fahrenheit (60 degrees Celsius) and remain warm for around an hour.

Why it works: When calcium chloride comes in contact with water, a chemical reaction occurs that breaks up the molecular structure of the crystals, releasing heat in the process.

For more information

BOOKS

Marks, Diana F. *Glues, Brews, and Goos: Recipes and Formulas for Almost Any Classroom Project.* Vol. 2. Westport, CT: Teacher Ideas, 2003.

PERIODICALS

Greenberg, Julia. "The Chemical Reactions That Make Hand Warmers Heat Up." *Wired* (December 26, 2014). Available online at http://www.wired.com/2014/12/whats-inside-hot-hands/ (accessed July 9, 2015).

Jackson, Joe. "What Are the Best Hand Warmers?" *Outside* (January 6, 2013). Available online at http://www.outsideonline.com/1785906/what-are-best-hand-warmers (accessed July 9, 2015).

WEBSITES

"How Do Handwarmers Work?" The Chemical Blog. http://www.thechemicalblog.co.uk/how-do-hand-warmers-work/ (accessed July 9, 2015)

"Winter Life in Japan: Ways to Endure the Cold." Trends in Japan. http://web-japan.org/trends/11_lifestyle/lif120322.html (accessed July 9, 2015)

Headphones

Headphones are small speakers that allow a user to listen to music or other media without bothering other people. In the most common design, the speakers are held together by a plastic headband and then placed over the listener's ears. The speakers in other models are inserted directly into the ear. Some headphones have extra padding around the ears to help reduce outside noise. Inside every pair of headphones are iron coils called voice coils. When they receive an electric signal from devices such as mobile phones, digital music players, or computers, the voice coils move back and forth. This makes parts called diaphragms inside the headphones vibrate and send sounds into the ear.

Although headphone prototypes (early examples that are later used as models for production) have existed since the 1880s, the invention is credited to Nathaniel Baldwin, a Utah engineer who mailed his design to the U.S. Navy in 1910. For the next several decades, headphones were used almost exclusively by telephone and radio operators. In 1958 John Koss produced the first pair of headphones specifically designed for listening to music. With the introduction of the Sony

Walkman in 1980, headphones transformed from heavy headsets to lightweight models suitable for wearing while walking or exercising. Earbuds are a result of this lightweight trend.

Headphones are important tools for many professionals, from musicians and engineers in recording studios to airline pilots needing to hear air traffic control. Research has found that music relaxes muscles, improves mood, and helps reduce blood pressure. These benefits explain why many office workers use headphones to help get them through the workday. Headphones are not only useful at work but also in any public place, such as subways or libraries, where people want to either block out surrounding noise or enjoy their favorite music or other media without disturbing others.

For operators and opera buffs

Long before they became associated with listening to music, headphones were used for a number of purposes, including radio and telephone communication. Starting in the early 1880s, telephone operators used a headphone-like device that rested on their shoulders. Weighing more than 10 pounds (4.5 kilograms), the device was made of one earpiece through which operators could hear the people who called them from another phone line.

In 1881 French engineer Ernest Mercadier (1836–1911) invented headphones that were similar to what would become earbuds. The result of his U.S. Patent No. 454,138, which promised "improvements in telephone receivers," were headphones weighing less than 1.8 ounces (51 grams) that could be inserted directly into the ear. Like modern earbuds, Mercadier's headphones had rubber covers designed for comfort and to block outside sounds.

Fourteen years after Mercadier's breakthrough, the British company Electrophone introduced the first headphones for listening to music. The Electrophone system was like a telephone that connected subscribers to live feeds of theater and opera performances throughout London. Subscribers wore a pair of bulky headphones that looked like a stethoscope. The earphones connected below the wearer's chin and were fastened together by a long rod.

The inventor in the kitchen

In 1910 U.S. Navy Lieutenant Commander A. J. Hepburn received a letter from Utah inventor Nathaniel Baldwin. The navy often received mail from inventors and scientists, but Baldwin's stood out because it was written in purple ink on blue and pink paper. Baldwin, who had an electrical engineering degree from Stanford University, had also included with his letter an invention: a pair of telephones converted into a headset.

Hepburn tested the headphones and realized they were significantly better than the navy's listening devices. The navy liked Baldwin's design so much that they waited while he built ten pairs of headphones at a time in his kitchen before shipping them off. Later the Wireless Specialty Apparatus Company worked with Baldwin to build a factory in Utah where his headphones were mass-produced.

A must-have for music lovers

Headphones were mostly used for radio communication until 1958, when musician and entrepreneur John Koss introduced the Koss Model 390 phonograph. Advertised as a private listening system, it included a portable (able to be moved around or carried) phonograph, attached speakers, and a pair of headphones. Koss teamed up with an audio engineer to design his headphones, which had 3-inch (8-centimeter) speakers set into foam ear pads that were held together by a metal headband. The Koss headphones were the first stereophonic listening device, meaning that the speaker in each ear delivered different parts of the music. This creates the feeling that the wearer is surrounded by sounds coming from different directions. Previous headphones were monophonic, meaning that the sound in each speaker was the same. Though large by modern-day standards, Koss's headphones were a lighter version of Baldwin's, which weighed more than 1 pound (0.45 kilograms).

When Koss introduced his phonograph system at a Milwaukee, Wisconsin, trade show in November 1958, his headphones, then called the Koss SP3 Stereophones, were an immediate hit. Music fans loved how the headphones delivered a clean sound, blocked outside noise, and comfortably covered the listener's ears. Other manufacturers started making headphones similar to Koss's design, but the Koss Corporation remained a major player in the headphone industry into the twenty-first century.

Shrinking headphones in a growing market

The Sony Walkman, a portable cassette player, was introduced in the United States in 1980. It changed the way many people listened to music. Lightweight, portable, and reasonably priced, the Walkman made it easy for listeners to take their music anywhere. An important part of the product was its headphones. They were much smaller and lighter than earlier models and did not cover the whole ear. This made it easier for users to remain aware of their surroundings. They were also easy to store or wear around the neck when not in use.

By the turn of the twenty-first century, the portable cassette player and its later version, the portable CD player, were replaced by the portable media player, particularly the iPod by Apple. The iPod included a pair of earbuds in a new shape that fit better than earlier versions. By 2012 Apple estimated that it had shipped about 600 million earbuds, meaning that one out of every twelve people on Earth owned a pair.

Because of advances in technology, headphones have not only gotten smaller since the 1950s, but they have also improved in terms of sound quality and other features. For example, in 1990 Koss introduced the first-ever cordless headphones, which allowed listeners to move around instead of remaining tied to a stereo system. Soon Recoton made its own cordless headphones that allowed listeners to travel as far as 150 feet (45.5 meters) from their music players. By the 2010s some listeners moved away from earbuds toward noise-canceling headphones. These devices use technology that reduces outside noise to improve the listening experience. Fairly large and covering the ear completely, noise-canceling headphones look similar to early headphone styles.

Raw materials

The headphones in Baldwin's day were constructed from materials such as copper, rubber, and leather. Most modern-day headphones are made of plastic and silicone, but, depending on the type of headphone, other materials may be used.

Parts of a Pair of Headphones

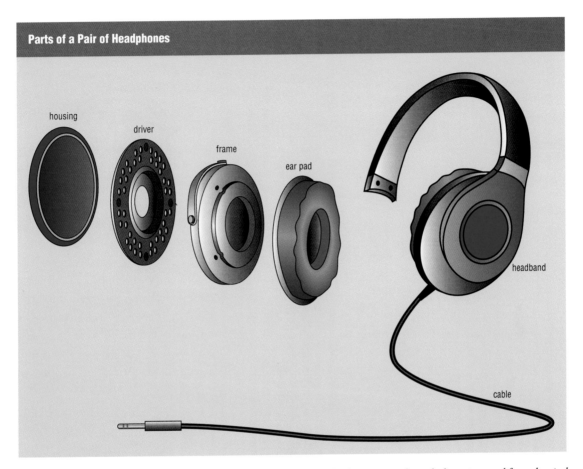

housing

driver

frame

ear pad

headband

cable

A circumaural headphone (which covers the ears) shows the placement of the driver, or speaker, which creates sound from electrical signals. ILLUSTRATION BY LUMINA DATAMATICS LTD. © 2015 CENGAGE LEARNING

Circumaural headphones, which cover the entire ear, are made from the greatest variety of materials, including polyurethane, real or fake leather, foam rubber, and textiles such as velvet and mesh. A metal or plastic band that bends around the head holds together the PVC (a synthetic plastic), rubber, memory foam, and artificial leather that make up headphones that cover just a portion of the ear.

Earbuds, which rest on the outer part of the ear canal, are usually made of polycarbonate and polyester, two strong plastics. In-ear headphones, which are partly inserted into the ear canal, are manufactured from synthetic rubbers, natural rubbers, or silicones that are designed to limit the spread of germs that can cause ear infections.

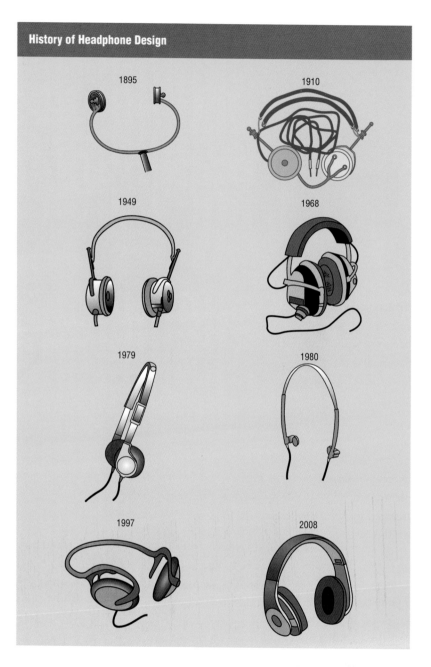

History of Headphone Design

1895

1910

1949

1968

1979

1980

1997

2008

Headphone design has been affected over time by technology, as well as trends in use and fashion. ILLUSTRATION BY LUMINA DATAMATICS LTD. © 2015 CENGAGE LEARNING

Design

The four main designs of headphones are circumaural (covers the outer ear), supra-aural (press against the ear), earbuds, and in-ear. In addition to knowing what kind of headphone they want to make, designers must know how it will create sound waves. This means choosing what kind of transducer, or speaker, will be used. The most common transducer is called a moving coil driver, or a dynamic transducer. It works by passing an electric signal through the voice coil, which causes the magnetic fields created by the small magnets inside the headphones to clash. This clashing causes the diaphragm, a thin polymer sheet (a membrane) stretched over the structure, to vibrate and produce sound waves.

In less common electrostatic transducers, sound signals produce electric fields that, when combined with air, create a sound wave. Electrostatic headphones have a far wider frequency range than dynamic transducers, but they are also more expensive.

Safety

Medical professionals believe headphones are the reason that roughly 20 percent of teenagers have some form of hearing loss. Headphones can only be as loud as the device they are connected to, which, in the case of most portable electronic devices, is 120 decibels, the same sound level as a rock concert.

Doctors recommend using headphones for a maximum of one hour a day at no greater than 60 percent of a device's maximum volume to prevent hearing damage. The length of time a person can safely use headphones increases as the sound volume decreases. This also means that a person can listen safely for less time if the volume is increased above 60 percent of maximum. Circumaural and supra-aural headphones are also recommended over earbuds or in-ear headphones, because headphones inserted into the ear can cause greater damage than headphones that rest on the ear.

The manufacturing process

The manufacturing process of most headphones follows the same general series of steps. The headphones' inner wiring is strung together and sealed into a diaphragm, which is then placed into the plastic casing that goes over the listener's ears. Lastly, the headband is attached to the headphone speakers. Materials and steps are slightly different for earbuds.

1 The process begins with headphones' plastic casings. An injection molding machine shapes plastic into the needed parts, which include plastic back covers and housings.

Think about It!

Blocking outside noise is great for listening to music in the comfort of your own home, but it can be dangerous in other situations, such as driving a car or bicycling through traffic. In response to the number of accidents caused by drivers wearing headphones, many states no longer allow people to wear them while driving. On the other hand, drivers in the European Union and some U.S. cities have been required to wear headsets if they are speaking on the phone because it allows them to have both hands on the wheel. Do you think people should be allowed to drive while wearing headphones? Why or why not?

2 While the casing is made, a computer-controlled machine winds thin copper wire hundreds of times around a cylinder to create the voice coil.

3 An assembly-line machine molds the diaphragm. A technician adds a bead of glue to the finished diaphragm and lines it up with the voice coil. A ray of ultraviolet (UV) light seals the two pieces together.

4 The magnets are inserted into the plastic housings, which are then joined together. This requires extreme accuracy, because the headphones' sound quality depends on the voice coil's position in the plastic housing. After this step the speakers undergo an audio check.

5 Technicians join the speakers together with a headband, if necessary. In high-end headphones, the curved wires that hold the headphones over a listener's ears and allow audio signals to move between the left and right speaker are clipped together. A connector for the headphones' audio cable is fastened in a plastic cord connector.

6 Next, the speakers are inserted into one half of the housing, and both halves are joined together and fastened with a plastic bracket.

7 The ends of the headband are attached to the speakers, and the wires in the speakers are joined to the wires in the headband.

8 A plastic grill is fastened over each speaker, and the headphones are ready to be packaged and shipped.

Quality control

After headphone speakers have been assembled and before they are encased in the plastic housing, they go through a series of tests to make sure that they correctly reproduce a full range of sounds. Technicians use a computer program to send sound waves into the headphones, testing everything from bass and treble balance to audio frequency range (high and low pitches). Speakers that fail these tests are thrown away.

WORDS TO KNOW

Casing: A protective outer covering.

Decibel: A unit of measure for how loud a sound is.

Distortion: The condition of something being altered from its normal or original condition or shape.

Media: A form of communication, information, or entertainment, such as radio, television, or newspapers.

Prototype: An early example of a product that is later used as a model for production.

Silicone: A nonmetallic element that conducts electricity under some conditions and resists it under others. Silicone does not allow water or heat to pass through it.

Stereophonic sound: An innovation in recording that allows for two or more independent channels of audio on a single recording.

Noise-canceling headphones require more testing. Many manufacturers have spent years studying the effects of sound leakage and even the density of the inner-ear bones of a typical listener, all of which is done to try to make headphones with as little sound distortion as possible. If outside sounds can be heard inside a pair of noise-canceling headphones, production ends.

Keeping the world independent yet connected

As portable devices such as smartphones and tablets become a major part of everyday life, headphones remain a necessary accessory for those who wish to enjoy music and other media without disturbing others. Many people own several pairs of headphones for different purposes. One pair may be good for exercising, and another pair of higher-quality headphones might be used when a person just wants to listen to music. Or, users may keep a pair of headphones at work and another at home.

As with most electronics, headphone technology continues to improve. Wireless headphones, once unusual, are becoming more common, and headphones of different shapes and sizes are made to meet individual needs and wishes. Some technology experts predict that future headphones may no longer need to plug into a device. Instead, cellular chips set in the headphones will connect listeners to streaming music channels and even incoming voicemail messages from smartphones and other devices.

A Wireless World

Walking into the first meeting of his high school's entrepreneurship club in New Rochelle, New York, Daniel Greenberg caught his headphone wire on a nearby object. Considering how much technology is now wireless, the experience made Greenberg wonder: why do headphones still need wires? Greenberg presented his wireless headphone idea to fellow students David Lopez and Avery Greenberg. Together the three worked for several months to create a prototype of their solution to the wire problem: the Spiro X1.

The Spiro X1 is a small circular device that turns any traditional pair of headphones into wireless headphones using Bluetooth technology. After disconnecting the wire on any pair of headphones, users can plug the Spiro X1 in its place. The device includes volume control and a button that allows users to answer phone calls. The product attracted attention from several Silicon Valley firms. Greenberg, who began his freshman year at New York University's Stern School of Business in the fall of 2015, remains hopeful that the Spiro X1 will get enough financial backing and soon be licensed by major headphone companies.

For more information

BOOKS

"Headphones." *World of Invention.* Farmington Hills, MI: Gale/Cengage, 2006.

PERIODICALS

Okyle, Carly. "These High-School Students Found a Way to Make Any Headphones Wireless." *Entrepreneur* (May 18, 2015). Available online at http://www.entrepreneur.com/article/246282 (accessed July 23, 2015).

Stamp, Jimmy. "A Partial History of Headphones." *Smithsonian* (March 19, 2013). Available online at http://www.smithsonianmag.com/arts-culture/a-partial-history-of-headphones-4693742/?no-ist (accessed July 21, 2015).

Thompson, Derek. "How Headphones Changed the World." *Atlantic Monthly* (May 30, 2012). Available online at http://www.theatlantic.com/technology/archive/2012/05/how-headphones-changed-the-world/257830/ (accessed July 21, 2015).

WEBSITES

Berkman, Fran. "Listen Up: Here's a Brief History of Headphones." Mashable. http://mashable.com/2012/09/26/headphones/ (accessed July 21, 2015).

High-Tech Swimsuit

Critical Thinking Questions

1. Based on information in the entry, what are the most important differences between high-tech swimsuits and other swimsuits? Why?

2. The section titled "The manufacturing process" explains that swimsuit logos are applied before the suits are assembled. Do you think that they could be applied after the suit is assembled? Why or why not?

High-tech swimsuits are designed to reduce drag, or resistance, in water and increase the ability to float (buoyancy), thus improving the race times of competitive swimmers. Made of fabrics that can repel (force away) water, high-tech swimsuits do not absorb water the way traditional suits do. These fabrics also sometimes trap tiny pockets of air, lifting a swimmer higher in the water. Stripes or grooves in the fabric, which help channel water around the suit, are designed as such to improve the swimmer's glide through the water. High-tech suits are worn very tight to the skin, and they come in both full-body and knee-length styles. Generally much more expensive than traditional competitive swimwear, some high-tech suits are priced at more than $500.

After decades of research into the development of efficient racing swimwear, high-tech swimsuits were first introduced in the mid-1990s. Although the suits sparked immediate interest among competitive swimmers, they were not widely used until the end of the twentieth century, when the introduction of the Speedo Fastskin significantly influenced the 2000 Summer Olympic Games in Sydney, Australia.

A total of thirty-three gold medals were awarded in swimming at the Sydney games, and twenty-eight of those were won by swimmers wearing high-tech suits.

The popularity and apparent success of high-tech swimsuits in high-level competitions caused the governing bodies that monitor competitive swimming to consider whether the suits should be allowed in competitions. Some critics of high-tech suits have complained that technical swimwear gives users an unfair advantage, going so far as to compare the use of such suits to the use of performance-enhancing drugs. Others insist that technological advancements occur in all fields of athletics and that the use of high-tech suits simply raises the level of accomplishment in the sport. In 2009, following an unusually high number of record-breaking performances by swimmers wearing technical suits at the World Swimming Championships in Rome, Italy, the Fédération Internationale de Natation (FINA, the International Swimming Federation) declared a ban on all full-body technical swimwear.

High-tech swimsuits are woven with tiny holes that prevent water from absorbing into the fabric, forcing the water to slide off the surface of the swimsuit.
© ISTOCK.COM/
PAVEL SAZONOV

The evolution of swimwear

Early swimmers in many societies found it most efficient and natural to swim naked. In ancient Greece and Rome, public bathhouses, where men and women generally bathed separately without clothes, were an important part of personal hygiene and social culture. During the Middle Ages (c. 500–c. 1500), many Europeans traveled to spa resorts in towns such as Bath, England, and Alet-les-Bains, France, where they soaked or swam in pools of mineral water that were believed to promote healing. As traditions of modesty developed, swim clothes became required.

Early swimwear was not designed for efficient movement in the water but to cover the body. Bathing suits were made of heavy canvas or wool, and weights were sometimes sewn into hems to prevent the fabric from floating up when in water. Other designs used fabric so stiff that it stood out from the body when wet rather than clinging to the skin in a revealing manner. By the beginning of the twentieth century, the increasing popularity of recreational bathing, along with more relaxed standards of modesty, sparked the introduction of more practical swimwear. Although less bulky, such suits still covered most of the arms and legs, as well as the trunk of the body. As social standards have relaxed, modern bathing suits have become both more revealing and more efficient, allowing the body to move through the water without dragging it down.

Building speed in the water

Modern competitive swimming began to develop in England during the mid-1800s. In early British swimming races, a controlled swimming stroke was as important as speed. With the development of more efficient strokes, such as the front crawl, in the early twentieth century, competitive swimmers began to seek ways to increase their speed. The heavy woolen suits worn by nineteenth-century swimmers weighed several pounds in water, making them a soggy burden to racers. In 1915 the Portland Knitting Company (later called Jantzen Knitting Mills) began to market the first commercial bathing suit. Made of a lightweight knit material, Jantzen suits were much faster and more comfortable than earlier suits.

In 1928 the Australian company MacRae Hosiery Manufacturers introduced a radical new concept in competitive swimwear: the racerback suit. Made of a thin, stretchy knit material, the racerback was designed to leave the shoulders and back free for swimming and to hug the body, decreasing drag in the water. Although some critics were shocked by the revealing new suit, competitive swimmers quickly adopted it. The suit's slogan, "Speed on in your Speedos," resulted in a new name for the racerback suit, and Speedo eventually became its own brand.

In addition to choosing streamlined suits and perfecting more efficient strokes, competitive swimmers have used a number of other techniques to increase their speed as they move through the water. For example, many competitive swimmers wear swim caps, stretchy caps made of latex or silicone. Swim caps are designed to fit tightly over the head, thus reducing the drag caused by a swimmer's hair. Competitive swimmers may also shave the hair from the exposed parts of their bodies in an attempt to drop fractions of a second from their racing times.

Swimming goes high tech

Swimsuit technology continued to develop as new synthetic (artificially made) materials were introduced. In 1938 DuPont, a U.S. chemical company, invented nylon, a strong, lightweight, silky fabric. In 1958 the company presented a durable rubbery synthetic called Lycra (also called Spandex or elastane). When woven together, nylon and Lycra produced a durable stretchy swimsuit that clung to the body and did not become overly heavy in the water. These nylon and Lycra bathing suits were sometimes called "paper suits" due to their light weight.

In the late 1960s West German swimmer Konrad Dottinger introduced the "Belgrad" suit, which was made of ultrathin woven cotton and was very tightly fitted, with a porous seam down the back to allow water to escape. Though it was not widely popular, Dottinger's suit was worn by the East German women's swim team during the 1969 FINA World Championships in Belgrade, Yugoslavia. The women won ten out of fourteen races and set seven world records.

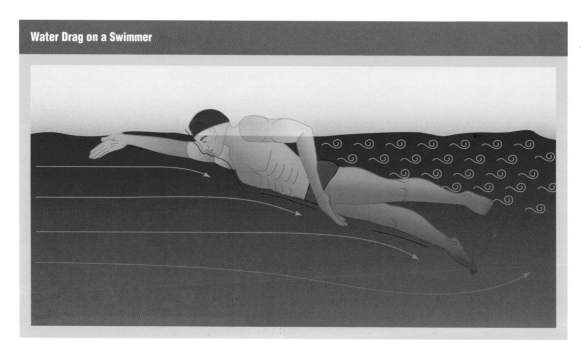

Water Drag on a Swimmer

As a swimmer moves through water, water flows around him or her, as shown by the arrows in the illustration. The contact of the water with the swimmer's body creates drag, or resistance that slows the forward motion of the swimmer. High-tech swimsuits cover the body with a material that produces less resistance against water than skin does. ILLUSTRATION BY LUMINA DATAMATICS LTD.

It *is* rocket science

In 1996 Speedo introduced a new type of tech suit: the Aquablade. Made from a polyester and Lycra blend in stripes of alternating smooth and rough texture, the suit was designed to move more smoothly and quickly through the water. In addition, the weave of the fabric was able to trap air, making the swimmer more buoyant. Speedo claimed that the Aquablade cut surface resistance by more than 20 percent compared with conventional suits. In 2000 the company launched the Fastskin, a full-body suit that attempted to mimic the water-shedding skin of a shark. It featured specially placed panels of rough fabric designed in a pattern of V-shaped ridges.

Other companies joined the rush to develop faster swimwear, introducing such suits as the Strush by Arena, the Jetconcept by Adidas, and the Tracer A7 by TYR Sport. Designers began to experiment with rubbery materials, such as neoprene and polyurethane, that were molded rather than woven to create a more efficient water barrier. Non-textile materials were created using compounds of light metal, such as titanium. Companies looked from marine mammals to aerospace technology as they attempted to design a suit that could shed water and reduce drag. In 2008 Speedo worked with the National Aeronautics and Space Administration (NASA) to produce the LZR Racer, an innovative seamless full-body suit with a tight fit, intended to hold the swimmer in the most aerodynamic position for buoyancy and glide. The LZR caused a sensation at the 2009 World Swimming Championships, when swimmers wearing it set forty-three new world records, more than twice the number set in 2007. At the 2008 Olympics in Beijing, China, 94 percent of swimmers who won gold medals wore Speedo LZR suits.

The apparent advantage provided by high-tech swimsuits caused concern among many swimming experts, who called the use of such suits "technical doping." FINA, the organization that governs competitive swimming internationally, banned full-length suits and suits of non-woven fabrics in 2009 but continued to allow waist-to-knee technical suits for men and shoulder-to-knee technical suits for women. Swimsuit makers continue to develop new designs that give swimmers a technical advantage while still meeting FINA requirements.

Raw materials

Following the FINA ruling in 2009, most high-tech swimsuits have been made from a variety of blends of nylon and latex. These synthetic fabrics

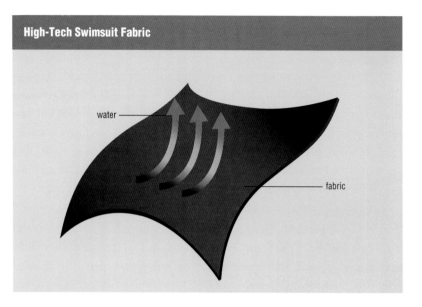

High-Tech Swimsuit Fabric

water

fabric

are hydrocarbons, compounds of hydrogen and carbon, and most come from petroleum, coal, or natural gas. Other hydrocarbons, such as keystone and alcohol, are also used in the construction of synthetic fabrics. Some manufacturers add silicone, silver, or natural or synthetic resins to create a smooth, slippery fabric.

Design

The basic element of high-tech swimsuit design is the composition of the fabric used to make the suit. Many high-tech suits are manufactured from patented blends of synthetic and natural materials that are specially formulated for each individual suit design. For example, for its revolutionary LZR suit, Speedo developed a new fabric, LZR Pulse, a blend of nylon and Lycra woven into a lightweight, water-resistant fabric with two-way stretch to provide both flexibility and compression (flattened by pressure). High-tech swimsuit fabrics are often woven with tiny holes that block water absorption and instead force water to slide off the surface of the suit. Many are made of microfibers, extremely fine synthetic fibers that can be woven into a soft, strong material with a greater ability to move water away from the body.

The most important feature of technical swimsuit design is a streamlined shape. Many suits are made with welded seams, which are created by applying heat to synthetic materials, resulting in a bond that is stronger and flatter than traditional sewn seams. This makes the suit smoother as it slides through the water.

High-tech swimsuits are meant to be worn very tight to the body in order to minimize surface space and hold the body in the best swimming position possible. A lining of compression fabric is often bonded inside the outer suit to provide an even tighter fit. Because high-tech suits are designed to fit so tightly, it can take fifteen to twenty minutes to put one on, and swimmers often need two helpers to dress for a race.

Other design features vary from suit to suit and may include textured panels, grooves, and outlines to direct water and increase flexibility while maintaining compression. The most effective high-tech designs are full-body suits that cover the legs, arms, and trunk. Abbreviated versions of this design, called kneeskins, leave the arms bare and extend only to the knees. Other tech suits look much like traditional suits, leaving both arms and legs bare.

The manufacturing process

The production of high-tech swimsuits begins with the manufacture of the specialized fabrics that give the suit its speed in the water. Fibers of durable nylon and strong, elastic Lycra are blended in a formula specific to each manufacturer. Sometimes very small fibers are used to create "microfiber" fabric. The resulting woven synthetic blend arrives at factories in large rolls, along with rolls of other materials, such as water-repellent polyurethane membrane. This may be used to make panels to cover parts of the body, such as the chest, hips, and thighs, that exert the most drag in the water.

1 Computerized design data is fed into a printer that creates a large sheet of swimsuit pattern pieces, laid out as closely together as possible to reduce waste of materials.

2 Fabric is rolled out on long tables, where it is inspected for flaws and cut by machine into workable pieces of the same length. The pieces are then stacked into thick piles for cutting.

3 The printed paper patterns are laid out on the stacks of fabric, where they are held in place by an air suction machine. Pattern pieces are cut out by workers with electric fabric saws.

At the 2008 Olympics in Beijing, China, American swimmer Michael Phelps (pictured) was unexpectedly defeated in the 200-meter freestyle by German swimmer Paul Biedermann, who was wearing a full-body, all-polyurethane swimsuit.
© MITCH GUNN/
SHUTTERSTOCK.COM

Think about It!

Champion swimmer Michael Phelps (1985–) found himself at the center of the high-tech swimsuit controversy at the 2008 Olympics in Beijing, China, when he was unexpectedly defeated in the 200-meter freestyle by German swimmer Paul Biedermann (1986–). It was Phelps's first loss at an international competition in four years. Although Phelps was wearing a waist-to-knee Speedo LZR, Biedermann used the Arena X-Glide, a full-body, all-polyurethane high-tech swimsuit that enabled him not only to defeat Phelps but to break the world record that Phelps had set a year earlier. Shock over the upset became a factor in the 2009 ban on full-body suits by Fédération Internationale de Natation (FINA, the International Swimming Federation). Do you think Phelps's loss was fair? Why or why not? If you were in charge of FINA, would you keep the ban in place or lift it?

4 Before the suits are assembled, workers apply brand logos to pattern pieces using a heat-transfer process. Logos may appear on the leg, chest, or waist of a suit, depending on the brand and design.

5 Most high-tech swimsuits are assembled with "sewing" machines, which use high-frequency vibrations to heat synthetic materials so that they can be bonded together without the use of needles, thread, or glue. Attachments on the machines use ultrasonic vibration to trim and seal fabric seams in order to prevent fraying.

6 Ultrasonic equipment may also be used to bond performance-enhancing features, such as polyurethane panels or silicone ribbing (raised lines), to specific parts of the high-tech swimsuit.

Byproducts

Modern swimsuit manufacture is generally efficient, as computerized pattern making helps to minimize waste. However, byproducts are created during the manufacture of the fabrics used to make high-tech swimsuits. The production of nylon, spandex, polyurethane, and other petroleum-based swimsuit materials releases a number of toxic compounds, such as ammonium sulfate and nitrous oxide, which may be harmful to the environment.

Quality control

Because high-tech swimsuits are used in competitions worldwide, manufacturers work to ensure that they meet high standards of excellence and dependability. Before production begins, all fabrics are tested by hand to ensure that they comply with specific guidelines for strength, stretch, color-fastness, and resistance to pool chemicals. Precision machinery is used during the production process so that materials are cut and joined according to exact specifications. One of the most important elements of quality control is user testing. Manufacturers enlist competitive swimmers to wear samples of completed suits for a period of time in order to test for fit and performance under normal use conditions.

WORDS TO KNOW

Aerodynamic: Designed to move most efficiently through the air.

Buoyancy: The upward force exerted by water that causes objects to float.

Drag: The force of resistance created when a body moves through air or water.

Hydrocarbon: Any of a number of compounds made up of only the elements carbon and hydrogen.

Hydrodynamic: Designed to move most efficiently through the water.

Microfiber: A fabric woven from very fine fibers, making it both soft and resistant to water.

Polymer: A substance whose molecular structure consists of a large number of similar units bonded together.

Polyurethane: A flexible yet strong material that can be used instead of rubber and other materials.

Porous: Having small holes, or pores, that allow liquid or gas to pass through.

Propulsion: The force that moves something forward.

Continuing innovation in swimwear

During 2008 and 2009, 196 new world speed records were set by swimmers wearing high-tech swimsuits. Subsequently the race to develop more effective suits continued, as manufacturers worked to design faster suits that conformed to FINA guidelines. In addition to developing new fabrics that slip through the water with increasing ease, companies have introduced changes in swim cap and goggle designs in an attempt to help swimmers shave fractions of a second off their race times.

In 2015 ten new tech styles were introduced, including the new Speedo LZR Racer X, the Arena Carbon Air, the Rocket Science LIGHT2, and the Aqua-Sphere MP Xpresso, which was designed with the assistance of Olympic champion swimmer Michael Phelps (1985–). Manufacturers continue to look to athletic and aerospace experts for design ideas. In 2009 Middle Atlantic Swimming (MAS), a branch of USA Swimming, pulled a prank on the swimming community by posting a mock article about an innovative new process through which swimmers could immerse themselves in a tank filled with a biodegradable liquid polymer, which would provide an overall slippery coating that could improve speed during a race and be toweled off afterward. Though it was intended to poke fun at the high-tech revolution, MAS's prank is an indication of how creative thinking may drive future developments in swimming technology.

Sharkskin, the Original High-Tech Suit

Researchers have studied high-tech swimsuits to determine whether their design elements really increase a swimmer's speed. One Harvard University study compared actual sharkskin with Speedo's Fastskin. The skin of a shark feels rough because it is composed of millions of tiny tooth-shaped structures called denticles, which direct the water around the fish's body, cutting down on drag and improving propulsion (the force that moves something forward). Speedo designers attempted to reproduce the shark's denticles in the nylon-Lycra fabric of its high-tech swimsuit. However, researchers were not convinced that the Fastskin fabric created the same effect as the shark's rough skin in the water. They concluded that it is the tight fit of the high-tech swimsuit, rather than texture design details, that makes the suit faster in the water. The compression of a tight tech suit can improve circulation while helping a swimmer maintain the proper stroke position, even when tired.

For more information

BOOKS

Lockyer, John. *Olympic Technology.* Huntington Beach, CA: Teacher Created Materials, 2009.

Ross, Stewart. *Sports Technology.* London: Evans Brothers, 2010.

Schmidt, Christine. *The Swimsuit: Fashion from Poolside to Catwalk.* New York: Berg, 2012.

PERIODICALS

Morrison, Jim. "How Speedo Created a Record-Breaking Swimsuit." *Scientific American* (July 27, 2012). Available online at http://www.scientificamerican.com/article/how-speedo-created-swimsuit/ (accessed July 16, 2015).

Nakrani, Sachin. "Racerback to Fastskin: Swimsuits That Rocked the Swimming Pool." *Guardian* (March 2, 2012). Available online at http://www.theguardian.com/sport/2012/mar/02/racerback-fastskin-swimsuits-swimming (accessed July 16, 2015).

Sterba, James P. "With These Swimsuits, the Issue Is Speed." *Wall Street Journal* (July 28, 1995).

WEBSITES

"Heritage." Speedo. http://explore.speedousa.com/heritage.html (accessed July 16, 2015).

"Record-breaking Benefits." NASA. https://www.nasa.gov/offices/oct/home/tech_record_breaking.html#.Va0bW_nw9x6 (accessed July 16, 2015).

Interactive Whiteboard

Critical Thinking Questions

1. Based on information in the entry, in what ways is an interactive whiteboard like a blackboard? In what ways is it different?

2. Other than the blackboard, what tool do you think most influenced the invention of the interactive whiteboard? What evidence from the entry supports your answer?

3. Based on information in the entry, do you think tablets will replace whiteboards in the classroom? Why or why not?

An interactive whiteboard, often known by the brand-name SMART Board, is an electronic version of the traditional whiteboard used in many classrooms to help teachers show information to the whole room. The word "smart," which originally meant quick-witted or intelligent, was redefined in the late twentieth and early twenty-first centuries to mean a device that has been redesigned to use computer technology, such as a smartphone, tablet, or smart watch. Interactive whiteboards are designed to look like traditional write-on display boards, but they are electronic screens that work similar to a computer monitor. Teachers can write on them directly using a special pen, or they can use a mouse or keyboard to enter information. Interactive whiteboards can also work with computer programs to display maps, pictures, and information. SMART Board was originally a trademarked brand of the Canadian company SMART Technologies, but the term is often used as a generic name for all interactive whiteboards.

The first interactive whiteboards were introduced during the early 1990s. The earliest boards used front or rear projectors to show

Interactive whiteboards look like traditional whiteboards found in classrooms but work with computer technology, such as a mouse and keyboard, smartphones, and tablets.
© RTIMAGES/
SHUTTERSTOCK.COM

information from a computer on a large screen for easy viewing. When flat-screen displays were invented, interactive whiteboards became smaller and lighter. The introduction of touchscreen technology, which allows users to click icons and move images with their fingers rather than a mouse, made the boards easier to use.

The use of modern touchscreen whiteboards has added interest and excitement to classrooms. Teachers and students can write, draw, and erase on the boards, much as they would on a traditional whiteboard or blackboard. Computer technology and software tools allow users to move words and images around the board, rearrange information, or answer questions, as well as enlarge, reduce, highlight, and use pictures and text in creative ways. In 2015 SMART Technologies reported that more than 3 million of its interactive whiteboards were in use worldwide, and a number of other companies, such as Promethean, eInstruction, Mimio, and Polyvision, have entered the market.

The blackboard improves teaching methods

As early as the 1300s, schoolchildren practiced their lessons by writing with chalk on pieces of slate, a gray, fine-textured rock that is easily split into thin layers. These erasable and reusable slate tablets were an affordable alternative to paper and ink, which at the time were expensive. At the beginning of the nineteenth century, a Scottish teacher named James Pillans (1778–1864) had the idea to put a number of slates together to form a writing surface large enough to show information to the whole class. Use of slate blackboards quickly spread throughout England and the United States, and by the mid-1800s almost every American school had chalkboards at the front of its classrooms.

The use of chalkboards greatly changed education, allowing teachers to illustrate lessons easily for the entire class to see at once. Students began to look up from their slate tablets to watch the teacher, and teachers began calling on students to come to the front of the class to write on the board. Most of these early blackboards were made of slate that was mined in Vermont, New York, and Virginia. Some schools made their own blackboards by coating wooden planks with a paint made from egg whites and charcoal. Manufactured blackboards made of wood covered with enamel paint began to appear during the mid-1800s. In the 1900s many manufacturers starting using green paint rather than black because green boards were easier to read and caused less eyestrain than blackboards.

In the 1960s a whiteboard was developed that could be written on with colored marking pens. Whiteboards did not become immediately popular because wiping off the ink was a messy process, but in the 1970s dry-erase markers, which are able to be wiped clean with a special eraser, were introduced, and use of whiteboards began to spread. Because dry-erase markers do not produce chalk dust, as writing and erasing on a blackboard does, whiteboards became the preferred choice in many schools.

Audiovisual in the classroom

At the same time that the use of the blackboard was spreading across the United States, other technologies were being developed to help teachers deliver lessons. The most common of these were the overhead projector and the slide projector. The overhead projector, which uses a bright light and mirrors to transmit an image from a horizontal surface onto a vertical wall or screen, was introduced by French inventor Jules Duboscq (1817–1886) during the 1870s. In the 1960s engineers at the 3M Company created a practical overhead projector that they marketed to educators and business leaders. Using an overhead projector, a teacher could display prepared lessons or write information during class that would be immediately projected onto a screen for everyone to see.

Slide and film projectors have also been commonly used as audiovisual aids in schools and businesses, and their history goes back even further than that of overhead projectors. The "magic lantern," which was popular during the 1700s and 1800s, was an early type of projector that used candles or oil lamps to project light through glass slides, casting images onto walls or screens. The invention of electricity led to improvements in projection technology, and during the 1930s the Kodak company introduced a slide projector that could project enlarged photographs onto a screen. A number of inventors, including Thomas Edison (1847–1931) and Woodville Latham (1837–1911) in the United States and Auguste Lumière (1862–1954) and his brother, Louis (1864–1948), in France, worked to develop a film projector at the turn of the twentieth century. Film projectors, which project moving images from a roll of film onto a screen, began to be used in classrooms during the 1920s and were commonly used as teaching aids until the 1980s. At this point they were replaced by videocassette players, which translate data recorded on magnetic tapes into images.

Thanks to these inventive technologies, teachers were able to present educational material in an interesting manner. However, these projectors were also somewhat awkward, requiring slides or films to be purchased or prepared in advance. The use of overhead projectors allowed teachers to create materials on the spot, but projected writing could be difficult to read, and the special lightbulb that produced the projection was expensive to replace.

Classroom demonstrations get smart

As the use of computers became increasingly widespread during the 1980s and 1990s, teachers began to use data projectors, which use special audio and video cables to connect to computers in order to project information onto a large screen. Like slide projectors and film projectors, data projectors were expensive and bulky, and SMART Technologies founder David Martin began to work to create a more useful computerized classroom aid. SMART introduced the interactive whiteboard in 1991. Early models used a front projector, much like a data projector, to transmit images to the board. By 1992 a rear projection model was introduced to streamline the board design and protect viewers' eyes from the bright projection beam.

By the early 2000s interactive whiteboards were able to record and play audio and video files from the Internet, and user interaction was improved. In 2003 the introduction of touchscreen technology made the use of interactive whiteboards even easier for students of all ages. By 2005 manufacturers offered larger screen sizes, and schools across the country began using the boards. As interactive boards became more popular, other manufacturers joined in to create increasingly user-friendly and effective boards that performed a wider variety of tasks.

Raw materials

Many of the materials used in computer construction are also used to make the computerized parts of interactive whiteboards. These include

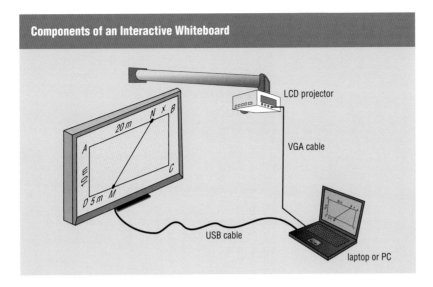

Components of an Interactive Whiteboard

LCD projector

VGA cable

USB cable

laptop or PC

An interactive whiteboard combines the benefits of a computer and a dry erase board, allowing teachers and students to share information.
ILLUSTRATION BY LUMINA DATAMATICS LTD. © 2015 CENGAGE LEARNING

elements such as silicon, aluminum, copper, lead, gold, nickel, beryllium, and cadmium, which are used to make the wiring, coatings, and contacts for circuit boards and to construct the transistors that control electric current in computer chips.

The outer casing of interactive whiteboards is generally made of petroleum-based plastic. The stiff backboard may be made of aluminum or hard plastic. Some companies use polyester-based plastic to construct the interactive front screen of their boards, and others use melamine-based plastic. Polyester is a synthetic, or artificially made, material created by combining acids and alcohols taken from petroleum. One of the common brand names of polyester plastic is Mylar®. Melamine is produced from petroleum and formaldehyde, a gaseous compound that can be found in nature. One of the common names for melamine plastic is Formica®.

Design

Interactive whiteboards are thin, rectangular computer screens designed to look like the whiteboards found in many schools and offices. They are generally hung on a wall, and many boards have a control panel that may be attached to a different wall, where the operator can see the screen while making changes from the panel. Like traditional whiteboards, interactive whiteboards have a flat screen enclosed in a plastic framework.

Teachers and students can write on interactive whiteboards in various colors. © PETER MACDIARMID/GETTY IMAGES

Modern interactive whiteboards are operated by touching the screen, and most use either resistive or electromagnetic technology. Resistive touchscreens have a thin plastic sheet and a hard backboard, which are coated with a film that resists the flow of electricity. The plastic sheet is placed over the backboard, with a tiny space between the two. When the screen is touched, the plastic sheet is pressed into the backboard, forcing the two surfaces together. A computer reads and displays the points of contact, which it then translates into writing, drawing, or instructions to open computer programs. Resistive touchscreens can be activated by any touching device, including fingers, pens, and pointers. Electromagnetic touchscreens have an electronic grid, surrounded by foam or other cushioning material, between two unbending sheets of plastic. When a user touches the surface of the plastic with a special electronic pen or stylus, the grid responds by producing lines and images.

Many interactive whiteboards designed by SMART include an electronic "pen tray" that has special properties. Similar to a tray on a traditional whiteboard that holds markers and erasers, the SMART electronic pen tray has places to hold a variety of markers and other tools that can be used to write on the board. However, on an interactive whiteboard, the tray itself has electronic parts that tell the computer screen what kind of mark to display on the screen. For example, a pen removed from the "red" section of the pen tray will expose a sensor that makes the text on the screen red. When the eraser slot on the pen tray is empty, any device, such as an eraser, a hand, or a tennis ball, will erase writing on the screen. The pen tray also features buttons that control a number of functions, including a help feature that assists users in navigating the board's programs.

Many interactive whiteboard designs also include a projector system to show computer images and a sound system with speakers.

Think about It!

Although many teachers and students have been excited to welcome interactive whiteboards into their classrooms, some experts believe that they might actually be harmful to the education process. Interactive whiteboards offer a wide variety of programs and options, and some educators are concerned that teachers spend more time learning to use the hardware and software than planning effective lessons. In addition, some critics of interactive whiteboards claim that the boards encourage an outdated way of teaching, in which a teacher lectures from the front of the room and students sit at desks facing the board. What do you think are some of the advantages and disadvantages of using an interactive whiteboard?

The manufacturing process

Because interactive whiteboard technology is rapidly changing, the processes used to manufacture them are regularly being updated. Sales and marketing of the boards is very competitive, and manufacturers are protective of their production procedures. Below is a brief overview of the construction of resistive interactive whiteboards.

1 A backboard made of unbending material, such as aluminum or hard plastic, is cut to size and coated with a thin layer of a resistive material (one that resists the flow of electricity), such as the metallic compound indium tin oxide.

2 The coated boards are inserted in special machines that place tiny plastic spacers, about the width of two human hairs, around the edges. A thin layer of adhesive is applied to hold them in place.

3 While the backboards are being prepared, other workers cut the thin, flexible plastic sheets that will be the front of the boards. These sheets are also coated with a layer of resistive film. A removable protective

WORDS TO KNOW

Circuit board: A board on which a number of electrical connections are organized for placement in electronic devices.

Data projector: A device that displays information from a computer on a larger screen.

Electromagnetism: The use of electrical current to create a magnetic field.

Interactive: Someone or something that responds to user input.

Prototype: An early example of a product that is later used as a model for production.

Resistive: Not conducting an electrical current.

Transistor: A device that regulates and controls electric current through the use of semiconductors.

Ultraviolet (UV) light: An invisible form of light produced by the sun. It can cause serious damage to the human eye.

---

covering is placed over the front of the board to prevent scratches during the manufacturing process.

4 An air vacuum machine stretches and holds the top sheets in position above an assembly line where the bottom sheets are ready to receive them.

5 As the bottom sheet is moved into place by a conveyer belt, the vacuum machine lowers the top sheet onto it and presses it into the adhesive around the edge of the bottom sheet. Heat lamps installed around the edges of the press area help quickly dry the adhesive.

6 The finished touchscreens are placed into metal frames called buss bars, which distribute electrical power to the screen.

Quality control

Even before production begins, design prototypes, or samples, of interactive whiteboards are put through numerous tests. A machine applies an abrasive to the screen one thousand times to make sure that it will not scratch. Other machines test the board's resistance to vibration and whether it can be dropped without breaking. Sample boards are also exposed to strong ultraviolet, or invisible, light to test their ability to resist discoloration or damage.

New directions in interactivity

Technology companies continue to develop and improve interactive display products. In 2014 SMART introduced the SMARTkapp digital

Creative Uses of Interactive Whiteboards

Imaginative teachers have found many uses for the advanced technology of interactive whiteboards. In *The Interactive Whiteboard Revolution: Teaching with IWBs* (2009), Nebraska teacher Katie Morrow describes a class project in which students used their classroom interactive whiteboards to create a news channel to report on school events. Board features helped students in every stage of production, including brainstorming and organizing ideas, working in groups to edit and rewrite stories, planning the broadcast, and filming the finished product. The interactive whiteboard was used as a teleprompter during filming, allowing students to read from a script while they appeared to be looking directly at the audience. Finished broadcasts could be viewed by the whole class on the interactive whiteboard.

Other teachers have used interactive whiteboards to take their students on virtual, or pretend, travels around the world. A program called Virtual Field Trips by SMART Technologies guides students on tours of foreign lands and famous museums and even allows them to travel under the ocean or back in time through video clips and colorful computer graphics.

capture board, which allows users to save materials created on the board and send them to smartphones and other devices. Teachers can use the boards to send classroom information and activities instantly to students who are not present in the classroom.

During the 2010s Mimio made interactive technology even more accessible and affordable by developing products designed to change regular whiteboards into interactive boards. In these products, a wireless transmitter is attached directly to a classroom whiteboard with magnets or adhesive strips, and the device communicates with a computer to project images onto the board. Using a stylus, teachers and students can write on the board and move images, much as they would on an interactive whiteboard.

Interactive whiteboards reached a peak of popularity in 2013, when industry sources reported that they were in use in 45 percent of classrooms in the United States, 37 percent in Canada, and 90 percent in the United Kingdom. However, some experts believe that the use of these boards may be decreasing as more schools provide students with personal tablets that allow them to participate in interactive learning in a more direct way.

For more information

BOOKS

Betcher, Chris, and Mal Lee. *The Interactive Whiteboard Revolution: Teaching with IWBs.* Victoria, Australia: Acer Press, 2009.

Dvorak, Radana. *SMART Board Interactive Whiteboard for Dummies.* Hoboken, NJ: John Wiley and Sons, 2012.

PERIODICALS

Akanegbu, Anuli. "Vision of Learning: A History of Classroom Projectors." *EdTech* (February 28, 2013). Available online at http://www. edtechmagazine.com/k12/article/2013/02/vision-learning-history-classroom-projectors (accessed July 30, 2015).

Manzo, Kathleen Kennedy. "Beyond Teacher Chalk Talk." *Education Week Digital Directions* 3, no. 2 (2010): 34–37.

WEBSITES

"The History of Smart." SMART Technologies. http://smarttech.com/us/About +SMART/About+SMART/Innovation/Beginnings+of+an+industry (accessed July 30, 2015).

"How Can a Screen Sense Touch?: A Basic Understanding of Touch Panels." EIZO. http://www.eizoglobal.com/library/basics/ basic_understanding_of_touch_panel/ (accessed July 30, 2015).

Orbaugh, Jason. "Lessons from the Downfall of Interactive Whiteboards." edSurge. https://www.edsurge.com/n/2013-10-22-lessons-from-the-downfall-of-interactive-whiteboards (accessed July 30, 2015).

Jeans

Critical Thinking Questions

1. Look at the illustration titled "Jean warp and weft." Does it help you understand this step? Why or why not?

2. How have your own perceptions of jeans changed over your lifetime? What events in the culture around you have affected this perception?

Jeans, also known as blue jeans, are casual pants manufactured from denim (a fabric made primarily of cotton) that has been dyed blue. The seams and pockets on a pair of jeans have an extra line of stitching and sometimes have metal rivets (a kind of pin with two flat ends) to make them last longer.

Jeans were first used as work clothes by gold miners in the American West. The pants became popular in the 1930s, when movie stars such as John Wayne (1907–1979) wore blue jeans in Western films. In the 1950s Hollywood stars such as James Dean (1931–1955) and Marlon Brando (1924–2004) wore denim when they played teenage rebels, and young people all over the United States started to wear blue jeans. Over the years different groups of people changed the style to fit their tastes, from the ripped jeans of punk rockers to the skinny jeans trendy among kids of the late twentieth and early twenty-first centuries.

Jeans are popular partly because they never need ironing and rarely need washing. As they get worn in, they become softer and more comfortable, and their color fades in a pleasing way. Cultural anthropologists

Jeans are popular in part due to their time-saving qualities. They never need ironing and rarely need washing.
© ROBERT_S/ SHUTTERSTOCK.COM

(people who study human culture) believe that jeans remind people of the past and of happy times and special places where they wore them.

The patent that paved the way

Denim, the main material in jeans, comes from Nimes, France. It was originally made of a mixture of wool and silk and was called *serge de Nimes* (surj duh neem). Around the middle of the nineteenth century, American textile mills (factories that made fabric) replaced the wool and silk, which were expensive to ship from France, with cotton. The word "jeans" was first used in the sixteenth or seventeenth century in Genoa, Italy, before the fabric denim was invented. The term referred to the clothes of working men and did not become popular in the United States until the 1930s.

Modern-day blue jeans were invented in the 1870s, when a woodcutter in Reno, Nevada, asked a local tailor, Jacob Davis, to make him a pair of sturdy, long-lasting pants. Davis decided to add copper rivets in certain places in the seams of the pants that wore out the fastest. Soon Davis's creation was in high demand among nearby workers, especially miners. When more and more people wanted to buy the pants, Davis decided he should apply for a patent, an official government document that stopped other people from copying and selling his invention. He asked his fabric supplier, the German immigrant businessman Levi Strauss, to supply money for the patent.

In 1853 Strauss (1829–1902) established Levi Strauss & Co. (LS&CO) in San Francisco. The store quickly became a center for gold rush miners who needed tents, blankets, and other necessary supplies. In 1873 Strauss and Davis registered a patent called "Improvement in Fastening Pocket-Openings." The two men split the profits from their popular workingman's pants, then known as waist overalls. It was not until 1960—a few decades after the rest of the country—that Levi Strauss & Co. began calling their pants "jeans."

Changing associations

For the next fifty years, waist overalls were the most popular pants for American men who worked at jobs such as farming and mining. By the 1920s jeans had also become fashionable in the western United States, where rodeos and dude ranches were common. Although Easterners associated this Old West fashion with ruggedness and strength, they also looked down on it as a small town and working-class style of dress. That did not stop many people from vacationing at dude ranches, where they could pretend to be cowboys by wearing jeans and riding horses. This connection between jeans and the American West continued well into the 1940s as movie stars such as John Wayne, Roy Rogers (1911–1998), and Gene Autry (1907–1998) spread the cowboy myth. Around this time photographs of World War II (1939–1945) soldiers wearing jeans during their downtime made other Americans relate jeans to freedom and leisure.

The American view of jeans changed in 1947, when *Life* magazine published photographs of motorcycle riders in jeans fighting with California police. The link between blue jeans and rebellion was made stronger by actors such as Marlon Brando in *The Wild One* (1953) and James Dean in *Rebel without a Cause* (1955). These films inspired many teenage rebels to choose a style of dress that included leather jackets, boots, white T-shirts, and jeans. In response, some schools, worried that jeans encouraged rebellious behavior, created dress codes that forbid students to wear them. These rules lasted until the 1980s. The ban only made jeans more popular, and by 1964 they were so strongly associated with America's antiestablishment movement (a movement against the traditional values of society) that the Smithsonian Institution in Washington, D.C., added a pair to its permanent collection.

Evolving styles and fits

The 1960s made blue jeans famous as a piece of clothing and also inspired the companies that made them to copy the ways young people changed their own jeans, including covering the fabric in patches and paint. In the decades that followed, clothing companies regularly changed their designs to follow youth trends. In 1976, when an album from the American rock group the Ramones showed the band members in ripped jeans, manufacturers rushed to bring

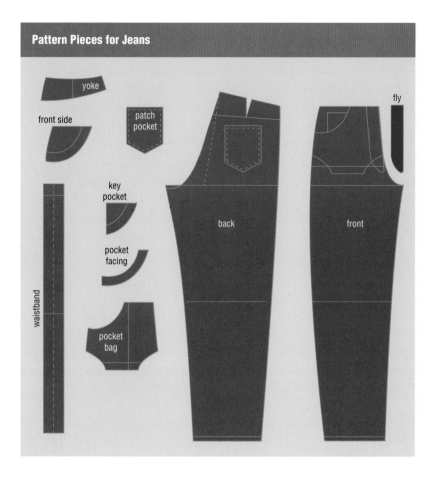

Pattern Pieces for Jeans

yoke

front side

patch pocket

fly

key pocket

pocket facing

back

front

waistband

pocket bag

A single pair of jeans requires many separate pieces, which are cut from a pattern.
ILLUSTRATION BY LUMINA DATAMATICS LTD. © 2015 CENGAGE LEARNING

pre-ripped jeans to stores. Later fads included acid-washed jeans (denim faded until it was nearly white) in the 1980s and scruffy jeans, inspired by the grunge look of bands such as Nirvana, in the early 1990s.

Just as the look of jeans changed over the decades, so, too, did the fit. Inspired by navy uniforms, bellbottom jeans, which were narrow down to the knee and then widened out at the bottom of the leg, were very popular in the 1960s and early 1970s. In the late 1970s, punk rockers rebelled against bellbottoms by wearing tight-fitting jeans, or skinny jeans, which came back in style after the beginning of the twenty-first century. In the 1990s, before the return of skinny jeans, many young people preferred baggy jeans with wide legs, which were inspired by hip-hop artists.

A textile worker sews blue jeans in the Chinese town of Xintang, nicknamed "the denim jeans center of the world." Jeans are sewn together in an assembly line by workers who are each assigned a different task, such as sewing leg seams together, attaching zippers or buttons, or sewing on a designer label. © LUCAS SCHIFRES/GETTY IMAGES

Once jeans became widely accepted as casual wear, name brands such as Calvin Klein and Guess introduced designer jeans, which were of higher quality and more expensive. Even Levi Strauss & Co. began making designer jeans that ranged in price from $45 to $150.

Raw materials

Although jeans are occasionally made from polyester blends, they are usually made from cotton denim. Their traditional blue color came from natural indigo, a plant used to make dark blue dye, until the twentieth century. After that time, jeans were colored with manmade indigo, a chemically manufactured blue dye. In addition to their cotton fabric, jeans include zippers, snaps, or buttons made from steel, as well as rivets made from copper. Designer labels on jeans are made from cloth,

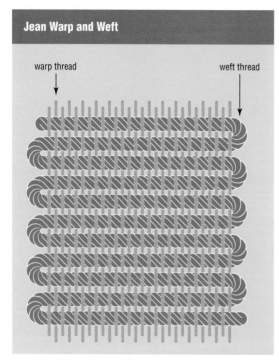

Jean Warp and Weft

warp thread

weft thread

As part of the jean manufacturing process, mechanical looms weave warp (long, vertical blue threads) and weft (shorter, horizontal white threads) together into fabric. ILLUSTRATION BY LUMINA DATAMATICS LTD. © 2015 CENGAGE LEARNING

leather, or plastic, and the designer name is often embroidered with cotton thread.

Design

Jeans are relatively simple. In addition to a fly that closes with a zipper or a series of buttons and a button at the waistband, jeans include pockets below the waistband and belt loops around it. They come in a variety of colors, from black and green to many shades of blue, and several styles, including skinny, slim, straight, and boot cut.

The manufacturing process

Over the years technological advances simplified the manufacturing process from a difficult single-person operation to a highly functioning assembly line. Still, the basics remain the same. Beginning with tufts of cotton, workers use factory machines to dye, twist, and stitch denim parts into brand-new pairs of form-fitting jeans.

1 The manufacturing process begins with workers ginning the cotton. Ginning consists of picking cotton from fields, processing it, and packing it into tight bales. From there each bale is inspected before it is separated into tufts, or bunches.

2 The tufts go through a process called carding. Using a machine with brushes fitted with bent-wire teeth, the tufts are cleaned, disentangled, straightened into threads, and gathered into slivers. The slivers are then entered into spinning machines, where they are stretched and twisted into balls of yarn.

3 Each ball of yarn is dipped several times into a mixture of synthetic indigo. Although this process is the same at all jeans manufacturers, each company keeps the ingredients of its specific dyes a secret. Once dyed, the yarn is slashed, which means it is coated with a starchy substance called sizing that helps strengthen and stiffen each thread.

4 After slashing, each strand of yarn is fed through mechanical looms, which weave long, vertical blue threads, called warp, and shorter, horizontal white threads, called weft, into fabric. The blue

warp threads are packed closer together than the white weft threads. This, along with the indigo dye, gives jeans their blue color.

5 Once woven, denim is finished during a series of steps that include brushing to remove lint and loose threads; skewing, which keeps the denim from twisting when it is made into jeans; and preshrinking, which prevents denim from shrinking more than 3 percent after three washings.

6 After the fabric is ready, designers choose what kinds of jeans they want to make by selecting from a series of cardboard or heavy paper patterns. Once the pattern has been chosen, 100 layers of denim are stacked on top of each other and cut with high-speed cutting machines into the pieces according to each design. A design usually consists of ten pieces, including pockets, leggings, and belt loops.

7 Pieces are sewn together in an assembly line by workers who are each assigned a different task, such as sewing leg seams together, attaching zippers or buttons, or sewing on the designer label.

8 After they have been assembled, jeans are prewashed in an industrial detergent that softens the denim. They may also undergo stone-washing, a process in which small or large stones are used to give the jeans a faded look.

9 As a final step, pressing machines are used to steam iron each pair of jeans for one minute. The jeans are then folded; separated by style, color, and size; and placed in boxes. These boxes are stored in warehouses, where they remain until they are sent by freight train or truck to stores.

Think about It!

When people use food trays and plastic bottles, they are usually having their lunch. However, a few years ago, Levi Strauss & Co. discovered something else you can do with food trays and plastic bottles: wear them. In 2013 the company launched Waste<Less, a line of jeans featuring denim made in part from recycled plastic bottles and trays. In 2013 alone these jeans contained nearly 3.5 million recycled bottles. What other recyclable materials could you use to make a pair of jeans?

Byproducts

The steps required for turning cotton into denim fabric, including dyeing and preshrinking, result in mostly biodegradable byproducts. Biodegradable waste can be broken down naturally with the help of microorganisms and other living things. The remaining byproducts are organic pollutants, primarily starch and dye. If dumped into streams or lakes, these pollutants would take up so much oxygen that none would be left for the animals or plants living in that body of water. As a result, denim

WORDS TO KNOW

Assembly line: A manufacturing process in which work passes from worker to worker or machine to machine until the product is put together.

Biodegradable: Able to be broken down naturally with the help of living things.

Cultural anthropology: The study of human culture.

Gin: To separate cotton fiber from cotton seeds and waste.

Patent: An official document that gives an individual or a company exclusive rights over the use of an invention.

manufacturers such as Levi Strauss & Co. process their own waste according to rules and regulations established by the government.

Quality control

Before denim is shaped and sewn into jeans, it must be tested to determine the fabric's strength and durability. These tests begin at the cotton stage, when each bale is examined to make sure it has the necessary color and fiber length. Each cotton fiber is then tested for strength by weighing it down and stretching it until it breaks, at which point the amount of force required to break that fiber is recorded.

Finished denim is inspected for defects and ranked on a four-point scale (one meaning only a few flaws; four meaning many flaws). Samples of denim are also washed and dried several times to make sure they remain durable and do not shrink too much. If denim passes all these tests, it is made into jeans, which are then put to another series of tests. If a problem is fixable, the jeans are resewn; otherwise, they are thrown away. All buttons, rivets, and snaps are inspected to make sure they can handle rust, and zippers are repeatedly opened and closed to make sure they remain durable.

Indestructible denim

The popularity of denim has lasted into the early twenty-first century and shows no sign of fading. Jeans have overcome their association with miners and cowboys, their rebellious reputation in schools, and their acceptance only on weekends or casual Fridays to become part of everyday attire. Comfortable, durable, and fashionable, jeans have kept up with all kinds of American cultural trends.

The Great Unwashed

When college professor Rachel McQueen mentioned her research on textiles and bacteria, University of Alberta sophomore Josh Le knew the perfect test subject: his jeans. Between September 2009 and December 2010—a total of fifteen months and one week, or 330 days—Josh wore the same pair of jeans without washing them. He carried around paper towels for dabbing stains, occasionally slept in his jeans to help them fade, and even stuck them overnight in his freezer when they started to smell. On Facebook and YouTube, Le charted the progress of his jeans as their color lightened and their denim began to crease.

When Le's trial finally came to an end, he and McQueen collected sample material from his jeans and then threw them in the wash. After thirteen days had passed (the average amount of time jeans go between washings), they took another sample. They found that there was no difference between the quantity of bacteria on Josh's jeans after fifteen months versus thirteen days. Though this experiment would need to be repeated many more times to be considered scientifically conclusive, Le and McQueen believe their trial is a good reminder that washing jeans infrequently (about once a month) extends their life and is good for the environment.

For more information

BOOKS

Hammer, Ferenc. "Jeans." *Encyclopedia of Consumer Culture*. Ed. Dale Southerton. Thousand Oaks, CA: SAGE Publications, 2011.

Hay, Ethan. "Jeans." *St. James Encyclopedia of Popular Culture*. Edited by Thomas Riggs. Vol. 3. 2nd ed. Detroit: St. James Press, 2013.

PERIODICALS

Hegarty, Stephanie. "How Jeans Conquered the World." *BBC News Magazine* (February 28, 2012). Available online at http://www.bbc.com/news/magazine-17101768 (accessed June 8, 2015).

WEBSITES

Hopper, Jessica. "Distressed Denim: College Student Wears Same Jeans for 15 Months." ABC News. http://abcnews.go.com/US/canadian-student-josh-le-year-washing-jeans/story?id=12722442 (accessed June 9, 2015).

"How Jeans Are Made?: Manufacturing Processes." History of Jeans. http://www.historyofjeans.com/jeans-making/how-jeans-are-made/ (accessed June 8, 2015).

Sternbenz, Christina. "GIFs Show How Raw Cotton Is Transformed into Blue Jeans." *Business Insider*. http://www.businessinsider.com/how-jeans-are-made-2013-11 (accessed June 8, 2015).

"Sustainability." Levi Strauss & Co. http://www.levistrauss.com/sustainability/enduring-brands/levis-less-platform/ (accessed June 9, 2015).

Lava Lamp

Critical Thinking Questions

1. What details from the entry support the claim that people in Great Britain take great pride in Mathmos lava lamps?

2. The lava lamp became popular because of changes in popular culture. What other products can you think of that have found new popularity because of historical events or trends?

3. How do the photographs add to your understanding of the lava lamp manufacturing process?

The lava lamp, introduced in the 1960s, is a symbol of youth culture. Also known as a liquid motion lamp, it is typically a long, clear globe placed on a base, which contains a lightbulb. The globe is filled with a brightly colored waxy substance in a liquid. When the lightbulb turns on, the globe lights up and becomes warm, causing the wax to move around in the liquid and change into different shapes.

Although invented in the United Kingdom in 1963, the lava lamp first became popular in the mid-1960s in the United States. Sales of lava lamps then took off in Europe and elsewhere around the world. Young people especially bought lava lamps, putting them in homes, college dorm rooms, and offices. Although sales dipped in the 1980s, they revived again in the 1990s. Over the years lava lamps have been associated with youth culture, but they have also appealed to adult buyers who remember them fondly from their younger days.

The value of the lava lamp comes not from the dim light it gives off but from its unusual appearance, which has been a source of entertainment and conversation. Its unique design and acceptance in popular culture have made it one of the most widely recognized lamps ever made. The British Design Council labeled it a "modern classic" in 2000, and the Smithsonian Museum in Washington, D.C., has a lava lamp on permanent display.

The lava lamp's inventor

British accountant Edward Craven Walker (1918–2000) first came up with the idea for the lava lamp in the 1950s. Craven Walker was inspired to make the lamp after seeing a strange egg timer at an English pub. An egg, along with a liquid-filled glass container with wax on the bottom, was put in a pot of boiling water. When the wax rose to the surface of the liquid, the egg was done. Craven Walker sought out the egg timer's inventor. When he found out that the man had died, he bought the patent from the man's widow. Craven Walker then spent a decade experimenting and perfecting a design for a lamp based on the egg timer. His early prototypes were made out of empty beverage containers. Eventually Craven Walker started the company Cresworth Ltd. in Dorset, England, to produce the lamp. The first models were sold under the name Astro Lamp in 1963.

The lava lamp, with its unique design and acceptance in popular culture, is one of the most widely recognized lamps ever made. It celebrated its 50th birthday in 2013. © STEVE BOWER/SHUTTERSTOCK.COM

Craven Walker meant for his lamp to be used in both homes and businesses, but sales got off to a slow start. People were not sure what to think of the strange-looking lamps, and stores were hesitant to stock them. Craven Walker and his wife, Christine, distributed their Astro Lamps out of a van and worked to come up with an advertising campaign that would attract buyers.

A new market and a new name

Although Craven Walker invented the lava lamp, he did not come up with the name. That honor belongs to Chicago entrepreneur Adolph Wertheimer and his business partner. The pair saw Craven Walker's Astro Lamp at a German trade show and recognized its potential for the American market. They bought the North American rights from Craven

How Everyday Products Are Made

Walker, formed the Lava Manufacturing Corporation, and began marketing the product to American consumers in 1965. Noting the resemblance of the lamp's colorful liquid to pāhoehoe, a type of lava known for its smooth, swirled surface, they named their product the Lava Lite (the company later adopted the name Lava Brand Motion Lamp, but consumers commonly called them lava lamps).

Lava Manufacturing Corporation began producing the Lava Lite at a promising moment in American history. By the late 1960s, a youth counterculture movement was growing. Around the country young people were rejecting the symbols of traditional society and embracing new forms of music, clothing, and experiences. The strange and unexpected appearance of the lamp, qualities that had initially made it difficult for Craven Walker to find buyers, made the Lava Lite appealing to American youth. The lava lamp quickly became associated with counterculture. As interest in counterculture grew, so did demand for lava lamps. Sales of the Lava Lite in the United States helped increase interest in Craven Walker's Astro Lite in Europe. The lamps became so popular that even Ringo Starr (1940–) and Paul McCartney (1942–), members

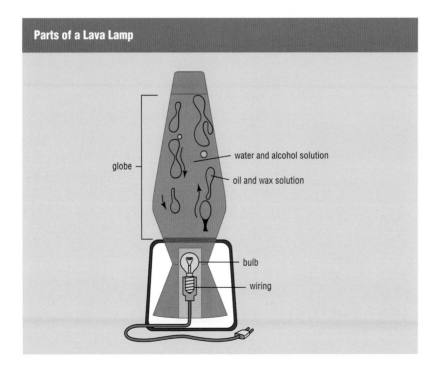

Parts of a Lava Lamp

globe

water and alcohol solution

oil and wax solution

bulb

wiring

Lava lamps are made of a globe that holds the liquid and the "lava" and a base that holds the bulb and wiring.

ILLUSTRATION BY LUMINA DATAMATICS LTD. © 2015 CENGAGE LEARNING

of the popular music group The Beatles, owned them. By the end of the 1960s, consumers were buying up to 7 million lamps a year.

Changing times, changing ownership

By the early 1970s, the lava lamp's popularity began to fade, and in 1973 Lava Manufacturing Corporation, branching out into new products, changed its name to Lava-Simplex Corporation. Three years later Chicago-based Haggerty Enterprises acquired the business. Under the leadership of Lawrence Haggerty (d. 1994), the company worked to keep the Lava Lite brand alive, despite limited sales.

In England sales of Craven Walker's Astro Lite also fell significantly. By the early 1980s, production had slowed to roughly a thousand lamps per year. In 1989, after lava lamps had suffered nearly two decades of slow sales, British antique dealer Cressida Granger (1963–) took an interest in vintage lava lamps. Convinced that the lamps had a promising future, she approached Craven Walker about buying his company. They agreed that Granger would become Craven Walker's partner and that she would eventually buy him out. Granger took over the company in 1992, although Craven Walker remained on as a consultant until his death from cancer in 2000. Granger renamed the company Mathmos and worked to make the lava lamp cool again. By 1998 Mathmos was selling 800,000 lamps a year.

In the 1990s sales also increased in the U.S. market, as consumers got caught up in a wave of nostalgia for the 1960s. In 1999 sales of the American-based Lava Lite were estimated at $49 million. In the early twenty-first century, sales widely fluctuated. In 2008, when Talon Merchant Capital bought the Lava Lite business from Haggerty Enterprises and renamed it Lava Lite LLC, sales were estimated at slightly more than $1 million. By 2013 sales had rebounded, topping $20 million.

Raw materials

The liquid that fills the globe of a lava lamp is traditionally made using water, isopropyl alcohol, paraffin wax, mineral oil, paraffin, and

Lava lamp owners can ensure their lamps are working properly by paying attention to the appearance of the lava.
ILLUSTRATION BY LUMINA DATAMATICS LTD. © 2015 CENGAGE LEARNING

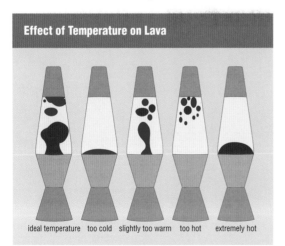

Effect of Temperature on Lava

ideal temperature   too cold   slightly too warm   too hot   extremely hot

carbon tetrachloride, a solvent. These raw materials are combined according to a secret recipe to create the perfect balance of liquid and lava. The base of the lava lamp is traditionally made of aluminum, although metal has been replaced with plastic in cheaper models.

Design

There has been little change to Craven Walker's original Astro Lamp design. The focal point of the lamp is the clear, elongated globe that holds the oil and wax solution and the liquid. A base, made from either metal or plastic, houses the lightbulb, wiring, and any additional heating elements. Craven Walker's original Astro Lamps featured a 52-ounce (1.5-liter) globe, and customers had a choice of red or white lava in either yellow or blue liquid. Eventually Craven Walker offered twenty color combinations, including five water and four wax colors. By 2015, in addition to many color combinations, Lava Lite LLC manufactured lamps in five sizes: Accent, 11.5 inches (29.2 centimeters); Classic, 14.5 inches (36.8 centimeters); Premier, 16.3 inches (41.4 centimeters); Designer, 17 inches (43.2 centimeters); and Grande, 27 inches (68.6 centimeters).

Lava lamps work because water and oil are immiscible, meaning it is impossible to mix them. A see-through glass or plastic container forms the globe of the lamp. Each lamp is filled with a delicate balance of two solutions: a water and alcohol solution and an oil and wax solution. Manufacturers of lava lamps carefully guard the exact recipes of their mixtures.

At room temperature the oil and wax solution is a solid and rests at the bottom of the globe. When the lamp is turned on, the lightbulb begins to heat the contents of the globe. As the oil and wax solution heats up, it expands, becoming a liquid and slightly less dense than the water solution. Because a substance that is less dense will float on a denser substance, the oil and wax solution rises in the water solution. As it moves away from the heat source, however, it begins to cool and contract. As it cools, it becomes less dense than the water solution and begins to sink back toward the heat source. As it moves closer to the lightbulb, however, it heats up again, and the process repeats itself. One thing that makes a lava lamp so fun to watch is that blobs of lava change shape as they move around the globe. The two solutions must be carefully balanced in order to keep the lava moving.

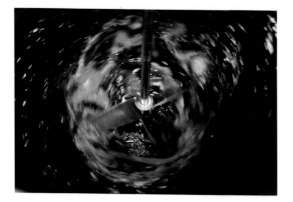

The oil and wax solution used to fill lava lamps is mixed at the Mathmos factory in Poole, Dorset, England. © MATT CARDY/GETTY IMAGES

Safety

Lava lamps are designed to be used only with the built-in heat source and must be treated with care. In 2004 attention was drawn to the potential dangers of lava lamps when a twenty-four-year-old man was killed after attempting to heat a lava lamp on his kitchen stove. Exposed to excessive heat, the glass globe exploded with enough force that a piece of glass punctured the man's heart. The incident was later replicated by the television show *MythBusters,* which confirmed that heating a lava lamp beyond recommended temperatures could lead to a forceful explosion.

The manufacturing process

In the early twenty-first century, Mathmos and Lava Lite LLC remained the most prominent manufacturers of lava lamps. After Craven Walker's patent expired in the 1990s, however, other companies began to mass-produce lava lamps outside the United States and Great Britain. Despite pressure to make lamps more cheaply by manufacturing them in China, Mathmos has continued to produce its lamps in England. Lava Lite LLC has moved its manufacturing to Asia, but in 2013 it announced plans to begin production of a line of upscale Lava Lite products in the United States. Although many lamps are now made in Asia, the manufacturing process has remained virtually unchanged since the 1960s.

1 Before production can begin, the two liquid components must be prepared. Isopropyl alcohol is added to water to create a solution in which the heated lava will float. Dyes and other additives are used to give the water solution the desired appearance. The second component is created from a combination of oil and wax. Like the water solution, it may be dyed to achieve the desired color.

2 The assembly process begins with the lamp's globe, which is usually manufactured separately and shipped to the factory where the lamps are made. A small heating coil is put into each globe, and the globe is sent down a conveyor belt.

3 In the next assembly phase, the desired color of wax liquid is measured into the globe. Although some manufacturers use machines to fill the globes, Mathmos lamps are still filled by hand. An average worker can fill 400 lamps a day. The lava is left to harden, usually overnight.

4 Once the lava has hardened, the colored water and alcohol mixture is added to the globe. Workers leave a small amount of room in each globe so the liquids have room to expand when heated.

5 Once the globes have been filled, they are sealed with a cap similar to the caps used to seal soft drink bottles. The decorative top of the lamp is fit over the cap.

6 Wiring is assembled inside the base, and the lightbulb is screwed into place. Most lava lamps use a 40-watt bulb. The globe is attached to the base.

Think about It!

How do you imagine life in a future space-age society? You might think about advanced technologies such as robots, holographs, or teleportation. In the late 1960s, the lava lamp was part of that vision for many television viewers. In a 1968 episode of the popular science-fiction series *Dr. Who*, large lava lamps were a major feature inside the spacecraft TARDIS. This product placement drew on the unusual newness of the lava lamp and helped to further the popular view of the lamp as a futuristic device. How has that perception changed over time?

Quality control

The chief objectives of the quality control process are to make sure that the globe contains the correct ratio of water and alcohol solution to oil and wax solution, that the electrical components have been properly sealed off from the liquid in the globe, and that there are no leaks anywhere in the lamp. A final check is made at the end of the assembly process to ensure that the lightbulb is firmly and properly tightened in the socket. Each lava lamp is packaged carefully to minimize the chance of damage during transport.

The Lava Lite website offers a frequently asked questions (FAQ) page (http://www.lavalamp.com/Faq) to help lava lamp owners troubleshoot problems with their lamps. The makers of the lamps warn that once the contents of a lamp's globe become cloudy, the condition is likely permanent. They warn against shaking, dropping, or moving the lamps while hot, as doing so can cause the liquid to turn cloudy. They recommend that owners turn off the lamp immediately and allow it to cool completely if they notice that the liquid is beginning to look cloudy.

WORDS TO KNOW

Counterculture: A subculture that rejects the values of the popular, dominant culture.

Density: The mass of a substance in a given space; the greater the substance's density, the tighter its molecules are packed in the space.

Immiscible: Incapable of blending.

Pāhoehoe: A type of lava that results from the movement of liquid lava under a cooling lava crust. Pāhoehoe is known for its smooth, swirled surface.

Solvent: A solid, liquid, or gas in which another solid, liquid, or gas is dissolved to create a solution.

Youth culture: A subculture created by and for young people that is noticeably different from adult culture.

A bright future

The lava lamp celebrated its fiftieth anniversary in 2013. Although the lamp's popularity has fluctuated since its introduction in 1963, production has never ceased, and lamps are widely available in retail stores such as Target and Walmart in the United States, as well as online specialty boutiques.

Beyond the traditional designs of the 1960s, lava lamps have evolved into new forms, including new sizes and colors, sound-activated lamps, nightlights, USB lamps, and even virtual lava lamps that serve as computer screen savers. Phone apps such as iLava and Ooze provide digital representations of the lava lamp and allow users to change colors with a swipe. Inspired by a local artist, the city of Soap Lake, Washington, began planning the world's largest lava lamp, which the city intended to build next to its lake in the manner of a lighthouse. Although the city was still raising funds in 2015 for the 60-foot-tall (18-meter-tall) lava lamp, the plans attracted worldwide press coverage, reflecting an ongoing curiosity with one of the most recognized products of 1960s youth culture.

For more information

BOOKS

Cameron, Schyrlet, and Carolyn Craig. *Ooey Gooey Science, Grades 5–8.* Greensboro, NC: Carson-Dellosa, 2012.

PERIODICALS

Anderson, Elizabeth. "How I Beat the Odds: Cressida Granger of Lava Lamp Pioneer Mathmos." *Management Today* (October 28, 2013). Available online

Try This!

Make a mock lava lamp

Although manufacturing traditional lava lamps requires specialized equipment and materials, you can make a mock lava lamp out of materials you probably have around your home.

You will need:

- liquid measuring cup
- 2½ cups vegetable or mineral oil
- ⅔ cup water
- 12 drops food coloring (bright colors work best)
- fizzing antacid tablets
- 20-ounce (0.6-liter) clear plastic bottle with a lid (an empty soda or water bottle works well)
- funnel

Directions:

1. Using the funnel, pour the water into the plastic container. Keeping the funnel in place, add the oil.

2. Once the oil and water are completely separated, add the food coloring. You will see the food-coloring droplets fall through the oil before dissolving in the water below.

3. Break up the antacid tablet and drop it in the bottle. Screw the lid onto the bottle.

4. Enjoy watching the lava move!

5. You can restart your "lamp" at any time by adding another antacid tablet.

at http://www.managementtoday.co.uk/news/1217039/ (accessed February 23, 2015).

Tucker, Abigail. "The History of the Lava Lamp." *Smithsonian* (March 2013). Available online at http://www.smithsonianmag.com/arts-culture/the-history-of-the-lava-lamp-21201966/?no-ist (accessed February 18, 2015).

WEBSITES

Lava Lamp: The Official Site of the Lava Lamp. https://lavalamp.com/ (accessed February 23, 2015).

Mathmos. http://www.mathmos.com/ (accessed February 20, 2015).

"Salt Volcano: Make Your Own Miniature 'Lava Lite.'" Exploratorium. https://www.exploratorium.edu/science_explorer/volcano.html (accessed February 18, 2015).

The Soap Lake Lava Lamp. http://www.giantlavalamp.com/ (accessed February 19, 2015).

LED Lightbulb

1. Based on information in the entry, why do you think the U.S. government wanted to encourage LED lightbulb development?

2. What connection does the author draw between LED lightbulb manufacturing and the manufacturing of solar cells? Why do you think the author includes this information?

3. What can you conclude about what is most important to consumers when they shop for lightbulbs?

LED lightbulbs are energy-efficient bulbs that screw into standard electrical sockets. LED stands for "light-emitting diode." A diode is an electronic device that uses a semiconductor to control the flow of an electric current. A semiconductor is a substance that has special properties when exposed to electricity, conducting electricity at high temperatures and resisting it at lower temperatures. Through a process called electroluminescence, LED technology uses semiconductors to convert electricity into light.

LED bulbs were first invented in the mid-1900s during the early development of the computer industry. Scientists had long noted that some substances released light when they came into contact with an electric current. By the 1960s electrical engineers were able to use this quality to power small colored lights on electronic devices. By the last decade of the twentieth century, a white-light LED powerful enough for household use was marketed to consumers. Development and improvement of LED bulbs has continued as researchers work to overcome the high cost, harsh

The long life and low energy consumption of LED bulbs make them a popular choice with energy-conscious consumers. © COPRID/ SHUTTERSTOCK.COM

quality of light, and high levels of heat produced by large clusters of LED bulbs, called arrays.

In the 2010s LED lighting, which uses less electricity than traditional bulbs, became one of the most promising new technologies for efficient and environmentally friendly electrical light production. LED bulbs have a significantly longer life, can be turned on and off repeatedly without damage, and are much less likely to break than incandescent and compact fluorescent lightbulbs. In addition, they contain far fewer toxic (poisonous) substances than compact fluorescent bulbs, which are filled with toxic mercury gas. The durability of LED lights, including their ability to handle temperature highs and lows, makes them especially useful in outdoor applications such as streetlights, signs, and scoreboards.

The pursuit of artificial light

The search for a simple electric light source began during the Industrial Revolution, a period of major invention and mechanization that spanned the eighteenth and nineteenth centuries. In 1800 English chemist Sir Humphry Davy (1778–1829) created one of the first artificial lights powered by electricity when he ran wires from a battery to a thin thread, or filament, of carbon, producing a glow. Others built on Davy's discovery. Most early lightbulbs had fragile filaments that burned out easily, making them unsuccessful for practical use.

In 1878 American inventor Thomas Edison (1847–1931) and his team of engineers in Menlo Park, New Jersey, joined the search for a practical lightbulb. Edison improved the carbon filament design to make it more durable and created a more perfect vacuum within the bulb. This allowed the filament to glow brightly without being consumed in flame. In 1880 Edison patented a bulb that could produce light for up to forty hours, and, with further improvements, its life was increased to more than 1,500 hours.

Alternatives to the incandescent bulb

The filament bulb developed by Edison and others was an incandescent light, meaning that it produced light by heating a substance until it

How Everyday Products Are Made

glowed. As these bulbs were improved, other scientists and inventors were working on another type of bulb that created light by directing an electric current through a gas. German glassblower Heinrich Geissler (1815–1879) built one of the first gas-tube lights in 1856, and in 1934 American chemists working for General Electric (GE) developed a working fluorescent lamp for consumer use.

Because fluorescent lamps had a longer life than incandescent bulbs and used less electricity, they were quickly adopted by businesses. However, most fluorescent bulbs required special fixtures with awkward electric regulators called ballasts. This made them less useful in homes designed for incandescent bulbs with screw-in bases. In the 1970s, in response to an increasing demand for less expensive energy options brought on by an energy crisis in the United States, GE engineer Edward Hammer (1931–2012) designed a compact fluorescent light (CFL) for use in standard light fixtures. Early CFLs were expensive and produced a low-quality light.

Semiconductors and the development of the LED

The modern LED light has origins as far back as 1907, when English engineer Henry Joseph Round (1881–1966) discovered that certain substances give off light when an electric current is applied. Several other scientists repeated Round's experiments, including Georges Destriau (1903–1960), who came up with the term "electroluminescence" to describe the way the metallic compound zinc sulfide releases light when exposed to electricity.

Little practical purpose was found for these discoveries until the mid-twentieth century, when the development of the computer industry led to the invention of transistors. Transistors regulate and control electric current through the use of semiconductors. When layers of different semiconductor materials are placed next to each other, they can be used to control the flow of electricity.

In 1961 American engineer James R. Biard (1931–) and inventor Gary Pittman (1930–2013) patented a diode that used semiconductor technology to produce invisible infrared light. The following year American engineer Nick Holonyak Jr. (1928–) created the first LED to give off visible light. Holonyak marketed a small red LED light that could perform functions inside a computer. The introduction of new semiconductor materials allowed the creation of green, yellow, and orange LEDs by the 1970s. However, LEDs were still largely limited to use inside computers and similar devices until the turn of the twenty-first century. In the 1990s Japanese physicist Shuji Nakamura (1954–) developed blue and white LEDs, leading to the introduction of LED for backlighting computer screens and televisions, as well as for use in traffic signals and flashlights.

In 2000 the U.S. government began encouraging the development of an LED bulb practical for popular use. In 2011 Philips Lighting North America won a government-sponsored competition with a 60-watt LED bulb. While the earliest LED bulbs were very expensive (some costing as much as $70 each), they have steadily decreased in price after 2008, while using almost seven times less electricity than conventional incandescent lights and avoiding the toxic disposal problems of CFLs.

A worker prepares an LED bulb housing for assembly at a Lumitec factory in Delray Beach, Florida. © MARK ELIAS/ BLOOMBERG/GETTY IMAGES

Raw materials

The most important raw material necessary for constructing an LED bulb is the semiconductor. It stimulates and controls the conversion of electricity into light. The most common semiconductors used in LED technology are compounds of the element gallium. A silver-colored metal that melts at approximately 100 degrees Fahrenheit (38 degrees Celsius), pure gallium is mainly used in thermometers. Gallium is most often found in combination with other elements, and it is the crystalline compounds gallium arsenide (GaAs), gallium phosphide (GaP), and gallium arsenide phosphide (GaAsP) that are commonly used in LED manufacture. These compounds are plentiful, in part because they are byproducts of the industrial processes that produce aluminum, copper, lead, and zinc.

Other chemicals are added to the semiconductor in small amounts both to stimulate electrical activity and to affect the color of the resulting light. These substances include zinc, nitrogen, silicon, aluminum, and tellurium.

How Everyday Products Are Made

Design

The basic components of an LED lightbulb are one or more LED chips with layers of semiconductor material attached to a circuit board; a heat sink, designed to spread the heat generated by the LED; a power supply, or driver, which converts the alternating current used by most household wiring to the lower-voltage direct power needed to power the LED; and a housing, usually made of glass, plastic, and metal.

The design of LED bulbs varies widely, as manufacturers have tried to create replacements for commonly used lightbulbs. Standard LEDs imitate the traditional shape of an incandescent bulb and have sockets to fit most light fixtures. LED bulbs are also made in shapes that are similar to specialty bulbs, such as round globes or teardrop bulbs for chandeliers. Reflector LEDs have the shape and appearance of a spotlight bulb, with a broad flat face narrowing to a standard socket. These bulbs have reflective surfaces behind the light source to produce a more powerful beam for outdoor purposes. LEDs have also been designed in the long tube shape used in fluorescent fixtures. Small LED bulbs may be placed in long strips to provide decorative accents or safety lighting for stairs and hallways.

The first generation of LED bulbs have a significantly different look than traditional bulbs. In order to provide a power supply and a heat sink suitable to cool the bulb as it works, these older LEDs have heavy plastic or metal bases with vents for air to escape. Although they produce far less heat than incandescent bulbs, LEDs do produce heat that could damage the interior of the bulb. Some large LED arrays require fans to remove the heat generated by the action of the bulbs' semiconductors. Even the glass part of many early LED bulbs have a different appearance from a standard lightbulb due to the arrangement of LED chips, which replace the traditional thin filament.

As research and development continues, manufacturers change and improve bulb design to more closely match the look of a standard bulb. Some designs have replaced flat chip arrangements with a tower design, while others have produced chains of tiny chips that look like a thick filament. The multinational corporation Cree Lighting produced an all-glass bulb in 2013 by introducing advances in heat sink design that removed plastic bases in favor of a process that circulates air through small vents in the top and bottom of the bulb. The following year Cree replaced the glass with lightweight clear plastic. In 2014 UgetLight in Beijing, China, introduced a sealed glass bulb with a liquid cooling system.

Safety

Although LED lights are considered safe and nontoxic, they do contain some dangerous substances. Red LEDs have been found to contain unsafe amounts of lead, and many white LEDs contain nickel, which causes allergic reactions in a significant number of people. Other materials used in LED construction, such as arsenic and copper, may be toxic to individuals and to the environment. Though the amount of these toxins found in one LED lightbulb is very small, they may present a hazard as increasing numbers of used bulbs enter landfills. In addition, if bulbs break, they can release toxic substances into the air. Protective gloves and a face mask should be worn when handling broken LED bulbs.

Some medical studies suggest that LED light, especially in the color blue, may be harmful to the eyes and skin and may cause health

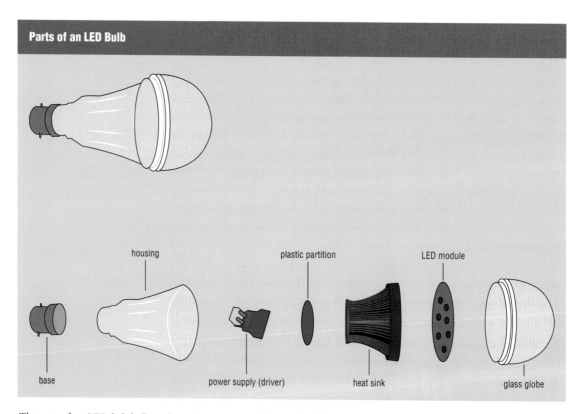

Parts of an LED Bulb

housing

plastic partition

LED module

base

power supply (driver)

heat sink

glass globe

The parts of an LED lightbulb work together to produce high-quality light. ILLUSTRATION BY LUMINA DATAMATICS LTD. © 2015 CENGAGE LEARNING

How Everyday Products Are Made

problems such as skin cancer. It is not safe to look directly into a bright LED light of any color.

The manufacturing process

Because of their reliance on semiconductor technology, the processes used in manufacturing LED bulbs is similar to those used to build motherboards, which contain the major circuits of a computer, and solar cells, which convert sunlight to electric power. The construction and use of LED is a growing industry, and the manufacturing process is quickly changing as new procedures are introduced to improve both factory technology and the efficiency of the finished product.

1 The first step in building an LED bulb is the creation of the semiconductor chip. A semiconductor material such as gallium arsenide is heated until it turns to vapor. The type of semiconductor used will determine the color of the light produced by the LED. A small piece of crystal, or seed, of the same compound is suspended in the melting pot. As the heated vapor begins to cool, it is deposited on the seed, forming a larger cylindrical crystal in the same shape. This cylinder, called an ingot, is about 4 inches (10 centimeters) in diameter.

2 Once it is removed from the pot, the ingot is sliced into thin wafers that are about .01 inch (.03 centimeter), or slightly thicker than two sheets of paper. These wafers are polished to a smooth surface to produce light at the maximum efficiency. They are then cleaned in a chemical bath and dried.

3 Next, specific contaminants (harmful substances that make something unfit for use) are added to the surface of the wafers in a process called doping to create the desired chemical reaction when an electric current is applied to the semiconductor. These materials may also be used to control the color of the LED light. Doping contaminants include compounds such as indium, gallium, and nitrogen, which are baked or melted onto the semiconductor wafer.

4 In order for the prepared wafer to conduct electricity, a specially designed grid of metal electrical contacts is applied and baked on at high temperatures. Wafers are then placed in a cutting machine, where they are separated into 60,000 to 100,000 tiny chips, called dies. The dies are the central light-producing element of the LED bulb.

Think about It!

Some companies have begun to sell wearable LED lights to add sparkle and individuality to personal fashion. A number of performers use LED strips to create robotic animation effects when dancing onstage in dim light. Korean designer and artist Soomi Park (1986–) has even invented LED eyelashes, a battery-operated strip of tiny LED bulbs placed below the eye and operated by a motion-sensor switch that turns them on and off with the motion of the wearer's head. Can you imagine an LED fashion that would appeal to you? What would it be? Where would you wear it?

5 LED bulbs are generally built on manual assembly lines. Workers glue LED dies into specially cast metal frames to form modules and solder electrical gold wires to the metal grid on each die.

6 Modules are glued into the heat sink, which is an aluminum cup produced by forcing molten metal into a form. The size and shape of the heat sink is determined by the design of the bulb and the number of LED dies that it uses. The LED modules are attached to the heat sink with a thermal adhesive, which transmits heat easily while serving as an electrical insulator. A power supply, or driver, which controls the electric current entering the bulb, is generally placed in a lower area at the back of the heat sink, with wires running to the LED modules.

7 The modules, heat sink, and power supply are sealed in a shell of plastic or metal and glass. A clear glass globe covers the LED modules and is attached by screws to a vented plastic or metal base. This protects the heat sink while allowing warm air to escape the bulb. A standard screw-in socket is wired to the power supply and attached to the base of the bulb.

Byproducts

Along with small amounts of toxic waste from the heavy metals used in the semiconductor assembly, the major byproducts of the production of LED bulbs come from the use of aluminum heat sinks. The mining and processing of aluminum creates a number of dangerous byproducts, such as sulfuric acid, which may be dangerous to the environment as well as to workers in processing plants.

Quality control

Government agencies that monitor energy efficiency and protect the rights of consumers require high standards of quality in LED manufacture. The U.S. Environmental Protection Agency's Energy Star program has set efficiency guidelines for LED bulbs. The U.S. Department of Energy's LED Lighting Facts Label program was launched in 2008 to make sure that claims made by LED producers are truthful and accurate.

WORDS TO KNOW

Diode: An electronic device that uses a semiconductor to control the flow of an electric current.

Electroluminescence: A phenomenon in which a substance gives off light when exposed to an electric current or field.

Gallium: A silver-colored element with a low melting point.

Heat sink: A mechanism that cools a device by driving away the heat.

Incandescent: Giving off light when heated.

Semiconductor: A substance that exhibits special properties when exposed to electricity, conducting it at high temperatures and resisting it at lower temperatures.

Transistor: A device that regulates and controls electric current through the use of semiconductors.

Other programs include Hong Kong's Energy Efficiency Labelling Scheme and the United Kingdom's Energy Savings Trust.

In order to be certified by the agencies listed above, manufacturers of LED bulbs must put their products through many complex testing procedures. Light-measuring machines called goniophotometers are used to test the angle and distribution of the light. Spectroradiometers measure color uniformity, output, brightness, and glare. Lights are placed in a testing chamber called an integrated sphere to test efficiency in a controlled environment. "Life tests" are given to determine how long LED bulbs will continue to provide high-quality light.

Ongoing innovations

As scientists and engineers have developed energy sources that use up fewer fossil fuels and have fewer negative impacts on the environment, the field of and uses for LED lighting has grown rapidly. Cities around the world have converted to LED street lighting, and LED video screens have become the standard. Organic light-emitting diodes (OLEDs), first developed in the late 1900s, use organic materials in their semiconductors. OLEDs have allowed for the creation of light-emitting polymers (LEPs), which are flexible LEDs that can be shaped into irregular forms for a number of unique uses, from accent lighting in the home to adding a strip of brightness to car dashboards and trunks. LiFi technology, introduced in the early 2000s, uses LED light to transmit information. TerraLUX, a lighting development company in Colorado, has

Teen Inventors and LED

Because the development of LED is a growing technology, it has been attractive to young minds. A number of young adults have come up with original and highly practical uses for LED bulbs. In 2013, at the age of fifteen, Canadian Ann Makosinski became a winner at the Google Science Fair with her invention of an LED flashlight powered by the heat of the hand holding it. In 2015 Adam Gibbs and Nick Bongi, two Massachusetts teenagers, were inspired by their love of night fishing to create the FISHinc. ProGlo+ Tackle System, a fishing tackle box with an LED tube light in the lid. The LED is powerful enough to light the contents of the box and act as an emergency cell phone charger. In 2012 thirteen-year-old Richard Turere, who lives with his family on a ranch in Kenya, designed an LED lighting system using bulbs from broken flashlights and a discarded automobile battery to deter lions from preying on livestock.

introduced responsive LED lightbulbs that can sense temperature and atmosphere. These lights can turn on automatically when people enter a room, control heating and cooling systems to a certain temperature, and warn of smoke or carbon monoxide in the air.

Though its long-term effects may not be known for decades, LED bulbs offer a number of advantages over other modern lighting technologies. These include cooler operation, less energy use, smaller amounts of toxic materials, and a much longer life that lowers cost over time.

For more information

BOOKS

Johnstone, Bob. *Brilliant!: Shuji Nakamura and the Revolution in Lighting Technology.* Amherst, NY: Prometheus Books, 2015.

PERIODICALS

Biello, David. "LED There Be Light." *Scientific American* (March 18, 2009). Available online at http://www.scientificamerican.com/article/led-there-be-light/ (accessed June 1, 2015).

"Lightbulb Frenzy in the 21st Century." *Scientific American* (January 2, 2014). Available online at http://www.scientificamerican.com/report/lightbulb-frenzy-in-the-21st-century-2/ (accessed June 1, 2015).

White, Martha C. "Light Switch: Why You'll Start Using LED Bulbs This Year." *Time* (April 25, 2013). Available online at http://business.time.com/2013/04/25/light-switch-why-youll-start-using-led-bulbs-this-year/ (accessed June 1, 2015).

WEBSITES

"The History of the Light Bulb." U.S. Department of Energy. http://energy.gov/articles/history-light-bulb (accessed June 1, 2015).

"LEDs and OLEDs." Edison Tech Center. http://www.edisontechcenter.org/LED.html (accessed June 1, 2015).

Lip Balm

1. Some lip balm manufacterers choose to emphasize the protective benefits of their product, while others choose to focus on its value as a cosmetic. How do you think this choice affects the design and manufacturing of lip balm?

2. Why do you think lip balm ingredients are melted separately before they are mixed? What do you think would happen if the ingredients were mixed before they were melted?

Lip balm is a waxy, semisolid ointment used to soothe dry and cracked lips. It is usually packaged and sold in a hard plastic, but it is also available in flat tins, round jars, and squeezable tubes. Lip balm comes in many flavors, colors, and scents. It is available at drugstores, supermarkets, hair salons, and other locations.

Lip balm dates to 40 BCE, when ancient Egyptians made a type of lip treatment with beeswax, olive oil, and animal fats. Centuries later, in the early 1880s, physician Charles Browne Fleet (1843–1916) created a lip balm shaped like a candle and wrapped in tinfoil. In 1912 entrepreneur John Morton bought the recipe from Fleet and developed it into the leading lip balm brand ChapStick. With ChapStick's success, other companies began to make lip balm, sometimes adding ingredients with medicinal, softening, or soothing qualities. Carmex, another early leading brand of lip balm, was created in 1936 by Alfred Woelbing (1901–2001).

Lip balm is valued because it seals moisture in the lips and protects them from cold temperatures, wind, dry air, and other environmental

factors that can have a drying effect. Unlike other areas of the body, lips have no oil glands, so they get dry quickly. Additionally, the skin of the lips is very thin, which means they can easily be damaged by sun or wind and makes them open to certain bacteria. Lip balm provides a thin protective layer that can keep lips from being damaged. It can also treat dry or cracked lips and has been used to treat cold sores, which are inflamed blisters near the mouth caused by infection from a virus.

The invention and marketing of ChapStick

Lip balm is usually packaged and sold in a hard plastic. It provides a thin protective layer that can keep lips from being damaged. © NAZZU/ SHUTTERSTOCK.COM

Fleet, a pharmacist from Lynchburg, Virginia, invented what he called "chap stick" in the 1880s. The word "chap" means a crack, sore, or roughness on the skin. When sales of his new product did not meet his expectations, Fleet sold the recipe to fellow Lynchburg resident Morton in 1912 for five dollars. Morton and his wife made the lip balm in their kitchen. Instead of wrapping the balm in tinfoil, as Fleet had, the Mortons cut the mixture into sticks that looked like pink candles and sold their product in tubes. They used the sales profits to found the Morton Manufacturing Company.

In 1936 commercial artist Frank Wright Jr. (1912–2008) designed the ChapStick logo (the name is written in cursive as one word with a capital "C" and a capital "S"), which as of 2015 was still in use. In the early 1960s, the ChapStick brand was purchased by the A. H. Robins Company, which added new products, including ChapStick sunblock and ChapStick petroleum jelly. Robins sold the ChapStick brand to American Home Products in 1988. In 2009 ChapStick was purchased by Pfizer, an international pharmaceutical company.

Carmex and other lip balms

Wisconsin native Woelbing created Carmex in 1936 to treat his cold sores. After discovering a formula that worked, he formed Carma

How Everyday Products Are Made

Laboratories in 1937 and began making the medicated lip balm in his kitchen. Woelbing poured the finished product into small glass jars with yellow tin lids and sold them out of the trunk of his car. He also visited pharmacies in person, giving them a dozen jars for free along with an order form. Sales grew steadily, and in 1957 Woelbing moved operations from his kitchen to a facility in Milwaukee, Wisconsin. In the early 1970s Woelbing stopped making personal sales calls, having established markets throughout Wisconsin, Illinois, and Indiana. In 1973 his son Don joined the business and began assembly-line production. Sales grew, and Carma Laboratories moved to Franklin, Wisconsin, which, as of 2015, remained its headquarters. By 2008 Carmex had sold 1 billion jars of lip balm.

Other notable companies that produce lip balm include Blistex, which was founded in 1947 by Charles Arch (1911–1990) and is still run by the Arch family, and Burt's Bees, a subsidiary (a company that is owned by a larger company) of Clorox. Burt's Bees was founded in Dover-Foxcroft, Maine, in 1984 by Roxanne Quimby (1950–) and Burt Shavitz (1935–2015). Some companies target their lip balm to specific groups. For example, Softlips, a lip balm made by the Mentholatum Company, aims its sales at young adult women. Autumn Harp, which is based in Burlington, Vermont, and uses only organic products in its cosmetics, tries to reach people who are concerned with protecting the environment.

Concerns about the side effects of lip balm

By the early twenty-first century, lip balm sales in the United States were more than $300 million a year. However, many consumers questioned whether lip balm actually moisturized lips, and some believed that the substance was harmful. Overuse of certain lip balms may cause an increase in chapping. Some lip balms contain phenol, menthol, or salicylic acid, ingredients that cause protective layers of dead skin to peel off the lips, exposing them to environmental factors that cause chapping. These ingredients also cause a pleasurable tingling sensation on the lips, which in turn leads many people to reapply lip balm often. This can make the dryness and cracking worse. Alum, an ingredient that is used in some lip balms to treat cold sores, can also dry and crack lips.

Some people have claimed that lip balm is addictive, meaning that people are so attached to it that they are unable to stop using it. However, most dermatologists (doctors who treat skin conditions) agree that lip balm

does not contain substances known to cause physical addiction. Continuous reapplication of lip balm, however, may indicate a psychological, or mental, addiction. Some groups have also raised concerns that lip balm can cause cancer, but there is no proof that lip balms contain carcinogens (substances known to cause cancer). It is worth noting that most lip balms do not contain ingredients that provide UV protection (protection from ultraviolet, or UV, light from the sun), so using lip balm instead of sunscreen can leave the lips exposed to the harmful effects of UV rays.

Raw materials

Lip balm formulas vary, but almost all brands use a base, or main ingredient, of petroleum jelly, beeswax, cocoa butter, camphor, lanolin, and cetyl alcohol. Most lip balms include some type of oil, most commonly olive, coconut, or castor oil. Some balms are flavored with ingredients such as vanilla, essential oils like tangerine, or herbs such as mint or rosemary.

Beeswax has been an ingredient in the making of lip balm since 40 BCE, when ancient Egyptians made a type of lip treatment with beeswax, olive oil, and animal fats. © MATIN/ SHUTTERSTOCK.COM

Design

Most lip balms come in hard tubes about 1.5 inches (3.8 centimeters) long with a 0.5 inch (1.3 centimeter) diameter. The small size makes the lip balm easy to hold and carry in a pocket or purse. Tubes are made of plastic and have a cap on the top and an adjustment knob on the bottom. As the lip balm is used, the knob is turned and more lip balm is pushed up through the tube. Lip balm is also available in small tins or jars and in squeezable tubes. The packages are usually decorated with different colors and patterns. Some companies design their packages for particular groups of customers. The packages of Eco Lips, for example, have symbols of different charitable causes, such as pink ribbons to support breast cancer awareness.

Safety

Some people use so much lip balm that a thick, waxy layer is created that can trap bacteria and cause lips to swell. People can develop contact dermatitis, a skin condition with irritated, swollen, cracked, and

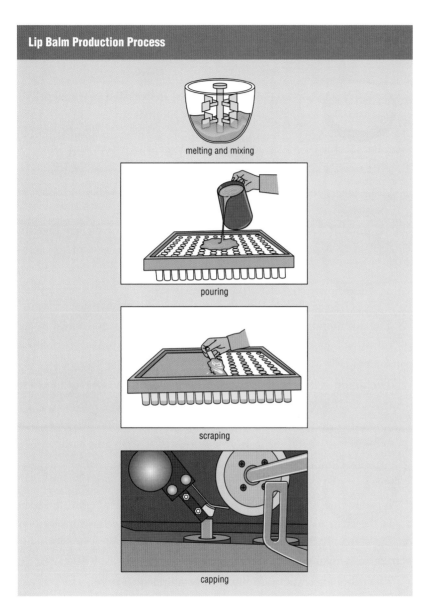

Lip Balm Production Process

melting and mixing

pouring

scraping

capping

After the ingredients for lip balm are melted in steel or ceramic containers, the liquid is poured into tubes. A capper machine puts the caps on the tubes. ILLUSTRATION BY LUMINA DATAMATICS LTD. © 2015 CENGAGE LEARNING

painful lips, or angular cheilitis, an inflammation of the corner of the mouth.

The manufacturing process

While most of the steps are now performed by machine, the most common form of lip balm, sold in hard plastic tubes, has the same basic process that the Mortons used in 1912. The steps involve melting and

Think about It!

Because lips can easily get chapped during cold weather, athletes who participate in winter sports have often been chosen as spokespeople for lip balms. In the 1970s model and Olympic skier Suzanne "Suzy" Chaffee (1946–) starred in a series of commercials for the product in which she told viewers to "call me Suzy Chap-Stick." The name stuck. If you were going to be a spokesperson for a product, what would it be? Would you like it if people started calling you by the product's name? Why or why not?

mixing the ingredients, pouring the mixture into tubes, and applying a label to the outside of the tubes.

1 Raw ingredients are weighed in batches. Different types of ingredients are melted separately in steel or ceramic containers. One mixture may consist of the oils used, such as olive oil, while another mixture contains the fatty or waxy material, such as cocoa butter or beeswax.

2 The different containers of melted ingredients are mixed together. Pigments (substances used to create different colors), flavorings, herbs, or other additives are added to the combined melted ingredients.

3 The hot liquid is stirred and mixed well, sometimes for hours, to get rid of any air bubbles and make sure that the texture and color are consistent.

4 The liquid is poured into tubes. Depending on the type of machine used, there may be as many as 2,400 tubes filled per hour.

5 The tubes go through a series of heating and cooling machines that help prevent the lip balm from cracking as it cools and hardens.

6 After the liquid has cooled and hardened, any extra balm is scraped away.

7 A capper machine puts the caps on the tubes. Machines put the labels in the right place on the tubes before labeling devices seal the labels on the tubes. Packaging methods vary greatly depending on what the particular company wants the label to look like.

8 The tubes are sorted into boxes to be shipped to stores.

Quality control

The Food and Drug Administration (FDA), the government agency responsible for making sure cosmetics (a product category that includes creams, lotions, and powders used on the skin) are safe and labeled properly, has strict rules for quality control for lip balm because it can be eaten or swallowed (in this case, usually accidentally) like a food. There are tests for all the ingredients (raw materials, fragrances, packaging) and

WORDS TO KNOW

Alum: An aluminum compound commonly used in making health products.

Carcinogens: A substance known to cause cancer.

Dermatologist: A doctor who specializes in the study of skin and skin diseases.

Ointment: A substance that is rubbed on the skin to help heal wounds and increase comfort.

Pigment: A substance that gives color to animals and plants or to another substance.

Post-consumer waste: Materials that people have thrown away. Post-consumer waste is often recycled into new materials.

for the manufacturing processes to make sure they meet FDA requirements and that the lip balm does not get contaminated. Manufacturers are required to save and store samples of every batch at room temperature for the life of the product. The color of lip balm is controlled with colorimetric equipment (machines that determine how much of each color should be added).

The continuing evolution of lip balm

Over time lip balm has gone through hundreds of changes in raw ingredients, colors, fragrances, and packaging. In the early twenty-first century, Carmex added flavors like pomegranate and expanded into other types of products, such as an ointment to help ease dry skin. Companies created new flavors, such as lavender and dark chocolate, and new colors, from sheer bronze to bright purple. Environmentally friendly companies such as Sweet Leaf Bath use recyclable containers made from post-consumer waste (materials that people have thrown away). Evolution of Smooth, or EOS, lip balm is made from 95 percent organic materials and is packaged in brightly colored globes that have appeared in music videos. Epic Blend makes a gluten-free lip balm for people who are sensitive to gluten, a substance found in grains such as wheat.

For more information

BOOKS

Romanowski, Perry. *Can You Get Hooked on Lip Balm?: Top Cosmetic Scientists Answer Your Questions about the Lotions, Potions, and Other Beauty Products You Use Every Day.* New York: Harlequin, 2011.

Try This!

Make your own lip balm

There are many lip balm recipes online, including recipes for traditional flavors, such as peppermint or coconut, and recipes for newer flavors, such as hemp and honey or coconut rose. Below is a recipe for a basic lip balm. Most ingredients can be found at craft stores or health food stores.

You will need:

- ¼ cup beeswax
- ⅛ cup coconut oil
- ⅛ cup shea butter
- 1 teaspoon vanilla, coconut, or almond extract
- 1 teaspoon sweet almond oil
- ¼ cup fresh or dried rose petals, other flowers, or herbs (optional)
- Lipstick shavings to add color (optional)
- Small saucepan
- Empty store-bought lip balm containers or small glass or plastic containers with lids

Directions:

1. Put all ingredients in saucepan and heat on low until everything is melted. Mix well.

2. If using flower petals, you can strain them out or leave them in. Add lipstick shavings if you want color (make sure shavings melt and are mixed well).

3. Pour into containers and let cool until hard. If you use store-bought lip balm, save the containers when they are finished and use them for your homemade balm. Otherwise, transfer the lip balm into small containers.

PERIODICALS

Atkinson, Nathalie. "Secret Gloss: A Brief History of Lip Balm, from Earwax to Clorox." *National Post* (June 12, 2014). Available online at http://news.nationalpost.com/arts/movies/secret-gloss-a-brief-history-of-lip-balm-from-earwax-to-clorox (accessed June 25, 2015).

Ferrier, Morwenna. "Are You a Lip Balm Addict?" *Guardian* (January 2, 2015). Available online at http://www.theguardian.com/fashion/fashion-blog/2015/jan/02/are-you-a-lip-balm-addict (accessed June 25, 2015).

WEBSITES

"15 Best Balms to Banish Chapped Lips." *Seventeen.* http://www.seventeen.com/beauty/advice/g839/best-winter-lip-balm/?slide=2 (accessed June 25, 2015).

Carmex. https://mycarmex.com/ (accessed June 25, 2015).

ChapStick. http://www.chapstick.com/ (accessed June 25, 2015).

Memory Foam

Memory foam is a soft plastic foam that can absorb high energy and impact. Best known to consumers for its use in mattresses and pillows, memory foam takes on the shape of a user's body and weight. It also adjusts its shape with movement. Memory foam is so named because it keeps an outline of its user even after he or she stops using it. After a short time, the foam returns to its original state, ready to react to the next person who uses it.

Memory foam was first developed by an aeronautical engineer at the National Aeronautics and Space Administration (NASA) as a way to keep astronauts safe during voyages away from Earth. Over time companies discovered that memory foam was also a good way to protect football players and other athletes from impact on the field, and consumers found it to be a comfortable alternative to traditional spring mattresses. As its popularity grew, memory foam was used in a wide range of items, including pillows, bath mats, mousepads, and even artificial limbs. By the early twenty-first century, more than 1.3 billion pounds (589.7 million kilograms) of memory foam was used each year in the United States.

Memory foam in household products such as mattresses and pillows provides comfort and support by distributing weight and pressure as it molds to the user's body. In cars, trucks, motorcycles, and airplane seats, memory foam makes traveling more comfortable and absorbs shock well in an accident. The military uses it for better protection in bulletproof vests and for ejection seats in military airplanes. Race car drivers and football players use memory foam in their helmets, and it is also used for packing material, providing particularly good protection for shipping fragile items.

An early discovery

Memory foam's origins can be traced to the work of German chemist Otto Bayer (1902–1982). In 1937 Bayer and his coworkers began working with polymers, substances whose molecular structure consists of a large number of similar units bonded together. Bayer believed that by mixing chemicals together in small quantities, he could create a dry foam. In 1941, after many experiments, Bayer produced polyurethane foam, or foam rubber, the basis for many later inventions, including memory foam.

Polyurethane foam was first manufactured for commercial use in the 1950s. In 1965 nurses at Lankenau Hospital in Pennsylvania tested a type of polyurethane foam for patients who spent long hours in hospital beds. These patients sometimes developed bedsores due to the pressure of the mattress on their bodies. The nurses found that placing a polyurethane foam pad on the bed prevented bedsores by gently reacting to the pressure of the patient's body on the bed.

Memory foam is so named because it keeps an outline of its user even after he or she stops using it. It is a common material in mattresses and pillows. © ISTOCK.COM/ EUROBANKS

From outer space to family homes

The product that came to be known as memory foam was invented in the 1960s by Charles A. Yost (1933–2005), an aeronautical engineer. Yost initially developed a polyurethane foam for cushions for Apollo space program astronauts. The cushioning was designed to help keep astronauts safe and comfortable during liftoff and return to Earth, when there is extreme pressure, known as g-force (gravity force), in the rocket. NASA was happy with

Yost's work and hired him to find a material that would improve the survival rate in airplane crashes. The result, a type of memory foam, was used in the manufacture of airplane seats. Its ability to absorb shock was useful in the event of a crash, and the support and softness the foam provided made seats more comfortable, especially for long flights. This first material was called "slow, spring back foam."

In 1969 Yost formed Dynamic Systems to sell a new version of the product that he had renamed temper foam. In 1974 he sold the formula for temper foam to Beckton-Dickinson, a medical technology company that wanted to use it to line football helmets. A few years later, Yost built a manufacturing facility for an improved version, called memory foam, in Leicester, North Carolina. Over the decades that followed, Dynamic Systems began to manufacture new types of memory foam that were more environmentally friendly and not as sensitive to temperature than the original temper foam. Major worldwide production took off in the 1980s. Among the best-known early manufacturers of memory foam was Fagerdala World Foams of Sweden, which produced the Tempur-Pedic Swedish Mattress. The first memory foam mattresses were very expensive, but over time the price came down, making them more affordable for the average family.

The original formula for memory foam has been changed over time to make it less sensitive to temperature, more resilient, more environmentally friendly, and less hazardous for manufacturers and consumers. New formulas have led to new uses. For example, in 2009 scientists at Northwestern University and Boise State University created a memory foam that could change shape when exposed to a magnetic field. This new material was also cheaper to make than similar products. Its applications include everything from surgical tools and car engines to printers and submarine sonar devices.

Polyurethane foam, a dry plastic foam, is the basis for memory foam. © CHARLES D WINTERS/GETTY IMAGES

Raw materials

The major components of memory foam are water; polyol, a type of alcohol with specific patterns of hydrogen and oxygen atoms; and diisocyanate, a chemical made of carbon, hydrogen, nitrogen, and oxygen.

Manufacturers may add other chemicals to create memory foam designed for specific uses. For example, fire-retardant (able to slow down the advance of fire) additives are used in the manufacture of shock-absorbing foam inserts for race cars because of the high risk of fire if there is an accident. Some manufacturers use non–memory foam substances, such as calcium carbonate, as fillers to reduce the cost of manufacturing memory foam. This allows them to offer consumers a lower, more competitive price.

Design

Memory foam can be designed to have more or less flexibility and softness. The firmness of the foam is measured by the Indentation Force Reflection (IFD) or the Indentation Load Deflection (ILD). The IFD/IFL shows how much support the foam has by measuring how many pounds it takes to indent a 4-inch-thick (10-centimeter-thick) piece of foam by 25 or 65 percent. The better the IFD/IFL, the more comfortable a person will feel if he or she is sleeping, sitting, or walking on a product made with memory foam.

Memory foam is also designed to be soft. The softness of the foam is measured by its density. Density is the mass of a substance in a given space. The greater the density of memory foam, the tighter its molecules are packed. The more chemicals used in the manufacturing process, the greater the memory foam's density. Fillers are sometimes used to increase density. However, memory foam products made with fillers are generally less comfortable and tend to break down more quickly than those made without them.

Safety

The U.S. Environmental Protection Agency (EPA), a government agency that protects human health and the environment, has classified some of the chemicals used in making memory foam as toxic. These include methylenedianiline (MDA) and vinylidine chloride, both of which are skin and eye irritants and are thought to cause cancer. Use of these chemicals presents a potential health hazard to the workers who make memory foam products.

The manufacture of memory foam can also present a safety hazard, as it produces a chemical reaction that gives off high heat. The liquid used to make the foam can reach temperatures of 140 degrees Fahrenheit (60 degrees Celsius) or higher. The heat reaction makes manufacturing foam dangerous. There is a high risk of explosions, fire, or the release of toxic gases. Manufacturers must find ways to cool the equipment to avoid accidents and health and environmental hazards.

Memory foam is highly flammable as a finished product and thus should not be placed near flames, cigarettes, or sources of intense heat, such as space heaters. Often manufacturers add chemicals to make memory foam flame retardant. Mattresses and upholstered furniture, for example, are required by law to be flame retardant. However, some scientists believe that polybrominated diphenyl ethers (PBDEs), a common flame retardant used in memory foam mattresses, negatively affects brain development. The European Union has banned PBDEs due to safety concerns.

Another possible hazard associated with memory foam are chemical smells, called volatile organic compounds, or VOCs. VOCs can be dangerous to people's health. Because different types of foams can have different amounts or kinds of VOCs, safety concerns differ by product. The term "off-gassing" is used to describe the process by which odors are released in memory foam. Off-gassing in memory foam is similar to the off-gassing present in a newly painted room. These odors can be particularly irritating to people sensitive to chemicals. In

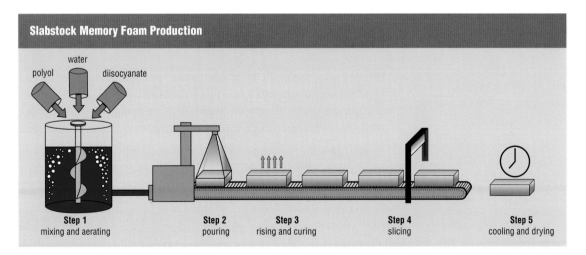

Slabstock Memory Foam Production

water
polyol   diisocyanate

Step 1
mixing and aerating

Step 2
pouring

Step 3
rising and curing

Step 4
slicing

Step 5
cooling and drying

To manufacture memory foam, chemicals are put into a mixer until they reach the correct consistency and then poured into molds. After additional processing, the mixture is sliced, cooled, and dried. ILLUSTRATION BY LUMINA DATAMATICS LTD. © 2015 CENGAGE LEARNING

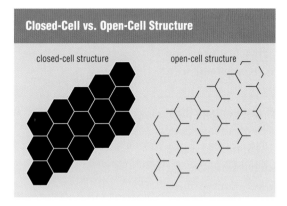

Closed-Cell vs. Open-Cell Structure

closed-cell structure   open-cell structure

In closed-cell foams, gases from the manufacturing process are trapped within the foam. Open-cell foams, such as memory foam, have open spaces that fill with the air around them, making them more springy. ILLUSTRATION BY LUMINA DATAMATICS LTD.
© 2015 CENGAGE LEARNING

experiments, VOCs have negatively affected the lungs of mice. As a result, anyone purchasing a new memory foam mattress should allow the room to air out until the odor goes away. This usually takes several days.

The manufacturing process

Although there is some variation in chemicals or methods for making memory foam, the basic manufacturing process is the same. There are two primary means of shaping the resulting memory foam: slabstock and molding. In the slabstock process, the chemical mixture is poured onto a plastic-lined moving conveyor belt where it expands to form a slab. Slabs are usually 2 to 4 feet high (0.6 to 1.2 meters high). After they cool the slabs are cut into "buns" and put away for 24 to 72 hours to set. The cured foam is then molded into different shapes depending on its intended use. When memory foam is shaped using the molding process, the chemical mixture is poured into a specifically shaped mold. The foam becomes the shape of the mold that is needed for a specific product, such as car cushioning.

1 The manufacturing process begins when water is mixed with specific amounts of two main chemicals, a polyol and a diisocyanate, in high-intensity mixers. When the water and chemicals are mixed together, a chemical reaction occurs, creating air bubbles. It takes about five minutes for the reaction to occur.

2 Any additional chemicals specific to the desired product, such as flame retardants or fillers, are added to the mixture. At this point the mixture is a liquid.

3 Air is stirred into the mixture, increasing the foam and resulting in a substance with the consistency of ice cream.

4 Depending on the process used, the foam is poured into molds or plastic liners, where it bubbles and expands.

5 Next, air is pumped out of the mixture, creating memory foam's open-cell structure. Unlike closed-cell foams, in which gases from the manufacturing process are trapped within the foam, open-cell foams such as memory foam have open spaces that fill with the air around them. The more air, the more springiness the material has. This springiness makes memory foam a good shock absorber.

6 The mixture is dried, cooled, and removed from the mold or plastic liner.

7 The foam is cleaned, dried, and inspected for quality.

Quality control

Manufacturers use many tests to measure the quality of memory foam. Flex or dynamic fatigue measures how long the foam can keep its original flexibility and softness. Foam samples are sometimes pressed thousands of times to see if they will maintain a good quality. Roller tear is a specific flex fatigue test in which a weight is rolled over a sample piece of foam from each direction as many as 25,000 times. Roller-tear testing is usually done for foam that gets a lot of use, such as carpet cushions or office furniture. Springiness or resilience is tested by dropping a steel ball onto a sample and seeing how high the ball bounces. Air-flow testing, which measures how quickly air flows through the foam, tests flexibility. The greater the air flow, the greater the flexibility. Foam is also tested to see how well it can resist tearing or shedding.

Quality control tests for combustibility, or how easily the foam will start a fire, are very important. Once memory foam catches on fire, it can burn very fast, creating high heat and potentially releasing poisonous fumes. Manufacturers, as well as wholesalers and retailers, have to be careful when storing or handling memory foam in bulk because of its high flammability. Depending on the purpose of the memory foam, manufacturers can add different fire-retardant chemicals, coatings, or fillers to make memory foam less flammable. No matter what the manufacturer adds, no memory foam is completely fireproof. It is always important to keep flames and space heaters away from anything made with memory foam.

Down on Earth and up in the sky

Memory foam was first developed for use in outer space, but its ability to withstand great force while retaining its softness has made it valuable on Earth as well. By the early twenty-first century, memory foam was

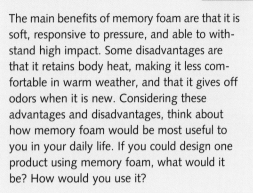

Think about It!

The main benefits of memory foam are that it is soft, responsive to pressure, and able to withstand high impact. Some disadvantages are that it retains body heat, making it less comfortable in warm weather, and that it gives off odors when it is new. Considering these advantages and disadvantages, think about how memory foam would be most useful to you in your daily life. If you could design one product using memory foam, what would it be? How would you use it?

WORDS TO KNOW

Density: The mass of a substance in a given space. The greater the substance's density, the tighter its molecules are packed in the space.

Flammable: Capable of being set on fire quickly.

Off-gassing: The potentially harmful release of chemicals from a substance.

Polymer: A substance whose molecular structure consists of a large number of similar units bonded together.

Polyurethane foam (foam rubber): A dry plastic foam.

Volatile organic compounds (VOCs): A group of chemicals that evaporate easily at room temperature and may pose health risks. VOCs do not always have an odor.

manufactured and sold by companies around the world. People from all walks of life, including athletes, medical workers, people with disabilities, and furniture makers, use it daily in some way. It is found in homes, offices, and hospitals and in cars, motorcycles, airplanes, and rocket ships.

As demand for memory foam products grows, so, too, does demand for safer manufacturing processes. Manufacturers have begun to experiment with different coatings to make mattresses flame retardant without using toxic chemicals. Some are using plant-based oils such as soy oil to make memory foam rather than relying on the more toxic petroleum-based oils typically used. Manufacturers have also experimented with adding gels to the foam to increase its softness and the speed with which it springs back after compression.

Memory foam also has a place in the world of art and design. It has been used to create new and innovatively designed furniture. Examples of such pieces have been displayed in the Museum of Modern Art and Cooper-Hewitt National Design Museum in New York City and the Smithsonian Institute in Washington, D.C.

For more information

BOOKS

Baker, David. *Scientific Inventions from Outer Space: Everyday Uses for NASA Technology.* New York: Random House, 2000.

"Polymers and Plastics." *Help Your Kids with Science: A Unique Step-by-Step Visual Guide.* New York: DK, 2014: 162–163.

NASA Inventions

Memory foam is just one of the many inventions that have been developed directly by the National Aeronautics and Space Administration (NASA) or that have been made possible by NASA research. For example, a water filter developed by NASA to make sure astronauts had access to clean drinking water in space was later adopted by many water treatment plants. NASA also developed insulation to keep instruments safe at high temperatures. These advances were later adopted by many construction contractors.

Many of NASA's technological innovations have helped drive advancement in the medical field. Infrared technology developed by NASA to measure the temperature of stars was later used to create ear thermometers, which register a patient's temperature much faster than traditional thermometers. NASA's work on sound and vibration sensors led to the development of the cochlear implant, a device that restores partial hearing to those who are deaf or severely hard of hearing. NASA has also funded research seeking to create better artificial limbs.

In a few cases, however, NASA has mistakenly been credited with inventions it did not develop. The most notable of these is Tang, an instant beverage that was invented by the General Foods Corporation in the late 1950s. It became forever associated with NASA in the 1960s when it was adopted by astronauts who used it to hide the bad taste of the drinking water on space missions. The use of Tang in space helped drive its popularity on Earth.

PERIODICALS

Cortesse, Amy. "The Sleep of Forgetfulness (and the Bed Remembers)." *New York Times* (September 12, 2004). Available online at http://www.nytimes.com/2004/09/12/business/yourmoney/12mattress.html?pagewanted=2 (accessed May 28, 2015).

Redd, Nola Taylor. "Space Tech That Makes the Super Bowl Possible." *Discovery News* (January 31, 2014). Available online at http://news.discovery.com/space/history-of-space/space-tech-that-makes-the-super-bowl-possible-140131.htm (accessed May 28, 2015).

Slater, Dashka. "How Dangerous Is Your Couch?" *New York Times* (September 6, 2012). Available online at http://nyti.ms/Q5qmdl (accessed May 28, 2015).

WEBSITES

"Forty-Year-Old Foam Springs Back with New Benefits." NASA Technical Reports Server. http://ntrs.nasa.gov/archive/nasa/casi.ntrs.nasa.gov/20060022025.pdf (accessed May 28, 2015).

"Memory Foam Mattress Information, Comparisons and Buying Tips." Memory Foam Mattress.org. http://www.memoryfoammattress.org/. (accessed May 28, 2015)

Polyurethane Foam Association (PFA). http://www.pfa.org/ (accessed May 28, 2015).

Mood Ring

Critical Thinking Questions

1. What connection does the author make between the "Me Generation" and the popularity of mood rings?

2. Based on information in the entry, does it matter if the ring band is made before or after the thermotropic crystals and stone? Why or why not?

A mood ring has a stone made of clear glass or quartz (a transparent mineral) that, according to manufacturers, changes color in response to the mood of the person wearing it. Blue, for example, could mean a person is calm, while yellow could mean excitement or tension. Mood rings are sold with a chart that explains which emotion each color represents. The bottom layer of a mood ring is a band of metal, silver or gold coating, or pure silver or gold, depending on the price. The stone contains thermotropic (temperature-sensitive) crystals or is placed on a thermotropic crystal strip. These crystals react to the body's temperature and change color, thus changing the color of the stone.

Mood rings became a worldwide fad in the mid-1970s, appearing on television and attracting such stars as singer and actor Barbra Streisand (1942–) and actor and philanthropist Paul Newman (1925–2008). Peppermint Patty, a character in the comic strip *Peanuts,* wore a mood ring. She once got so mad at the main character, Charlie Brown, that her mood ring exploded. Although sales of the mood ring declined after a few years, production continued, and other "mood jewelry," such as bracelets and necklaces, was created. Over the decades mood rings have experienced increases in popularity.

A mood ring from the era in which they were first introduced reflects the fashion of the time, featuring an oval stone placed in a metal setting.
© SHANNON WEST/ SHUTTERSTOCK.COM

Most mood rings are inexpensive novelty items and are especially popular with young girls. Although the "science" behind mood rings is not supported by scientific studies and the color shifts are affected by factors such as air temperature, body temperature often does change when mood changes. An excited person usually has more blood flow to the hands, making the fingers warm. This warmth might change the color of a mood ring to yellow.

Invention of the mood ring

According to one story, a jeweler in California named Marvin Wernick came up with the idea of the mood ring in the 1960s during an emergency room visit with a friend who was a doctor. The doctor used a thermotropic strip to take the patient's temperature; the thermotropic strip changed colors as it registered the temperature. Wernick recognized that he could use a small thermotropic strip to make a ring that would change colors when a person's body temperature changed slightly, but he did not get a patent for his idea.

The invention of the mood ring has often been credited to entrepreneurs Josh Reynolds and Maris Ambats of New York, who in 1975 began selling rings as a way for people to monitor their moods. The 1970s have been called the "Me Decade," a time when people were moving away from large social concerns such as the Vietnam War (1954–1975) and the civil rights movement (1955–1968) and beginning to think about how to improve themselves. At the time, Reynolds was teaching methods for reducing stress and, according to Kelly Boyer Sagert in *The 1970s* (2007), was searching for "ways in which we could all cut back, mellow out, check hypertension and learn to become aware of stresses and moods." Mood rings allowed wearers to become more aware of how they were feeling.

Some mood rings were produced as trinkets and sold for as little as $2, but more expensive gold versions were also made. Within a year of the mood ring's introduction, more than $15 million had been spent on them, and other companies were producing their own versions.

The chemistry of mood rings

Color is created when light is absorbed and reflected by molecules, the smallest parts of any physical matter. The color is determined by the position of the molecules. Molecules in a mood ring's crystals are sensitive to temperature. When there is even a slight change in temperature, the molecules in the crystals "twist" and change position. As the positions of the molecules change, light is reflected differently by the liquid crystals, affecting the color. A change in body temperature can cause the crystals in the mood ring to twist, thus changing color.

What color is your mood?

Mood rings are sold with a chart that identifies which moods each color reflects. The glass or quartz stones usually display as a greenish color when placed on the skin at its average temperature (82 degrees Fahrenheit, or 28 degrees Celsius). Sometimes a mood ring turns black when it is no longer working. Rings can be damaged by moisture, humidity, or cold temperatures. Higher-quality rings are sealed so moisture does not leak into the liquid crystals.

Raw materials

Depending on the quality and price of the mood ring, its band might be crafted of pure gold or silver; of sterling silver, which is usually 90 percent silver with another metal mixed in; or of brass, copper, or other inexpensive metal, which may be plated, or covered, with a thin layer of silver or gold. The stone is usually quartz or clear glass. Heat-sensitive liquid crystals are placed in the stone, or a strip of liquid crystals is attached to the band below the stone. Stones are sometimes sealed with a chemical agent to keep out moisture.

There are different types of natural and artificially made liquid crystals. Most rings have crystals made from cholesteryl benzoate, an organic substance with liquid crystal properties that can be taken out of plants or sheep's wool, for example.

Design

Mood rings come in many designs, reflecting differing preferences in fashion. Some have a metal band with a round or oval stone placed on the top. On

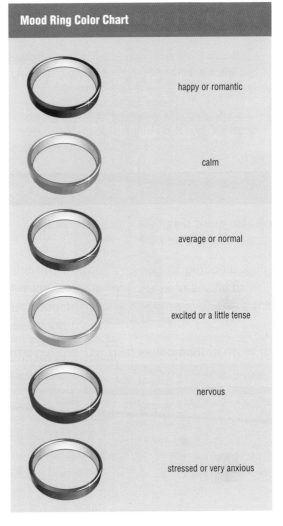

Mood Ring Color Chart

happy or romantic

calm

average or normal

excited or a little tense

nervous

stressed or very anxious

Most manufacturers use some version of the original mood ring color chart. ILLUSTRATION BY LUMINA DATAMATICS LTD. © 2015 CENGAGE LEARNING

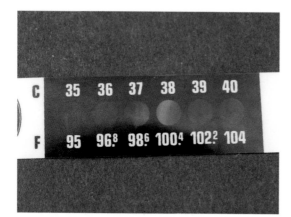

C	35	36	37	38	39	40
F	95	96.8	98.6	100.4	102.2	104

According to one account, the inspiration for a mood ring came from a thermotropic strip, which is sometimes used by doctors to take a patient's temperature. The strip changes colors as it registers the temperature. © MITZY/ SHUTTERSTOCK.COM

other rings, stones circle evenly around the band. Metal bands might be simple or fancy. Stones might display a solid color or a blend of colors.

Although many mood rings are sold in general discount and toy stores and on the Internet, there are also costly and extravagant mood rings made of precious metals and real gemstones. Some mood rings reflect a traditional style, such as art deco, and others have playful designs with stones set to look like butterflies or cats. Stones are sometimes imprinted with hearts, peace signs, or other images.

Safety

Mood rings are generally considered safe, but there have been concerns about the amount of lead in the metal of some styles. Exposure to high levels of lead can lead to serious health problems such as delayed growth and development, damage to the brain and nervous system, high blood pressure, and more. In 2006 the chain store Dollar Tree and the U.S. Consumer Product Safety Commission (CPSC) recalled 580,000 pieces of children's jewelry, including mood rings and mood necklaces, because of high lead content. A recall is a request to return a product because it is or might be dangerous. In 2010 D & D Distributing-Wholesale Inc. and CPSC recalled about 19,000 mood rings and 4,000 mood necklaces that were manufactured in China. Although there were no reported health problems, the commission ruled that children were at risk for lead poisoning.

The manufacturing process

The manufacturing process for a mood ring includes the production of the band and the addition of the thermotropic liquid crystals and the stone. Manufacturing is similar among different companies, but there are variations in materials and designs.

1 The production of the band is begun by placing metal scraps in a melting pot. The scraps are heated and melted together. The melting point of each metal is different. The melting point of silver, for example, is 961.8 degrees Fahrenheit (516.5 degrees Celsius).

2 The melted metal is poured into molds, usually rectangular in shape. While the metal is still hot, it is taken out of the mold and dipped into acid to clean it and then into water to cool it. The metal is then squeezed through a press many times to flatten and lengthen it.

3 The metal is heated again to help it maintain its shape and to keep it from getting weak and brittle. The metal is again squeezed through the press many times until it becomes a long piece.

4 The long piece is cut by a machine into small pieces that are worked into circular ring shapes. Rings that are custom made are stretched over a metal rod or bar and hammered into the desired shape.

5 Edges are smoothed out, and the rings are polished. Often the rings are again dipped in acid to remove extra material and then rewashed.

6 Thermotropic crystals are generally microencapsulated, or enclosed with a protective coating of tiny capsules, usually made of a polymer resin. Resin is a clear, liquid plastic product that hardens to form a thick, long-lasting coating. The diameter of a microcapsule for thermotropic crystal sheets is usually between a few microns and a few millimeters. There are 25,400 microns in 1 inch (1,000,000 microns = 1 meter).

7 The thermotropic crystal coating is dried, and a black ink is applied on top of it. Changes in color can be seen through the uncoated side of the strip. Sometimes a clear coating is applied on top of the dry thermotropic crystal coating, and sometimes another agent is applied to help protect the crystals from being damaged by ultraviolet light or other damage, such as scratches.

8 The coated crystals are placed inside either the ring's stone or on a thermotropic strip. These strips generally have a thin film of liquid crystals between a transparent polymer sheet and a black absorbing background, usually also made of polymer. Polymers are substances whose molecular structure consists of a large number of similar units bonded together.

9 The stones are usually attached to the jewelry with a strong glue made with resin.

Think about It!

Although manufacturers claim that mood rings reveal the moods of the people who wear them, there is no scientific proof that mood rings work. Even so, some people buy them with the hope that the rings do display their emotions. Would you want to wear a ring that truly exposed your moods? What if everyone in your class, including your teacher, wore a mood ring and you could know at any moment if someone was calm, excited, or nervous?

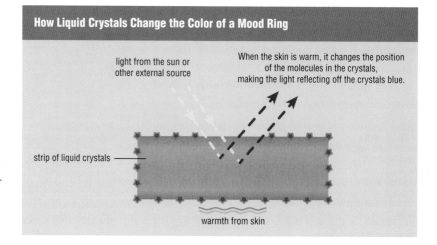

How Liquid Crystals Change the Color of a Mood Ring

light from the sun or other external source

When the skin is warm, it changes the position of the molecules in the crystals, making the light reflecting off the crystals blue.

strip of liquid crystals

warmth from skin

The color of a mood ring is determined by the warmth of the skin. ILLUSTRATION BY LUMINA DATAMATICS LTD. © 2015 CENGAGE LEARNING

Quality control

Quality control for making jewelry generally involves inspecting raw materials, such as metals, for cracks and other flaws and making sure that machines and tools are in good and safe working order. For mood rings, testing must be done to determine the quality of the seal between the stone and the ring. In addition, because resin-based adhesives used in the process can be health hazards when inhaled or touched, factories must have proper ventilation, and workers must wear protective clothing when handling toxic resins. Originally mercury was used in the production of mood rings, but manufacturers stopped using it because of the health hazards associated with it.

Thermotropic crystals can easily get damaged, particularly from ultraviolet light. Coating the capsules, or microencapsulating them, is an important part of manufacturing good-quality mood rings.

The mood ring in the world of new technology

In the early twenty-first century, mood rings were created by toy manu-facturers, fine jewelers, and even hip young designers. Mood bracelets, mood necklaces, and mood earrings were also produced. Some people bought mood beads to design and create their own mood jewelry. In addition, mood jewelry was not just for people. Companies made dog and cat collars with mood stones, which were designed to help owners monitor the moods of their pets.

Molecule: The smallest part of any physical matter.

Novelty: Something that is unusual or new.

Patent: An official document that gives an individual or a company exclusive rights over the use of an invention.

Plated: Covered.

Polymer: A substance whose molecular structure consists of a large number of similar units bonded together.

Thermotropic: Temperature sensitive.

Ultraviolet (UV) light: An invisible form of light produced by the sun. It can cause serious damage to the human eye.

Mood rings and other mood products are being developed with new technology. The Finnish company Moodmetric introduced a mood ring in 2015 that sends information over Bluetooth to a phone app and records different moods throughout the day. Instead of crystals reacting to skin temperature, the ring uses a sensor that measures electricity on the skin, which Moodmetric claims reflects a person's state of mind. According to the company, the ring and the app help people figure out what makes them feel good during the day and what brings on stress, leading to better mental health.

Another new mood device is the Gemstone Cap, introduced by London design studio THE UNSEEN. Worn on the head, it is a stylish headpiece made with 4,000 Swarovski gemstones. It monitors brain activity, reflected by heat generated at specific areas of the head, and the gems change colors in response.

Even these new mood rings and devices, developed with new technology, have not been confirmed by scientific studies. However, like the original mood rings of the 1970s, they attract buyers looking for ways to accessorize and become more self-aware, and they lead at the very least to curiosity and conversations about emotions.

For more information

BOOKS

Overbeck Bix, Cynthia. *Fad Mania!: A History of American Crazes.* Minneapolis: Lerner Publishing Group, 2014.

Sagert, Kelly Boyer. *The 1970s.* Westport, CT: Greenwood Press, 2007.

PERIODICALS

Elliot, Andrew J., et al. "Color and Psychological Functioning: The Effect of Red on Performance Attainment." *Journal of Experimental Psychology* 136, no. 1 (February 2007): 154–68.

Color and Emotion: Is There Really a Connection?

Mood rings were introduced in the mid-1970s. However, thousands of years ago people saw a relationship between color and mood. Ancient Chinese and Egyptians used colors as a kind of therapy to treat mood and physical ailments. Blue (which on a mood ring represents calm) was used in these ancient cultures to lessen pain and soothe a patient. They believed yellow (which expresses excitement on a mood ring) could stimulate the nerves.

Although modern scientists and psychologists are doubtful of such ideas, researchers have continued to explore the emotional meaning of color. A study reported in 2007 in the *Journal of Experimental Psychology* studied the relationship between the color red and student performance

in tests focusing on intelligence, task selection, and stimulation of certain areas of the brain. In one part of the study, students were shown black, green, or red just before a test. Students who were shown the color red performed more poorly. According to the study, "Red is hypothesized to impair performance on achievement tasks, because red is associated with the danger of failure in achievement contexts and evokes avoidance motivation."

Despite suggestions that color and mood are connected, scientists generally believe that the relationship is influenced by cultural and personal factors. In Asia, for example, white is commonly associated with mourning. In the West white is often considered pure and innocent.

"Kent State Uses Mood Ring Technology to Help Diabetics." *Targeted News Service* 3 (April 2015). Available online at http://go.galegroup.com/ps/i.do?id=GALE%7CA408078427&v=2.1&u=eugenepl&it=r&p=STND&sw=w&asid=f643d121ca9c14686f473629dae0d397 (accessed June 9, 2015).

Shimbun, Yomiuri. "Blue Streetlights Believed to Prevent Suicides, Street Crime." *Seattle Times* (December 11, 2008). Available online at http://www.seattletimes.com/nation-world/blue-streetlights-believed-to-prevent-suicides-street-crime/ (accessed June 29, 2015).

WEBSITES

"Uses for Liquid Crystals?" JVC's Science Fair Projects. http://scienceprojectideasforkids.com/faqs/uses-for-liquid-crystals/ (accessed June 9, 2015).

Paintball

1. Charles Nelson's paintballs became a success when he received help from a drug company that had experience making gelatin capsules. Can you think of another invention that benefited by borrowing from an unrelated product or industry?

2. Why do you think companies choose paintball as an activity for a corporate retreat?

3. Most of the improvements in the sport of paintball have come from changes to paintball guns or how the game is played. Can you imagine a change to the paintballs themselves that would make the game more exciting?

A paintball is a small paint-filled capsule made of colored gelatin. Paintballs are the ammunition for a special air gun and are designed to explode when they come into contact with someone or something. Unlike traditional firearms, which use a chemical propellant (a substance or device that causes something to move forward with force), air guns use compressed air for a less dangerous release of ammunition. Paintballs come in a variety of colors and are most commonly found in the sport of paintball.

Paintballs were originally used in forestry and cattle herding as a short-term way to mark trees and animals. At first workers marked trees and animals by hand, but when the paintball was invented in the 1960s, they realized how much easier it was to make markings with a paintball gun. Since then, however, paintballs have become almost entirely used for the game of paintball, which was developed in the 1980s. The game's

A paintball, used in the game paintball, is a small paint-filled capsule. It is fired from an air gun. © ISTOCK.COM/ MORDALEZ

inventors wondered whether aggressiveness in the workplace translated to aggressiveness on a playing field. They created paintball as a hunting game that would show players' competitive abilities without causing injury.

The game of paintball is much like the game Capture the Flag. Each team has an area where their flag is located. The goal of each team is to capture the other team's flag and return with it to their home territory. Paintball offers the added excitement of being able to tag opponents with paintballs. Once a player has been tagged, he or she is out of the game. Most games of paintball are played on large obstacle courses, either indoors or outside, although games are sometimes played in privately owned wooded areas. Paintball is a growing sport that, despite its aggressive beginnings, is safer than many other sports. It causes fewer injuries per player each year than football, soccer, or tennis. With the game's popularity in the United States and around the world, paintball pellets remain in high demand.

From paint squirters to paint guns

As a recreational sport, paintball began in the 1980s, but its roots are in forestry and cattle herding. In the forestry business, trees must be tagged for cutting or clearing or to mark hiking trails. For many years this was done by workers who carried buckets of paint around, which was difficult and sometimes dangerous. Cattle owners also needed to identify their cattle with a unique mark. Instead of branding livestock with a hot iron, owners sometimes used oil-based paints or chalk to identify animals that were ready for breeding or those that were being sold.

Charles and Evan Nelson imagined a paint squirter that would simplify the forestry-marking process. The brothers and business partners started the Nelson Paint Company in 1940 in Kingsford, Michigan. They created a paint squirter that fired a narrow stream of paint into spots that were difficult to reach by hand. However, the squirter did not become popular with the forestry industry, and sales were low.

In the early 1960s Charles decided that an air gun that fires a small pellet filled with paint might be even more effective than the paint squirter. His paintball prototypes, or experimental models, used wax capsules. When he was ready for mass production, he got help from R. P. Scherer, a drug company that had pioneered the gel capsule used in many medications. Nelson's first paintballs used the same capsules as drugs for livestock, which were made out of soft gelatin. Gelatin is a substance that can be eaten and is made from collagen, a protein in the tendons and ligaments of various animals.

A member of the Los Angeles Ironmen professional paintball team holds an air gun in a competition. © ROBERT GAUTHIER/LOS ANGELES TIMES/ GETTY IMAGES

Nelson Paint asked Crosman, an air gun company, to design a gun that would shoot the paintballs. However, after a few years of poor sales, Nelson switched to air gun manufacturer Daisy. Because Nelson did not own the Crosman paintball gun design, the company had to start from scratch. Daisy created the Splotchmaker paint gun, which was later renamed the Nelspot 007. It could shoot paintballs accurately up to 75 feet (23 meters). By 1969 Nelson paintballs were being used for animal marking. Gamekeepers in South Africa used them to identify animals that were being studied, and biologists marked and identified penguins in the Antarctic with the guns.

From animal marker to game time

In 1976 friends Hayes Noel and Charles Gaines talked about creating a survival game. Noel was a Wall Street stockbroker and Gaines was an author and outdoorsman. They wondered if they each had an instinct that had caused them to do well in high-stress, competitive environments. They also wondered if their instincts in the modern world would work in a survival situation. In 1981, when Noel and Gaines saw an advertisement for a Nelspot 007 paint gun, they asked their friends George Butler and Bob Guernsey to help them create the rules for a survival game using the paintball gun. The result was a game much like Capture the Flag, only using Nelspot guns and oil-based paintballs. Twelve people paid $175 each for materials to play the first game on 125 acres (51 hectares) of New Hampshire woods.

Sports Illustrated featured an article about paintball in the summer of 1981. The article caused an explosion in paintball's popularity, and soon the sport was a popular choice for birthday parties and corporate team-building retreats. Weekend leagues also became common, and land-owners willing to rent space out to players created obstacle courses. By 1999 paintball production reached 3 billion per year.

According to American Sports Data, paintball was the third-largest alternative sport in the United States in 2006. More than 10 million people played the game at least once that year, and nearly 2 million people played fifteen times or more. The largest paintball event in the United States, the D-Day event in Wyandotte, Oklahoma, was first held in 1997 and reenacts battles from the Normandy invasion in World War II (1939–1945). The event attracts several thousand participants every year from all around the world.

Raw materials

Paintballs are made of an outer, gelatin shell, just like a medicine capsule, with a mixture of water and different-colored liquids inside. The gelatin shell is thinner than that of a medicine capsule so it will explode easily on contact. Sometimes a sweetener is added to the capsule. All ingredients used in paintballs are food grade, because the finished product looks like a gumball and may be attractive to children. The shell is filled with a mixture of food dye, propylene glycol (a colorless liquid with a slightly sweet taste), and crayon wax to give the paint a thick consistency.

Design

Paintballs are manufactured in several grades. The lowest-grade paintball is a recreation-grade paintball. These paintballs can vary slightly in size, and some are oblong rather than perfectly round or have dimples or visible seams. Because of their lower quality, they are sold at a cheaper price. Mid-grade, or tournament-grade, paintballs are inspected to make sure they all have the same size and shape. They usually contain a higher-quality paint that is thicker and has more pigment to lessen confusion about who has been hit. The gelatin-based outer shell of a tournament-grade paintball explodes easily on impact, whereas a recreation-grade paintball might have a thicker shell that could sting players on impact.

Paintballs only work when they are shot out of specially designed air guns. These guns have a long valve tube that runs from a barrel to a

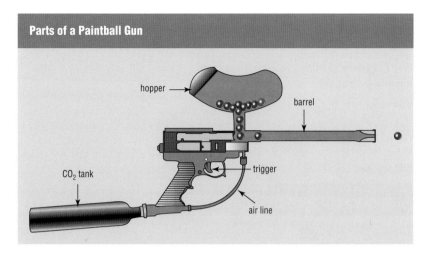

Parts of a Paintball Gun

hopper

barrel

CO₂ tank

trigger

air line

In a paint gun, when the bolt slides back, the paintball falls into the barrel. Pulling the trigger releases the hammer from the bolt, releasing gas from the tank that sends the ball flying toward its target.
ILLUSTRATION BY LUMINA DATAMATICS LTD. © 2015 CENGAGE LEARNING

chamber, passing through a bolt, a spring, a hammer, and a valve seat. Each part plays an important role in launching the paintball toward its target.

First, paintballs are loaded into the barrel of the paint gun either by hand or by using a device called a hopper, which is a container that holds many paintballs and delivers them one at a time to the barrel. The front of the barrel is open, and the other end is blocked off by the valve seat. The bolt goes through the barrel and blocks the entry of a paintball until the trigger is cocked (pulled back). When the player cocks the gun, the bolt is pulled backward. This pushes the spring so the bolt is pressed against the hammer.

When the bolt slides back, the paintball falls into the barrel. On the bottom of the hammer is a latch called a sear. The sear turns on a small pin and grabs the bolt when it is pressed against the hammer. The sear basically connects the bolt and the hammer so that they move at the same time.

Pulling the trigger of the paintball gun releases the hammer from the bolt and the spring catapults the hammer backward. This propels the valve tube backward fast enough that the side openings on the tube are uncovered, allowing the pressurized gas from the gas cartridge to rocket forward. This sends the paintball flying at speeds up to 300 feet (91 meters) a second, the legal limit for paintball guns in the United States.

Safety

Paintballs are designed to be shot with a velocity, or speed, of no more than 300 feet (91 meters) per second in the United States. The United

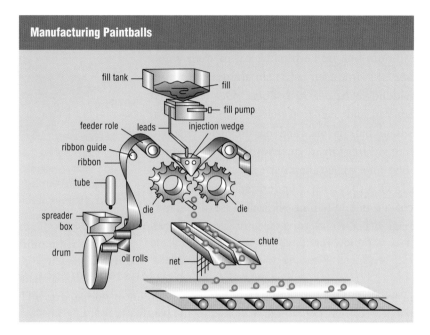

Manufacturing Paintballs

The machinery used to make paintballs ensures that each ball is round and the same size.
ILLUSTRATION BY LUMINA DATAMATICS LTD. © 2015 CENGAGE LEARNING

Kingdom allows a maximum velocity of 280 feet (85 meters) per second. While paintballs are designed to explode on impact, players who are shot at close range can suffer bruises. For that reason, protective gear such as masks or goggles, heavy pants, and a heavy-weight shirt are required in public paintball arenas. Overall, paintball is a fairly safe sport, resulting in 45 injuries per 100,000 participants per year. The most serious are eye injuries, which can cause blindness. These usually happen when a player refuses to wear eye protection or takes his or her goggles off during game play. Paintballs themselves are nontoxic and present no safety issue if accidently eaten.

The manufacturing process

The paintball manufacturing process involves several steps, including the making of the paint and the capsule and enclosing the paint into the capsule.

1 The contents of a paintball differ from manufacturer to manufacturer, but they typically include polyethylene glycol, crayon wax, and a food dye colorant. To manufacture the paint, these ingredients are heated well and mixed together.

How Everyday Products Are Made

2 The outer capsule of a paintball is made out of edible (safe to eat), nontoxic materials including liquid gelatin. To manufacture the capsule, the gelatin is melted for thirty minutes with a sweetener and other ingredients before it is filtered into a hot container called a gel tote. The filter keeps unmelted chunks of gelatin from entering the gel tote. The contents are mixed for about twenty minutes, and a dye is often added so that the capsule matches the color of the paint inside it. Workers may manually stir the mixture, depending on the manufacturer.

3 The gelatin mixture is flattened to the correct thickness on a machine. Next, the gelatin is dropped into two thin ribbons that are passed over a rotating die, or mold. These two pieces form the top and bottom halves of the capsule.

4 The two halves are pressed together, and the paint filling is injected inside while the gelatin shell is still warm. Once the filling is injected, the hole is pressed closed, and the paintball is complete.

5 The gelatin capsules are rolled into a tumble dryer so that they stay round as they harden. Finally, they are placed on a drying rack to finish hardening.

Think about It!

Despite the excitement of a paintball competition, the number of paintball players dropped from 5.5 million players in 2007 to 3.5 million players in 2011. One of the main reasons behind this may be the cost to play the sport. Buying a paintball gun, paint pellets, a hopper, an air compressor, and safety gear can cost a new player $1,000 or more. What are some ways that the sport could become more affordable while remaining safe?

Quality control

Once paintballs are dried, they are inspected visually by workers before they are shipped. Several paintballs from each batch are tested more thoroughly to make sure that they will break under the proper amount of pressure but are not so fragile that they will break before being released from a paintball gun.

Because paintballs are filled with liquid, they expand and contract naturally as temperature changes. The paintball factory must stay at a constant temperature and humidity to maintain product quality. A temperature of approximately 72 degrees Fahrenheit (22 degrees Celsius) and a humidity below 65 percent is considered ideal. Many manufacturers recommend that players refrigerate their paintballs on hot days.

WORDS TO KNOW

Air gun: A gun that uses compressed air instead of an exploding propellant for a less dangerous discharge of ammunition.

Capsule: A thin, rounded outer shell, usually of gelatin, that is used for packaging something.

Gelatin: A thickening agent obtained by processing the bones and skin of animals, usually cows or pigs.

Propellant: A substance or device that causes something to move forward with force.

Prototype: An early example of a product that is later used as a model for production.

The future of paintball

Given that paintball technology is quite basic, it has stayed mostly the same since its invention in the 1960s. While the quality and grade of materials used in the paint and gelatin capsule have improved slightly over time, no major changes have been made to the design of the product. The main improvements related to the paintball industry have been in the technology of paintball guns and in the evolution of the game itself.

As of 2015 paintball was played all over the world and at many different levels, from small parties or corporate events to national and international tournaments played by athletes who train for the sport. In 2013 the first international paintball tournaments took place, including the Paintball World Cup in Paris, France, and the Naza World Cup Asia, which were aired on live television.

Despite some decrease in paintball participation, the paintball industry remained strong in the early twenty-first century. According to IBIS Market Report, revenue from paintball fields in the United States alone brought in more than $600 million in 2014 to those who owned and rented paintball fields. That year the sale of paintball equipment, including paintballs, totaled $132 million in the United States.

For more information

BOOKS

Davidson, Steve. *A Parent's Guide to Paintball.* Vancouver, BC: Creative Guy Publishing, 2009.

Dell, Pamela. *Paintball for Fun!* North Mankato, MN: Capstone, 2008.

Policing: A New Use for Paintballs

Paintball may soon be more than just a game. In July 2015 the police force in Willimantic, Connecticut, became the first in the United States to use a new gun model produced by Belgian manufacturer Fabrique Nationale de Herstal. The FN 303 is basically a paintball gun with bullets that mark the target with paint. Able to hit a suspect from more than 160 feet (49 meters) away, it was designed to help police officers identify a potential criminal who is trying to run or to slow him or her down. More forceful than common paintball guns, the gun's instructions warn users to avoid aiming for the head, spine, groin, or kidneys.

The use of the FN 303 is part of a general trend in the United States toward non-deadly weaponry, such as rubber bullets. While paintball guns are still projectile weapons, they are designed to cause discomfort rather than serious injury. The hope is that tools such as paintball guns, which still work at a distance, can cut down on fatal shootings between police officers and suspects.

Manière, Romain, Ritch Telfor, and Fabien Cuviliez. *Paintballer: The Paintball Book.* Paris: DTB, 2012.

PERIODICALS

Adkisson, Kevin. "WWII Inspires Paintball Game in Wyandotte, Oklahoma." *NewsOK* (June 1, 2008). Available online at http://newsok.com/wwii-inspires-paintball-game-in-wyandotte-discover-oklahoma/article/3250266/ (accessed August 28, 2015).

Alo, Mohammed S. "Has Paintball Technology Reached a Plateau?" *Paintball Times* (n.d.). Available online at http://www.paintballtimes.com/Article.asp?ID=160 (accessed August 15, 2015).

Conn, J. M., J. L. Annest, J. Gilchrist, and G. W. Ryan. "Injuries from Paintball Game Related Activities in the United States, 1997–2001." *Injury Prevention* 10 (2004): 139–43. Available online at http://injuryprevention.bmj.com/content/10/3/139.long (accessed August 28, 2015).

Ho, Melanie. "Locals Hope to Leave Their Mark in Paintball." *Washington Post* (June 21, 2006). Available online at http://www.washingtonpost.com/wp-dyn/content/article/2006/06/19/AR2006061901270.html (accessed August 28, 2015).

Ratliff, Jamie. "Willimantic Police First in State to Use Less-Lethal Weapon." *NBC Connecticut* (July 29, 2015). Available online at http://www.nbcconnecticut.com/news/local/Willimantic-Police-Less-Lethal-Weapon-Training-FN-303-319741411.html (accessed August 28, 2015).

Venter, Dewald. "Participating in Paintball: Adventure or Extreme Sport?" *African Journal of Hospitality, Tourism and Leisure* 3, no. 1 (2014): 1–11.

WEBSITES

"How Are Paintballs Made?" Blast Zone Paintball. http://www. blastzonepaintball.com/how-are-paintballs-made/ (accessed August 22, 2015).

"How It's Made: Paintballs." YouTube. https://www.youtube.com/watch?v= 3AKrzgUSsoA (accessed August 22, 2015).

"Paintball Statistics." Minnesota Paintball Association. http://www.paint-ball. org/paintball/statistics.htm (accessed August 22, 2015).

Personal Watercraft (PWC)

Critical Thinking Questions

1. How would personal watercraft design change if there was no drag?

2. Kawasaki, one of the most famous makers of personal watercrafts, is better known as a motorcycle manufacturer. What do these two products have in common? What are the major differences between them?

3. Do you need to carry out the Try This! experiment in order to learn from it? Why or why not?

A personal watercraft (PWC), sometimes known as a water scooter or by the brand name Jet Ski, is defined by the U.S. Coast Guard as a boat less than 13 feet (4 meters) in length that is propelled by a jet of water pumped inside the bottom of the watercraft and then sent out through the stern (rear end). PWCs are capable of speeds of up to 80 miles (130 kilometers) per hour. Most personal watercraft are made for one or two passengers and are ridden like a motorcycle, with hands placed on handlebars and thighs gripping a seat attached to the craft's hull (body or frame). Some PWCs can be driven from a standing position, and some hold as many as four passengers.

Although PWCs were developed as early as the 1940s, they did not become popular until the internal jet-propulsion system was perfected in the 1970s. Since then they have been enjoyed by millions all over the world in water environments ranging from small lakes to big oceans. This

A personal watercraft is commonly called a Jet Ski, one of the most popular brands.
© EDDIE PHANTANA/
SHUTTERSTOCK.COM

popularity has a price, however. In some areas PWCs have become so numerous that people have questioned their effect on the environment.

A personal watercraft lets the user glide over the water's surface at high speeds. In addition to general recreational use, PWCs can be used for obstacle courses in sporting events or to explore a coastline. The feeling of riding a PWC is similar to that of water-skiing, but with a higher degree of user control.

Action and reaction

Newton's third law, known as the law of action and reaction, was expressed by English scientist Isaac Newton (1643–1727) around 1666. It describes the way that objects apply force on one another. Newton observed that for every action there is an equal and opposite reaction. The object that receives a force also returns force. For example, when you push against a wall with your hand, the wall must exert force back, or else it falls over. The force applied by the wall is the force of resistance.

Newton's third law applies on land as well as water and explains the concept of water propulsion that powers personal watercraft. In designing PWCs, engineers have taken advantage of Newton's laws of motion. They understand that, because water has a high degree of resistance, viscosity (resistance to flow), and surface tension, craft moving through water must have enough power—and the right shape—to overcome these forces.

All watercraft, whether small or large, wind- or motor-powered, must account for the way that motion is affected by water. Watercraft are designed to cut down on drag (a force that acts on an object moving through a fluid, slowing its movement), maximizing forward movement by minimizing resistance. The principles of designing watercraft are similar to those used to design aircraft. However, although wind resistance and water resistance act similarly, water resistance has a greater strength.

PWCs take in water through a valve on the bottom of the hull and expel it with great force. Therefore, the craft moves forward under a

How Everyday Products Are Made

force equal to that of the expelled jet stream. Jet-powered airplanes work in a similar way but on a much greater scale. Multiperson PWCs can weigh as much as 1,000 pounds (450 kilograms) and need strong propulsive force to move at their common speeds of up to 60 miles (97 kilometers) per hour.

Early aquatic devices

After World War II (1939–1945), when the economy was growing, consumer interest in personal recreational vehicles increased, not only for motorcycles and snowmobiles but also for personal watercraft. One of the first PWCs was built by the Californian inventor Theodore R. Drake (1928–1989) in 1940 and patented in 1942. Named the Aquatic Device, it was designed for the driver to sit in like a car and featured an internal combustion (fuel-burning) engine located inside the craft's hull just in front of the driver's seat, also like a car. Floats located in the front and back of the craft were connected by a ridge element that allowed for steering.

While the Aquatic Device never took off as a consumer product, the German-made Lepel Wave Roller had some success in the mid-1950s. However, this PWC was only 59 inches (150 centimeters) long, weighed only 65 pounds (29 kilograms), and could go only 8 miles (13 kilometers) per hour. The Wave Roller was more of a beach toy than a watercraft. The 1.5-horsepower engine was located in a compartment under the driver's seat and received fuel from a 1-quart tank. The 1955 Amanda Water Scooter, a small propeller-driven personal watercraft produced by the British Vincent Motorcycle Company, also had some success on the consumer market. It sold about 2,000 units in the United States, Europe, and Australia.

The Water Ski Skooter was patented by Julius Hamori (1937–1998) in 1968. This small personal watercraft was inspired by traditional water skis. It was designed to tilt backward when used so that the craft would glide over the surface of the water with little contact, minimizing drag. The front of this PWC was supported by skis on supports, and the craft was powered by an inboard propeller motor.

Beginning in the mid-1960s, Australian inventor Clayton Jacobson II experimented with PWCs powered by internal pump-jet systems. His work led to a discovery in jet propulsion that changed the PWC market. A fan of motocross racing, Jacobson eventually quit his job as a banker in Byron Bay, Australia, to work on his watercraft. He created a working jet-powered aluminum-hull prototype in 1965. A prototype is an early example of a product that is later used as a model for production. He received a patent for his "power-driven aquatic vehicle" in 1969.

Jacobson's vehicle, often considered the first modern PWC, was designed for the driver to stand and hold onto handlebars similar to those of a motorcycle. The two-part hull was designed to work partly in and partly out of the water. Jacobson switched the hull material from aluminum to fiberglass, a sturdy plastic that is reinforced with glass fibers. His revolutionary internal pump-jet motor system made the watercraft truly unique.

Market competition

The first company to successfully market a jet-propelled PWC was Kawasaki, a Japanese firm that began as a shipbuilder in the late nineteenth century and later became known for motorcycles. Kawasaki PWCs were first sold in the United States in 1972 under the brand name Jet Ski, and the company has remained one of the leading PWC manufacturers. Due to the popularity of the Jet Ski in the United States, Kawasaki built a production facility in Lincoln, Nebraska, in 1975 to supply the market. Kawasaki continued to improve PWC design, releasing new models in 1977 and 1982. In these early years Kawasaki PWCs were designed to be operated from a standing position, which is more physically difficult and requires more skill than later seated models. They were also made for only one rider.

In the late 1960s Bombardier, a snowmobile manufacturer in Quebec, Canada, that later became a multinational aerospace corporation, produced a personal watercraft based on Jacobson's design. In fact, Bombardier had been the first to market a PWC with jet propulsion. However, the product was discontinued due to lack of sales, and the company did not return to personal watercraft manufacture for many years. Its Sea-Doo model, which was introduced in 1986 and allowed users to operate the craft from a sitting position, quickly took over the market because it was easy to drive.

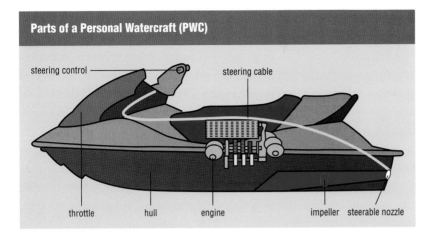

Parts of a Personal Watercraft (PWC)

steering control

steering cable

throttle   hull   engine   impeller   steerable nozzle

Personal watercraft hulls, made out of lightweight, high-strength fiberglass, are shaped like traditional boat hulls with the addition of grooves to lessen water resistance. ILLUSTRATION BY LUMINA DATAMATICS LTD.
© 2015 CENGAGE LEARNING

Since then many other seated-use PWCs have joined the market, including Kawasaki's Jet Ski, Yamaha's WaveRunner, Honda's Aqua-Trax, Polaris's Sealion, and Arctic Cat's Tigershark. Movie audiences were introduced to PWC by the James Bond film *The Spy Who Loved Me* (1977), in which Bond pilots a unique "water motorcycle" produced specifically for the film by Spirit Marine, a division of Arctic Cat. By the 1990s PWCs were popular worldwide.

Raw materials

The raw materials used for PWC manufacture include fiberglass and polyester epoxy, a waterproof, salt-resistant substance used as a protective paint and sealant, for the hull; rubber for foot grips, straps, and padding; metal, plastic, and rubber for the engine; and paint and vinyl decals for decoration and branding.

Design

All PWCs are designed for user comfort, fuel efficiency, and hydrodynamics. Hydrodynamics is the study of the motion of fluids and bodies submerged in fluids. PWC hulls, made out of lightweight, high-strength fiberglass, are shaped like traditional boat hulls with the addition of grooves to lessen water resistance and make forward motion easier during high speeds. Hull design differs depending on the purpose of the watercraft (for example, based on the number of passengers and whether passengers are seated or standing).

Modern PWCs are constructed with innovative, high-intensity jet engines that use water pressure to propel the hull through the water. While in use, the PWC jet-propulsion system takes in water through a large grate on the bottom of the craft. The gasoline engine inside the craft powers an impeller, or water pump. In the impeller, a three-blade stainless-steel propeller fitted inside a 6-inch- (15-centimeter-) diameter pipe, increases the water's speed. The water is expelled out the end of the pipe with increased force. A nozzle at the end of the pipe further pressurizes the jet stream and also forms the basis of the craft's steering system. A swiveling nozzle, controlled by the handlebar steering mechanism, controls the direction of the jet spray. Because the jet spray decides the watercraft's direction, it is easier to steer PWCs at higher speeds when the spray is more forceful.

PWC engines need to have a significant amount of power to overcome water resistance and reach high speeds. Large PWCs often have four-cylinder engines like those used in many cars or large motorcycles. PWCs also need a fuel tank, often as large as 20 gallons (76 liters) in volume, located within the hull.

Safety

Most PWCs are equipped with safety cords or "kill switches" that cut off power if the rider falls off, which can happen easily at high speeds or when riders hit a rough wake or wave. For that reason, all drivers and passengers should always wear a life vest. Riders should also wear helmets, especially if they are riding at very high speeds or around other watercraft or obstacles. A PWC is capable of emitting sounds of more than 100 decibels, almost as loud as a chainsaw. At this level, sustained exposure can lead to permanent hearing loss.

PWCs should never be operated while a person is under the influence of alcohol or drugs, and all drivers should follow safety rules similar to driving a car. Many states have age restrictions on driving a PWC. For example, some states do not allow children under fourteen to drive PWCs, and those between fourteen and sixteen must have a valid boating safety certificate and stay within 100 feet (30 meters) of a parent or guardian. According to the National Transportation Safety Board, more than 90 percent of PWC accidents are caused by operator error.

PWC can be dangerous if operated carelessly. Florida and California, the states with the highest number of PWCs and the highest PWC accident rates, have introduced the toughest operator guidelines and, as a result, have seen a significant drop in the number of accidents. In 2005 the U.S. Coast Guard enacted the Personal Watercraft Act to limit reckless driving, which it defines as including becoming airborne, weaving through boating traffic, driving faster than a no-wake speed within 100 feet (30 feet) of a shoreline or an anchored vessel, or driving too close to another vehicle.

Despite these guidelines and serious consequences for not following them, many people are injured or killed each year due to PWC accidents. According to the U.S. Coast Guard, in 2012 personal watercraft accidents caused 721 injuries and 58 deaths.

Think about It!

A number of people use PWCs, snowmobiles, or all-terrain vehicles (ATVs) to travel to isolated wilderness locations. How does traveling through wilderness areas in a motorized vehicle change the experience of being there? What does this type of transportation add to recreational wilderness exploration? Do you think using PWCs detracts from the fun of being on the water?

The manufacturing process

PWCs are manufactured in factories, where workers use heavy machinery to assemble their various components. Manufacturing operations are similar to those used in car manufacturing. Engine assembly and hull casting and molding are completed before final assembly.

1 The molded fiberglass deck and hull pieces arrive at the factory fully painted. Workers apply identifying decals to the deck piece at the beginning of the assembly process.

2 Workers attach rubber treads to the footholds molded into the hull. A robotic system drills holes in the fiberglass hull for drainage and exhaust.

3 The hull is flipped over to allow workers access to the craft's interior. Workers install rubber straps to hold internal parts in place.

4 Before the engine is lowered into the craft, workers place a rubber pad against the hull to cushion it. Then they attach plastic motor mounts to secure it.

5 The engine is lowered into place. Workers connect the intake and exhaust tubes and then install and connect the battery.

6 The jet pump is connected to the engine through the driveline and then is attached to the hull. The gas tank is placed inside the hull

PWC races and rallies became popular in the late twentieth and early twenty-first centuries as the vehicles could perform at increasingly higher speeds.
© NICK STUBBS/
SHUTTERSTOCK.COM

before being connected to the engine, the drive-line, and the exhaust system.

7 A robotic system applies adhesive to key locations inside the hull. More support straps are glued in, and the deck and hull pieces are pressed together. They are clamped together while the adhesive sets.

8 The hood and steering column are installed. The seam between the joined deck and hull pieces is covered by a plastic bumper.

Quality control

PWC hulls are scanned by an ultrasound machine to make sure they do not have any leaks. The engine of each unit is also tested in water before the completed PWCs are shipped to sellers.

Beach bombing

PWCs are used by millions of people all over the world. In 2014 PWC sales in the United States reached 47,900, down from a record high of 92,000 in 2000. As of 2015 the international PWC market was dominated by Kawasaki, Bombardier, and Yamaha. Although both Yamaha and Kawasaki continue to sell standing PWC models, seated watercraft are far more common. High-performance models with increased speeds were popular throughout the late twentieth and early twenty-first centuries, with PWC races and rallies growing in popularity as sporting events. High oil and gas prices in the 2000s affected PWC sales, but the vehicles continue to be found on many lakes, oceans, and other bodies of water.

The popularity of PWCs has raised several environmental issues. Their loud engines disturb not only other boaters and those enjoying the water or beach but also fish, water birds, and other coastline wildlife. For that reason, many lake and beach communities have either banned PWCs or limited their use to certain hours of the day to limit noise pollution. The turbulence produced by the jet-propulsion system can disturb sediment on lake beds that in turn damages the environment of fish and other marine organisms. In addition, because PWCs run on gasoline, they give off exhaust that contributes to air and water pollution.

How Everyday Products Are Made

WORDS TO KNOW

Drag: The force of resistance created when a body or object moves through air or water.

Expel (verb): To drive or force out.

Fiberglass: A durable material made of threads of glass. Fiberglass is widely used in manufacturing and is often used to reinforce plastics.

Hull: The main part of a watercraft that is immersed in water, including its sides and bottom.

Hydrodynamics: The study of the motion of fluids and bodies immersed in fluids.

Patent: An official document that gives an individual or a company exclusive rights over the use of an invention.

Prototype: An early example of a product that is later used as a model for production.

Viscosity: Resistance to flow.

The environmental impact of PWCs is still being studied, but evidence suggests that they have a greater effect on the environment than other types of watercraft.

For more information

BOOKS

Thompson, Luke. *Jet Ski.* New York: Children's Press, 2001.

PERIODICALS

Miller, Joshua Rhett. "Danger on the High Skis: Fatalities Bring Renewed Calls for Personal Watercraft Safety." *Fox News* (July 13, 2012). Available online at http://www.foxnews.com/us/2012/07/13/high-profile-crashes-create-perfect-storm-for-recreational-boating-safety/ (accessed August 25, 2015).

WEBSITES

Asplund, Timothy R. "The Effects of Motorized Watercraft on Aquatic Ecosystems." Wisconsin Department of Natural Resources. http://dnr.wi.gov/topic/ShorelandZoning/documents/201301041052.pdf (accessed August 21, 2015).

Benson, Shellie. "How Sea-Doo Launched the Personal Watercraft Industry." Popyachts.com. https://www.popyachts.com/how-seadoo-launched-the-personal-watercraft-industry-blog-post-130 (accessed August 14, 2015).

"Dangerous Sports: The Personal Watercraft Industry." *Insider Exclusive.* http://www.insiderexclusive.com/justice-in-america/dangerous-sports-the-personal-watercraft-industry (accessed August 21, 2015).

Try This!

Hero's Engine

The classic experiment "Hero's Engine" was first conducted by the scientist Hero of Alexandria around 60 CE and demonstrates Isaac Newton's third law of motion. Following the steps below will help you understand how moving water can change the motion and direction of an object.

You will need:

- craft knife
- plastic cup
- string
- 2 plastic bendable drinking straws
- modeling clay
- water
- sink or bucket

Directions:

1. Use the craft knife to carefully cut two small holes on opposite sides of the cup, near the top rim.

2. Thread and tie the string through these holes, so that the cup can hang from the string.

3. Make two larger holes on the sides of the cup, near the bottom, making sure the cuts are opposite to each other.

4. Cut the straws, 1.5 inches (4 centimeters) below the bendable part.

5. Slide the cut straws into the lower holes in the cup. The bent ends of the straws should both be facing in a clockwise direction.

6. Use the modeling clay to create a water-tight seal where the straws pass through the cup.

7. Hang the cup over an empty bucket so it can move freely when you pour water into it. When you fill the cup with water, gravity forces the water downward, causing it to flow out through the straws. This low-pressure water jet causes the "engine," or cup device, to spin in a clockwise direction, demonstrating Newton's third law of motion.

8. Experiment with the direction of the straws to see what happens when you move them in a counterclockwise direction, or have them tilt toward or away from each other. How does this relate to Newton's third law of motion?

"Noise Pollution in Ears of Beholder." Minnesota Sea Grant. http://www.seagrant.umn.edu/newsletter/1998/06/noise_pollution_in_ears_of_beholder.html (accessed August 21, 2015).

"Performance Wave Runners." Yamaha. http://www.yamahawaverunners.com/performance (accessed August 15, 2015).

Popping Candy

Critical Thinking Questions

1. How does the process of making popping candy affect the shape of the candy pieces? Would it be possible to change the shape of the candy? Why or why not?

2. According to the entry, what happens to a batch of popping candy that has a carbonation rating of seven? Would you rather eat popping candy rated seven or fourteen? Why?

Popping candy is a hard candy filled with bubbles of carbon dioxide (CO_2) gas. The gas is released as the candy melts, making pieces pop and fizz in the mouth. Popping candy is made from sugar, lactose (a type of natural sugar found in milk products), and other sweeteners and flavorings. Carbon dioxide is added to the sugar mixture during manufacturing. The individual pieces are small, uneven in shape, and usually pale or light in color. Popping candy is usually sold in single-serve paper packages.

Developed by General Foods Corporation in the 1950s, "gasified" or popping candy was first sold to the public in the 1970s under the brand name Pop Rocks. The unique treat quickly became a hit. In fact, Pop Rocks were so popular in the late 1970s that the candy is often still associated with that period of time. By the early 1980s, popping candy had become the subject of a popular urban legend, a widely believed story that is not actually true. The legend says that eating popping candy while drinking a carbonated soda results in a potentially deadly explosion in the stomach. Although this myth spread widely, it did not affect sales of the candy, which is perfectly safe to eat.

Popping candy, a type of hard candy that fizzes in the mouth, is available in many colors and flavors. © THOMAS RIGGS & COMPANY

Popping candy is unique because it affects the senses through taste, sound, and touch. The candy starts to fizz when the heat and moisture inside the mouth melt the sugar mixture and release the CO_2 trapped in the small bubbles inside it. These bubbles, no larger than half the diameter of a human hair, are created in the candy during a high-pressure manufacturing process. The CO_2, once released, makes loud popping noises. The popping effect can be so extreme that it makes the candy jump around in the mouth. The unique experience of eating popping candy sets it apart from other treats.

A popping patent

The carbonation technique behind popping candy was first patented in 1957 by research chemist William A. Mitchell (1911–2004) of General Foods. Mitchell experimented with including compressed, or pressurized, CO_2 in foods for several years. In 1956 he found a way to capture compressed CO_2 that allowed him to create ice cubes with bubbles of CO_2 inside them. When the ice cubes melted, the CO_2 escaped, instantly carbonating any drink to which they were added. In order to create Pop Rocks, Mitchell had to find a way to hold CO_2 inside something that could be eaten, a process that was much more complicated than freezing water around the gas. He eventually came upon sorbitol, a form of sugar alcohol, as an edible (safe to eat) means of trapping CO_2. Sorbitol is naturally sweet, so it made sense for Mitchell to use it in candy.

Mitchell made small batches of popping candy beginning in 1957. Among the first people to taste test the new candy were Mitchell's administrative assistant and his four children, all of whom enjoyed the suprising sensation of the popping candy. Although these early testers all said they enjoyed the candy, it was not immediately produced at General Foods. The company was not in the candy-making business and did not have the system necessary to sell it. Instead, hopeful that the company could develop a self-carbonating line of the popular flavored drink mix Kool-Aid, General Foods asked Mitchell to explore the use of CO_2 in powdered drinks. Although Mitchell continued to make batches of his popping candy for his family and friends, it was nearly twenty yeras before General Foods returned to popping candy as a marketable product.

Perfecting the process

One thing standing in the way of popping candy making it to stores was the complicated process of creating CO_2 bubbles inside the candy. Getting enough compressed CO_2 into a food product is difficult. If not done properly, the process can result in "dud" candies that do not have much pop. It was one thing for Mitchell to make small batches of the candy for his family and friends, but it was an entirely different thing to produce the candy in large quantities while maintaining high quality control and consistency standards. In 1957, when Mitchell patented gasified candy, making the candy on a large scale seemed impossible.

In the 1970s Paul A. Kirkpatrick, another General Foods developer, returned to the idea of carbonated candy. He improved Mitchell's production process, adding steps to keep the CO_2 bubbles in the pieces of finished candy intact when big blocks of it were shattered as part of the manufacturing process. Kirkpatrick filed a second patent for General Foods for the production of gasified candy in 1977. By that time Pop Rocks was already a hit.

The Pop Rocks craze

General Foods began using Kirkpatrick's improved process to make popping candy as early as 1975. At first the candy was only sold on a limited or trial basis. Early locations for Pop Rocks sales were Seattle, Washington, and cities throughout Canada. Pop Rocks went on sale to the general public in 1976. Almost immediately the candy took off in an explosive way. In the first 18 months, 500 million packages of Pop Rocks were sold to consumers in the United States. The original price was fifteen cents per packet, and the candy was available in three flavors: cherry, orange, and grape. Between 1976 and 1982, more than 2 billion packets of Pop Rocks were sold, making it one of the best-selling treats in the country. General Foods also sold a powdered carbonated candy, known as Cosmic Candy or Space Dust, made with the same formula and carbonation process as Pop Rocks.

As popping candy grew in popularity, stories sprang up about the effects of carbonation. Urban legends about kids exploding after eating Pop Rocks, or after combining Pop Rocks with carbonated drinks, were exciting to children, though they were not actually true. These tall tales continued to spread by word of mouth no matter how many statements General Foods issued about the candy's safety. In one popular version of

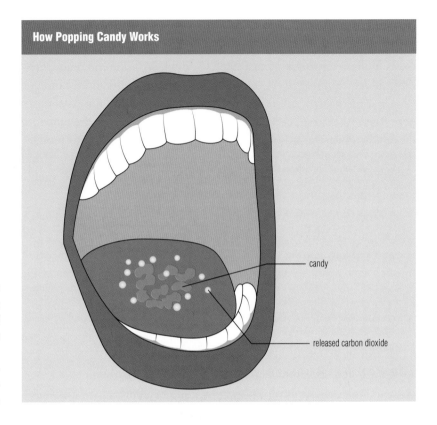

How Popping Candy Works

candy

released carbon dioxide

Heat and moisture inside a person's mouth melt popping candy, releasing trapped bubbles of carbon dioxide gas with a popping sound.
ILLUSTRATION BY LUMINA DATAMATICS LTD. © 2015 CENGAGE LEARNING

the Pop Rocks urban legend, the person who exploded after eating Pop Rocks was identified as a boy named Mikey, who had been the central character in a popular commercial for Life cereal in the late 1970s.

General Foods worked hard to reassure people that Pop Rocks were safe, taking out full-page ads in as many as forty-five major publications in the late 1970s and early 1980s. The company also sent mail explaining the candy's safety to school principals around the United States. When distribution issues that had led to expired packets of Pop Rocks being sold in stores caused General Foods to stop producing Pop Rocks in 1983, the candy's removal from shelves further spread the urban legend. Many people were convinced that the candy had been pulled because of a real risk to the public.

Carbonated candy was back on the market within a few years, and sales quickly returned due to continued interest in its unique taste and popping sensation. Kraft Foods started selling Action Candy in 1985 and licensed the brand to Spanish company Zeta Espacial, which is based in Barcelona. Zeta Espacial began selling carbonated candy around the world under a number of different product names, including Pop Rocks, Peta Zetas, and Fizz Wiz. The company also produced a carbonated chewing gum, Magic Gum.

Raw materials

The main ingredients in popping candy are sugar, corn syrup, lactose, and other flavorings and preservatives. CO_2 is added to the candy under high-pressure conditions.

Design

The design of popping candy is consistent across brands. It comes in many small pieces that are all about the same size. Pop Rocks packaging has kept many elements from the original 1970s product design, including the candy's bubble-font logo. The Pop Rocks brand has grown to include many new flavors of popping candy, including green apple, watermelon, tropical punch, and strawberry. Sugar-free formulas of the candy have also been developed. Peta Zeta, the similar carbonated candy sold by Zeta Espacial outside of the United States, features a cartoon of a character with his tongue out, eyes popping with surprise, as part of a colorful package design.

Carbon dioxide, the gas that makes popping candy pop, also gives cola its fizz. © COFFEE LOVER/SHUTTERSTOCK.COM

The manufacturing process

Popping candy is made in two stages. First, the hard candy base is heated and mixed. Then CO_2 is added to the candy in high-pressure containers. Once the candy has cooled and hardened, the containers are opened, removing the pressure. The candy reacts to the drop in pressure by shattering into small pieces. Each of these pieces contains air bubbles that hold the CO_2 that creates the candy's fizzy, popping qualities.

1 The candy is mixed in large quantities by factory machinery. Sugar, corn syrup, flavoring, and water are combined and then heated until the mixture boils. The candy is boiled until all the water has evaporated, leaving a pure sugar syrup with a temperature of about 300 degrees

Think about It!

Although the urban legend about exploding Pop Rocks caused General Foods to stop selling the candy in 1983, the same tall tale is a major reason why kids still want to buy popping candy today: to test the legend out and see if it is true. Why do you think that doing something that feels dangerous but is known to really be safe, like riding a roller coaster or eating popping candy and drinking soda, is often so much fun?

Fahrenheit (149 degrees Celsius). This hot sugar mixture is the medium, or the "matrix," in which the CO_2 will be stored.

2 The hot liquid candy is placed in high-pressure containers, where it is allowed to mix with CO_2. The candy and gas are kept at a pressure level of 4,137 kilopascals, or 600 pounds per square inch, about forty times the amount of pressure naturally present in the atmosphere, until the candy has had time to cool and harden.

3 When a container is opened, the sudden lowering of pressure causes the lump of candy to shatter into many small pieces.

4 The small pieces are run through a sieve, a container with holes in it that allows smaller particles to pass through it while larger ones are held back, to make sure that each piece of candy is roughly the same size.

5 The pieces of candy contain small bubbles that hold CO_2. The bigger the bubble, the more highly carbonated the candy. Each batch of popping candy is rated for level of carbonation on a scale of zero to fourteen, with fourteen being the most intense level of fizz. If a batch scores below a seven on this scale, it is thrown away.

6 After batches have been inspected, the candy is packaged by an automated system. The most commonly sold package contains 0.3 ounces (9.5 grams) of individual small candy pieces. Packs of candy are sealed, boxed, and shipped to distributors all over the world.

Quality control

Quality control measures include the inspection of raw ingredients, careful maintenance of factories and machines, and tests of each batch of candy before it is packaged. The Zeta Espacial factories in Spain, where most Pop Rocks candy were made as of 2015, follow European Economic Community technical and sanitary regulations and use a state-of-the-art safety inspection program.

Safety

Popping candy is as safe to eat as any other candy. The candy does not contain enough CO_2 to cause harm and does not combine explosively

WORDS TO KNOW

Carbon dioxide (CO_2): A colorless and odorless gas that can be dissolved in water.

Carbonated: Containing dissolved carbon dioxide.

Matrix: A substance in which another substance is held.

Novelty: Something that is unusual or new.

Patent: An official document that gives an individual or a company exclusive rights over the use of an invention.

Urban legend: A story, usually about an unusual event, that is believed to be true even though it has little basis in fact.

with other carbonated substances. The total amount of CO_2 contained in a packet of popping candy is only about one-tenth of the amount in a single mouthful of a carbonated soft drink.

The Pop Rocks legend

In the early twenty-first century, Pop Rocks are sold as a novelty candy and nostalgia item, meaning the candy appeals to people from an earlier generation, sometimes with limited-edition twists such as the Pop Rocks chocolate bar. Other brands of carbonated candies are sold around the world. HLEKS, a company based in Turkey, has been the international market leader in the development of new popping treats since 2000. Australian company Cadbury Schweppes Pty. Ltd. began selling Marvellous Creations Jelly Popping Candy Beanies in 2012. The treat is a mixture of candy-covered chocolate, jelly beans, and popping candy. Fancier adult treats using popping candy have also been created, notably by British chef Heston Blumenthal (1966–), who won awards for his spiced popping candy chocolate tart.

The Pop Rocks urban legend is also still active. In 2003 the "mixing Pop Rocks and soda" legend was one of the first myths tested on the popular Discovery Channel television show *MythBusters*. On the show, Adam Savage (1967–) and Jamie Hyneman (1956–) combined six packs of Pop Rocks and six cans of carbonated soda inside a stomach from a pig. They chose a pig's stomach for their experiment because it holds about the same amount of liquid as a human stomach. Even when they added acid to more correctly represent an active human digestive system, the stomach did not explode, and the show exposed the myth as "busted."

Still, as long as popping candy is startling to eat, the sense of excitement and danger that surrounds it will remain. Kids want to try popping candy

Try This!

Fizzy fun

Although there is not enough carbon dioxide (CO_2) contained within a package of popping candy to inflate a balloon, with the added help of carbonated soda, you can use popping candy to create a fizzing (CO_2) inflation system. Follow the directions below to see the candy's carbonation in action.

You will need:

- uninflated balloon
- funnel
- popping candy
- bottled soda or other carbonated drink

Directions:

1. Insert the narrow end of the funnel into the neck of the balloon.

2. Using the funnel, pour the popping candy into the balloon.

3. Stretch the balloon over the mouth of the drink bottle, making sure that the candy in the balloon does not fall out.

4. Empty the candy out of the balloon into the soda bottle. As the soda reacts with the candy, you should see the balloon start to inflate.

to experience the legend for themselves, and then they want to share the thrill with their friends. Even adults are fond of the unique popping candy.

For more information

BOOKS

Leavitt, Loralee. *Candy Experiments 2.* Kansas City, MO: Andrews McMeel Publishing, 2014.

Rudolph, Marv. *Pop Rocks: The Inside Story of America's Revolutionary Candy.* Sharon, MA: Specialty Publishers, 2006.

PERIODICALS

Levine, Elise Hilf. "Confectionery Chemistry." *Science Teacher* 63, no. 5 (1996): 18.

"What Common Gas Do Swiss Cheese and Pop Rocks Have in Common?" *Kids Discover* (November 15, 2013). Available online at http://www.kidsdiscover. com/quick-reads/common-gas-swiss-cheese-pop-rocks-common/ (accessed July 18, 2015).

WEBSITES

Hudak, Diana. "Pop Rocks: A Discussion of Children's Culture and Candy Consumption." Candy Favorites. http://www.candyfavorites.com/shop/pop-rocks-history.php (accessed July 18, 2015).

"Pop Rocks FAQ." Pop Rocks. http://www.pop-rocks.com/f-a-q/ (accessed July 18, 2015).

Roller Coaster

1. Based on information in the entry, would you rather ride a Russian Mountain or the Scenic Railway? Why?

2. What connection does the author draw between the Matterhorn Bobsleds ride and the revival of roller coasters? Based on other details in the entry, what other events or factors do you think contributed to this increase in popularity?

3. Because of the risk of serious injury, quality control is especially important when manufacturing a roller coaster. What other products can you think of that require a similar level of quality control?

Roller coasters are amusement park rides with linked, wheeled cars that speed across a wooden or steel track full of steep drops, sharp twists and turns, and, in some cases, inversions (loops). At the beginning of every coaster ride, a motorized chain pulls cars to the top of a towering hill. From there gravity pushes the cars down the first major drop at speeds that continue until the ride returns to its starting point. Roller coasters do not have engines like cars or trains. Instead, they rely on the conversion of potential energy, the energy built up as the cars climb the first hill, to kinetic energy (the energy of motion), which the cars release as they go downhill and move toward the next rise. Because the roller coaster never has more potential energy than at the top of the first hill, each hill is lower than the one that came before it.

Roller coasters originated in seventeenth-century Russia and first gained popularity in the United States in the late nineteenth century

Roller coasters originated in seventeenth-century Russia and first gained popularity in the United States in the late nineteenth century. © GOBOB/ SHUTTERSTOCK.COM

with the rides of inventor and businessman LaMarcus Adna Thompson (1848–1919). Thompson's Switchback Railway, which amazed visitors to Coney Island in Brooklyn, New York, in 1884, was the first in a series of gravity-defying rides that were introduced over the next half-century, peaking with the so-called "golden age" of roller coasters in the 1920s. After the Great Depression (1929–1941) and World War II (1939–1945), interest in roller coasters had faded away, and many were destroyed. The opening of the Matterhorn Bobsleds ride at Disneyland in 1959 inspired a renewed interest in roller coasters, which are now probably the most popular amusement park attraction.

Thrill seekers enjoy the towering heights, plunging drops, and high speeds of roller coasters. The Kingda Ka at Six Flags Great Adventure in Jackson, New Jersey, for instance, rockets from 0 to 128 miles (0 to 206 kilometers) per hour in only 3.5 seconds. Roller coasters are also loved for their creative designs, which range from coasters with cars that dangle from overhead tracks to coasters that let riders feel like they are flying by lying parallel to the ground below.

From icy hills to guided tracks

The earliest roller coaster prototype was dependent on winter weather. In the seventeenth and eighteenth centuries, upper-class Russians from St. Petersburg traveled to "Russian Mountains," massive ice hills that were built into sled rides. From the top of a 70-foot (21-meter) wooden tower, riders went down a 600-foot (183-meter) ice ramp that took them past valleys and hills.

French inventors created their own Russian Mountains in 1812 using a wheeled bench fitted to a grooved track. In the following decades, the French made several improvements to the ride, including designing wheels that locked securely to tracks (1817) and adding a first-ever loop (1846).

The Scenic Railway

In the United States, roller coasters began not as fun rides but to fulfill a practical need: improving the efficiency of coal mining. Along Pennsylvania's

How Everyday Products Are Made

Mauch Chunk Switchback Railway (built in 1827), train cars full of coal were sent down a mountain, followed by train cars with mules that would be used to carry the cars back to the top of the mountain after the coal was unloaded. In 1844 the Switchback was equipped with a steam-powered cable railway that pulled cars back up the mountain. It remained in operation until the mines expanded into nearby mountains.

By 1870 the Switchback was converted into a tourist attraction called the Scenic Railway. The ride, which reached speeds of 65 miles (105 kilometers) per hour, carried passengers past scenic views of the Poconos Mountains. The Scenic Railway became a popular attraction, with 35,000 passengers annually in the 1870s. The attraction inspired U.S. inventors to create their own rides. In 1878 Richard Knudsen patented the "Inclined-Plane Railway," a ride in which a car would go down one set of tracks before a lift pulled it back to the top on a parallel track. Knudsen's ride was never built.

The birth of the modern coaster

Thompson, nicknamed the "father of gravity," adapted Knudsen's system to create Coney Island's Switchback Railway. Introduced in 1884, the coaster, which cost one nickel to ride, earned $600 a day and paid for itself in only three weeks. Within five years Thompson had built

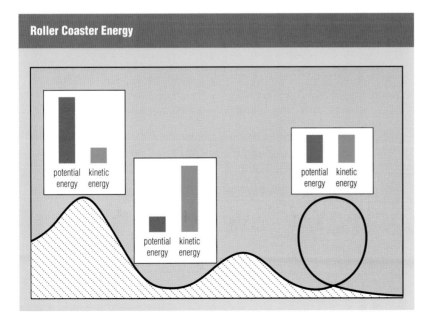

Roller Coaster Energy

potential energy / kinetic energy

potential energy / kinetic energy

potential energy / kinetic energy

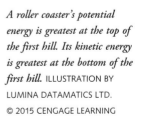

A roller coaster's potential energy is greatest at the top of the first hill. Its kinetic energy is greatest at the bottom of the first hill. ILLUSTRATION BY LUMINA DATAMATICS LTD.
© 2015 CENGAGE LEARNING

nearly fifty roller coasters in Europe and the United States, including rides that plunged into dark tunnels.

In the following decades, such roller coasters, including the Mystic Screw, which twisted passengers through a 75-foot (23-meter) helix, or corkscrew spiral, and the Flip-Flap, which had a 30-foot-high (9-meter-high) loop, dominated Coney Island. Roller coasters also became international sensations. Starting in 1912, one such coaster in Luna Park in Melbourne, Australia, served between eight thousand and ten thousand passengers every Saturday night.

The golden age of scream machines

By the 1920s U.S. amusement parks were home to approximately fifteen hundred roller coasters, which thrilled riders with faster drops and higher heights. The fastest at that time went 61 miles (98 kilometers) per hour; the tallest stood 138 feet (42 meters).

By the 1930s and 1940s, however, due to the Great Depression and World War II, most people no longer had the money or time for amusement parks. By the time the war finally ended in 1945, roller coasters had become a thing of the past. Many were torn down, and by the 1960s, the number of roller coasters in the United States had dropped from fifteen hundred to two hundred.

The roller coaster revival

The roller coaster regained popularity thanks to Walt Disney (1901–1966), who hired the Arrow Development Company to build the Matterhorn Bobsleds ride at Disneyland in 1959. Unlike past coasters, the Matterhorn was made with steel tracks, which resulted in a smoother, quieter experience. In 1975 Arrow opened the Corkscrew at California's Knott's Berry Farm. It was the first roller coaster that let passengers travel fully upside down, thanks to two loops.

In the late twentieth and early twenty-first centuries, roller coaster creators raced to top their past designs and those of their competitors. For example, the Colossus in England's Thorpe Park has ten inversions. Superman: Escape from Krypton at California's Six Flags Magic Mountain imitates freefalling with a 415-foot (126-meter) vertical drop.

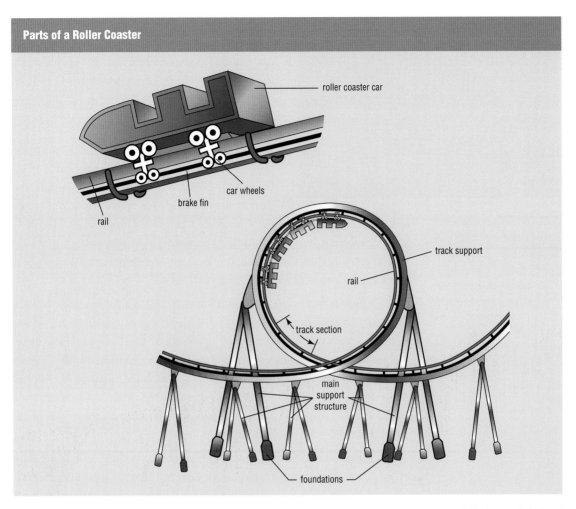

Parts of a Roller Coaster

roller coaster car

car wheels

brake fin

rail

track support

rail

track section

main support structure

foundations

The supports for steel roller coasters are manufactured in factories, then delivered to the construction site, where they are bolted and welded to their connector plates. ILLUSTRATION BY LUMINA DATAMATICS LTD. © 2015 CENGAGE LEARNING

Raw materials

There are two general categories of roller coasters: wooden and steel. Wooden roller coasters are supported by trestle-style structures (a series of horizontal beams attached to a pair of legs) held together with bolts, nails, and steel plates. Steel roller coasters are also supported by trestle-style structures, but they are made from thick steel tubes that are welded together. All coasters have tracks and lift chains made from steel. Roller coaster cars have bodies that are fashioned from aluminum or fiberglass,

with wheels usually made from polyurethane, a synthetic composite used in the manufacture of many durable items. The axles, or bars on which the cars' wheels turn, are typically made of steel.

Design

Determining a roller coaster's rider is an important early step in the design process. A ride made mostly for children will have slower speeds and gentler drops. A ride for teens and adults might take advantage of extreme speeds and heights. Designers also have to consider the amount of ground and air space they have to work with, the soil and wind conditions, and the location of nearby structures such as power lines and other amusement park rides.

Designers must select the right kind of car and track for their coaster. Wooden coasters are often designed so passengers sit in pairs, facing forward, in cars with wheels attached to the track. Steel construction allows for variations, such as cars that require passengers to stand rather than sit, or cars rolling free through a trough (like a bobsled) instead of attached to a track. Designers have also experimented with everything from adding more twists and loops to creating higher, longer climbs up the lift hill before the coaster's first big drop.

Many elements of a roller coaster's design are flexible, but all must follow to the same laws of physics to offer an exciting, safe ride. Because coasters gather energy on their climb up the lift hill, every coaster's first hill must be tall enough for cars to generate enough energy to make it all the way through the ride. Additionally, the coaster's support structure must be strong enough to handle the amount of force cars put forth on the track, and the track's every turn and loop must be banked, or tilted, at the correct angle so that cars can safely cross them. After using three-dimensional (3D) modeling programs to plan out every aspect of these coasters, designers create a prototype, or model, to test out their ideas before building the final ride.

Safety

Safety considerations are the most important part of roller coaster design. The force used by loaded cars on the track is calculated at every point of the ride to make sure that the roller coaster's support structure is strong enough. All materials used in the ride must meet government-regulated strength requirements, and the ride must pass daily safety inspections. All roller coasters have a passenger restraint system—either a lap bar or an over-the-shoulder harness. All aspects of a roller coaster's operation are monitored by computers, which make sure that all restraint systems are locked before departure, control the speed of the ride, and maintain the proper distance between the individual cars.

The manufacturing process

Designers are responsible for planning the roller coaster, but construction crews do the actual building. These teams follow the designers' blueprints piece by piece to assemble each coaster. The type of coaster determines how long each project takes. Wooden coasters usually require about nine months to complete, and steel coasters take anywhere from a year and a half to five years. Though the project time varies, the steps every crew follows are roughly the same.

1 Before any part of the roller coaster can be assembled, the area where it will be built must be prepared. That means that any existing structures or vegetation must be removed, holes must be filled with dirt, and the ground must be completely level.

2 Once the land is ready, holes for the foundation of the coaster's support structure are drilled or dug. If the ground is soft or sandy, large wooden columns are driven into the holes to make sure the coaster's foundation does not sink or move over time. Modern coasters often have as many as two thousand such holes, which are also known as foundation points.

3 Mixer trucks fill the holes with concrete. Before the concrete dries, a heavy metal plate, called a connector plate, is set into the concrete. The tops of these plates stick out of the concrete so that the coaster's main supports can later be attached to the foundation.

4 Workers build the main support structure, which must handle the weight of the coaster. Starting with the lower supports and making their way to the upper supports, workers lift each support piece with cranes, arrange it in its proper place, and attach it to the connector plates. For wooden coasters, the supports are cut on the worksite from unfinished lumber and attached to the connector plates with bolts and nails. The main supports for steel coasters are manufactured in factories, driven to the construction site, and then bolted and welded to their connector plates.

Think about It!

In the late eighteenth century, Russian leader Catherine the Great (1729–1796) was said to have enjoyed the popular Russian Mountain ride so much that she had one constructed for her personal use. The version built for her was designed for use in summer weather, with wheeled carts and a grooved track in 1784. Imagine you were as powerful as Catherine the Great. What amusement park ride would you have built for yourself and your friends? What special features would you add?

5 Workers now lay down the roller coaster's track on top of the support structure. Just like their main supports, the track sections for steel coasters consist of steel tubes made in factories that are assembled at the worksite and then attached to each other and the main support structure. Wooden coasters also have steel tracks, but these steel rails are mounted in parallel rows on top of six to eight layers of wood.

6 Workers add walkways and handrails, which provide easy access for maintenance crews when working on the coaster and allow passengers to safely exit the ride if there is an emergency.

7 The lift chain and anti-rollback mechanism are installed. The lift chain pulls cars up the coaster's lift hill, and the anti-rollback mechanism prevents the cars from rolling backward down the lift hill.

8 The coaster's brake system must be installed in the track. Most coasters rely on a computer-controlled mechanism, a fin brake, in which a fin installed on the bottom of the car brings that car to a complete stop whenever it encounters enough friction. Some newer roller coasters rely on magnetized brakes, where a strong magnet on the bottom of each car brings the car to a stop when it passes over oppositely charged magnets on the track.

9 Workers add cars to the roller coaster. Each car is held to the track by three kinds of wheels: wheels that guide the cars along the coaster's path, wheels that support the weight of each car, and wheels built underneath the track that lock the cars to the track.

10 Workers add finishing touches. Electrical wiring is installed to light the ride, the coaster is painted, its boarding station is installed, and signs and landscaping are added around it.

Quality control

Before laying the foundation of a new roller coaster, workers inspect all materials to make sure that each piece is sturdy enough to support the combined weight of the ride and its riders. Government inspectors frequently visit the worksite to make sure each phase of construction follows government safety rules.

How Everyday Products Are Made

WORDS TO KNOW

Axle: A bar on which a wheel turns.

Density: The mass of a substance in a given space. The greater the substance's density, the tighter its molecules are packed in the space.

Electromagnetism: The use of electrical current to create a magnetic field.

Fiberglass: A durable material composed of threads of glass. Fiberglass is widely used in manufacturing and is often used to reinforce plastics.

Kinetic energy: The energy of motion. An object has energy when it is in motion.

Patent: An official document that gives an individual or a company exclusive rights over the use of an invention.

Potential energy: Energy that is built up as a result of position. For example, as cars in a roller coaster climb the initial lift hill, they build up potential energy.

Prototype: An early example of a product that is later used as a model for production.

Once the roller coaster has been constructed, its cars are loaded with dummies or sandbags that simulate the weight of riders. Then the ride is tested several times to make sure everything functions safely and properly. In addition to government investigators who inspect the finished ride before it opens, each roller coaster undergoes a daily inspection by amusement park workers before anybody can ride it.

The future of roller coasters

In the past, roller coaster lovers had to choose between wooden or steel rides, but passengers now can ride both at once thanks to wooden-and-steel coaster hybrids. The year 2013 marked the premiere of several looping wooden hybrids, including the Iron Rattler at Six Flags Fiesta Texas. Even more looping hybrids are planned for parks in Ireland, China, and Sweden. Future coasters will also likely depend more on electromagnetic technology, in which magnetic waves drive cars across the coaster's track. Roller coaster designers are hoping to use this technology to create magnetically soaring coasters that would proceed without any bumps or noise at all.

For more information

BOOKS
"From Blueprint to Ride: Building a Coaster." In *Roller Coasters*. Edited by Jenny MacKay. Detroit: Lucent Books, 2013.

A Backyard Roller Coaster

Frisco High School seniors Nathan Rubin and Ian Mair built a roller coaster in Rubin's Texas backyard for an independent study project. The eighteen-year-old engineering students worked with mentors from amusement park company Six Flags as well as employees of roller coaster and engineering companies. The two also relied on more than $1,000 in donations from Home Depot and other local businesses to help pay for nearly $1,500 worth of supplies, including 4,000 screws.

After five hundred hours of hard work, which included puzzling over math equations and coating their coaster's car in black and green paint, they were finally ready to test out the Predator, a 10-foot-high, 60-foot-long (3x18-meter) roller coaster. The Predator, whose car launched down an initial 9-foot (3-meter) drop before continuing over two smaller humps, remains one of the few successful backyard coasters to ever exist in the United States. By the time he left for college, Rubin needed to break down the coaster, but it was worth it: the Predator earned him scholarship money to help pay for his college tuition.

"Roller Coasters." In *Encyclopedia of Play in Today's Society.* Edited by Rodney P. Carlisle. Vol. 2. Thousand Oaks, CA: SAGE Publications, 2009.

PERIODICALS

MacDonald, Brady. "Get Ready for the Next Wave of Looping Wooden Coasters." *Los Angeles Times* (October 1, 2014). Available online at http://www.latimes.com/travel/themeparks/la-trb-looping-wooden-coasters-next-wave-20140929-story.html (accessed June 10, 2015).

Meyers, Jessica. "Liberty High Seniors Build Roller Coaster in Frisco Back Yard." *Dallas Morning News* (May 27, 2010). Available online at http://www.dallasnews.com/news/education/headlines/20100527-Liberty-High-seniors-build-roller-coaster-5219.ece (accessed June 12, 2015).

WEBSITES

"A Century of Screams: The History of the Roller Coaster." American Experience. http://www.pbs.org/wgbh/amex/coney/sfeature/history.html (accessed June 10, 2015).

Crockett, Zachary. "The Business of Building Roller Coasters." Priceonomics. http://priceonomics.com/the-business-of-building-roller-coasters/ (accessed June 10, 2015).

"Roller Coasters." BBC. http://news.bbc.co.uk/cbbcnews/hi/find_out/guides/trends/rollercoasters/newsid_1578000/1578955.stm (accessed June 22, 2015).

Shaving Cream

Shaving cream is a grooming product that is used to make hair removal more comfortable. Invented in the early twentieth century as an alternative to shaving soap, shaving cream is typically made of water, oil, and soap or soaplike substances called surfactants. It is packaged in tubs, tubes, or aerosol cans and is available in a variety of fragrances, colors, and consistencies. Shaving cream that comes in tubs or tubes may need to be lathered with a brush or fingertips. Canned shaving cream comes out of the can as foam or gel, which begins to foam as it is heated by the skin.

Archaeologists (scientists who study ancient humans and their cultures) believe shaving was around before recorded history. Recovered relics and cave paintings suggest that prehistoric humans used clam shells, knives made of flint (a hard mineral), and shark teeth to remove unwanted hair as long ago as 30,000 BCE. Ancient Sumerians and Egyptians used animal fats, oils, and simple forms of soap to lessen the discomfort of shaving. As soap evolved, it became used most often for shaving. Common soap was used throughout Europe for shaving until the early nineteenth century, when soap designed just for shaving was introduced first in England and later in the United States. Shaving soap became less popular a century later when shaving cream hit the market.

A key tool in the shaving process, shaving cream helps prevent cuts and skin irritation such as razor burn by lubricating (to make smooth or slippery) the skin. This allows the razor to glide more easily. Shaving cream also swells (increases in size) and softens individual hairs so they can easily be cut by the razor blade. Shaving creams that produce a thick lather can also show which parts of the skin have been shaved and which still need attention. The film that the cream leaves behind after the shaving process helps soothe freshly shaved skin.

Soothing soap

The first known use of shaving cream is credited to the Sumerian civilization in Iraq about 4,000 years ago. Ancient Sumerians mixed wood ashes with animal fat to create a simple soap that could then be applied to the area meant for shaving. Ancient civilizations around the world had different recipes for soap making. A Babylonian recipe for soap made from water, alkali, and cassia oil dates to around 2200 BCE. According to the Ebers Papyrus, a medical text from 1550 BCE, Egyptians used a mixture of alkaline salts and animal or vegetable oils to create a soaplike product. One of the most famous soap recipes comes from the ancient city of Aleppo in Syria. Made from olive oil, sweet bay oil, water, and lye, Aleppo soap became a popular product along the Silk Road, an ancient trade route that linked China and Rome, Italy.

During the Middle Ages (c. 500–c. 1500) Crusaders (European Christians who fought against Muslims over land) brought Aleppo soap back to Europe, where it became popular. The recipe was changed over time, and castile soap made in Spain soon became the most sought-after variation of Aleppo soap. Castile soap was traded throughout Europe and finally entered the English market during the mid-1500s. As soap became more common, it changed grooming practices in Europe and was often used as a shaving aid. Its thick lather helped keep moisture and created a cushion between the razor and the skin. Although most shaving was done by men wishing to remove their beards, both men and women began shaving their heads in the 1700s to wear the popular powdered wigs of the time period. It was around this time that shaving tools such as the shaving brush and mug began to appear.

By the early 1800s, soaps designed specifically for shaving began to appear in England. Introduced in 1840, Vroom and Fowler's Walnut Oil Military Shaving Soap became one of the most widely available shaving soaps on the market. Sold as a tablet, the shaving aid created a luxurious foam when combined with water, offering moisture-holding properties that made it more useful than the simple soaps of the past. Around the same time, Connecticut-born James Baker Williams (1818–1907) developed Williams' Genuine Yankee Soap, which became a very popular product in the United States. Shaving soap was also available in sticks and powders in the mid- to late 1800s.

Cream of the crop

Creating a thick lather with shaving soaps could take time and be difficult, so a number of inventors tried to lessen the hassle of shaving with soap, a brush, and a mug. In 1914 the U.S. company Colgate invented the first brushless shaving cream, known as Rapid-Shave. Unlike shaving soap, shaving cream did not require lathering with a brush and could be applied directly to the face. Shaving cream was also a better lubricant than soap and left a thin coating of oil on the skin that reduced irritation and made the skin softer.

Colgate's Rapid-Shave was followed five years later by Barbasol shaving cream, a product that remained popular into the early twenty-first century. Its thick, creamy formula was packaged in collapsible tubes. In 1925 Burma-Shave hit the market. Demand for the product was low at first, but a quirky marketing campaign featuring wacky, rhyming billboards saved the day. Between the 1920s and the 1960s, more than 7,000 billboards along U.S. highways advertised Burma-Shave.

The market for shaving cream truly exploded with the invention of the aerosol spray can, which had been used during World War II (1939–1945) to spray insecticides (chemicals used to kill insects). After the war the U.S. secretary of agriculture allowed U.S. companies to use the aerosol patent. Aeroshave, the first instant shaving cream in an aerosol can, was introduced in 1947, followed by Carter-Wallace's Rise shaving cream in 1949. In the 1950s Barbasol replaced its tubes of shaving cream with the new aerosol cans, which produced a fluffy foam. Because this shaving cream contained soap, men no longer had to wash their beards before shaving. Shaving foam in a pressurized can soon became the most popular shaving aid on the U.S. market.

In 1970 S. C. Johnson & Son introduced Edge shaving gel, which was a better skin lubricant than foam and offered better protection from skin irritation. In 1993 Proctor & Gamble patented a shaving gel that turned into a foam after it was applied to the skin, thus combining properties of both foams and gels. After this the market for post-foaming shaving gel increased greatly while shaving foam sales dropped. In 2008 retail sales for men's shaving foam totaled $49 million; post-foaming shaving gel was $131 million. Some companies, including Colgate, stopped manufacturing shaving foam.

Raw materials

Although each brand of shaving cream has its own secret formula, most contain the same basic ingredients: water, oil, and soap. Shaving creams are 80 percent water, which is used to dissolve and evenly separate ingredients while also making the shaving cream easy to spread. Oil and soap are added to provide moisture, create viscosity (resistance to flow), and produce lather. Soap is a surfactant, meaning it has parts that attract dirt and grease and other parts that attract water. Surfactants commonly used in shaving cream include stearic acid, palmitic acid, coconut fatty acids, triethanolamine, and sodium lauryl sulfate (a foam stabilizer). Oils are types of humectants that help lubricate and hold moisture to the skin. Common humectants and conditioners found in shaving cream include mineral oil, lanolin, glycerin, guar gums, and polyoxyethylene sorbitan monostearate. Glycerin is a solvent and an emollient, a substance that leaves skin soft.

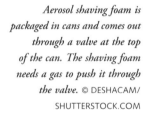

Aerosol shaving foam is packaged in cans and comes out through a valve at the top of the can. The shaving foam needs a gas to push it through the valve. © DESHACAM/ SHUTTERSTOCK.COM

Some manufacturers add aesthetic components to shaving cream such as fragrance, essential oils, aloe, vitamin E, colorants, and antiaging ingredients. Sometimes menthol is added for fragrance and to create a cooling sensation on the skin.

Design

Nonaerosol shaving cream is packaged in tubes and tubs made of plastic, though some tubes may be made out of metal. Shaving cream is scooped out of tubs, and collapsible tubes are squeezed to dispense (to give out) the product. Lathering shaving cream must be used with a shaving brush; non-lathering creams can be applied directly to the area intended for shaving.

How Everyday Products Are Made

Aerosol shaving foam and post-foaming gel are packaged in steel or aluminum cans and are dispensed through a valve at the top of the can. Both types of shaving cream need a propellant (a gas) to help dispense the product. Common propellants are butane, isobutene, pentane, and propane. For shaving foams, the soap mixture is placed directly in the can, the can is sealed with a valve, and then propellant is added through the valve. When a small amount of shaving cream is dispensed, it expands into a rich foam.

Post-foaming shaving gels do not expand as much as shaving foams when they are dispensed. The foaming action takes place once the gel is heated by the skin. Post-foaming shaving gel also includes a moisturizer that helps protect the skin before and after shaving. In a "bag-in-can" system, the shaving gel is poured into a bag that is supported by the neck of the can. A valve is placed on the can, securing the bag. A propellant is inserted into the cavity between the bag and the can wall through a hole in the base of the can. In the "pouch-on-valve" system, a pouch is sealed onto the bottom of the valve, which is then placed inside the can. Before the valve is secured, the space between the pouch and the can wall is pressurized. The product is then introduced to the can through the valve.

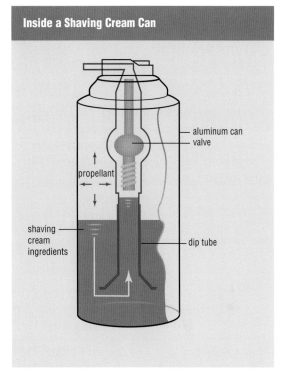

Inside a Shaving Cream Can

propellant

aluminum can
valve

shaving cream ingredients

dip tube

When the top of the can is pressed and the valve is opened, a gas propellant pushes the shaving cream up and out of the can. ILLUSTRATION BY LUMINA DATAMATICS LTD. © 2015 CENGAGE LEARNING

Safety

Most aerosol shaving cans are labeled with a warning telling users to keep the product away from sources of heat and to store the cans at room temperature. Consumers are also warned not to put a hole in or burn the can. Some of the chemicals used, including lauryl sulphate, have been linked to cancer.

The manufacturing process

The manufacture of shaving cream is a carefully monitored process and may differ from brand to brand. Post-foaming shave gel is the most

Think about It!

Oils and animal fats were the first substances used as shaving aids. Why do you think they became less popular when soap, shaving soap, and soap-based shaving creams were introduced? Why might soap and soap-based products be better than the oils of plants or animals for shaving?

popular shaving cream on the modern market. The manufacturing process for most post-foaming gels is similar.

1 A surfactant such as castor oil is added to a mixer along with any fragrances.

2 The mixture is heated to 100 degrees Fahrenheit (40 degrees Celsius) and mixed until well blended.

3 Another surfactant, such as 50 percent lauryl glucoside, is heated to the same temperature and added to the mixer while stirring.

4 Water is heated to the same temperature and is slowly added to the mixer while stirring. Stirring continues until the resulting substance is well blended.

5 A colorant is added to the mixer, and the mixture is stirred until the color is well blended. A preservative is added to the mixer and stirred until dissolved.

6 The contents of the mixer and a post-foaming agent such as isopentane are cooled separately to 40 degrees Fahrenheit (4 degrees Celsius).

7 The post-foaming agent is added to the mixer slowly while stirring. Stirring continues until contents are well blended.

8 The product is poured into the packaging, and the valve is set in place.

9 The container is pressurized through a hole in the base using a propellant. A small cork is placed in the hole to prevent the propellant from leaking.

Quality control

Shaving cream is manufactured under strict quality control and is regulated by various federal agencies, including the U.S. Food and Drug Administration (FDA). Batches of shaving cream are tested both at the manufacturing site and in a laboratory. Among the things tested are pH value (the acidity or alkalinity of the product), the height of the foam when sprayed, and water quality. Some manufacturers use a microbiologist (a scientist who studies microscopic life forms) to test the water and the final product for contaminants

Aerosol: A substance kept under pressure in a container, often a can, and released as a spray.

Biodegradable: Able to be broken down naturally with the help of living things.

Carcinogen: A substance known to cause cancer.

Emollient: A substance that soothes or softens.

Groom: To clean and care for the appearance of a person or thing.

Humectant: A substance that promotes moisture retention.

Lubricant: A substance that reduces friction when applied between surfaces.

Lubricate: To make smooth or slippery, often with the application of oil or grease.

Microbiologist: A scientist who studies microscopic organisms.

Patent: An official document that gives an individual or a company exclusive rights over the use of an invention.

Solvent: A solid, liquid, or gas in which another solid, liquid, or gas is dissolved to create a solution.

Surfactant: A substance that reduces the surface tension of water, promoting foaming.

Viscosity: Resistance to flow.

(harmful substances that make something unfit for use). The ingredients in shaving creams are also examined for their potential to cause skin or eye irritation or allergic reactions. Aerosol shaving products are put into water in order to detect leaks.

Growing concern for the environment

Aerosol shaving creams are the most popular shaving aids on the market, with post-foaming gel taking the lead over shaving foam. However, shaving soaps and hand-applied creams have made somewhat of a comeback in the early twenty-first century. Consumers trying to avoid harmful chemicals and carcinogens (substances that can cause cancer) have turned to soaps and creams made from natural, organic, and biodegradable (able to be broken down naturally with the help of microorganisms and other living things) ingredients. Recipes for homemade shaving cream using household products are also widely available.

For more information
BOOKS
Ditchfield, Christin. *The Story behind Soap.* Chicago: Heinemann-Raintree, 2011.

Try This!

Shaving cream marbling

Aerosol shaving cream foam can be used to lubricate squeaky hinges, remove stains from carpets and clothing, and prevent steam from collecting on mirrors and eyeglasses. It can also be used in classrooms as a teaching aid, particularly for students who learn better by doing. When mixed with cornstarch, shaving foam turns into a substance similar to modeling clay. Aerosol shaving cream foam can also be used in arts and crafts projects, such as the one below.

You will need:

- aerosol shaving cream foam (not post-foaming gel)
- jelly roll pan or tray with a lip
- rubber spatula (optional)
- several colors of food dye or liquid watercolor paints
- toothpick
- piece of white paper
- ruler or other flat edge

Directions:

1. Spread shaving cream foam on the surface of the pan or tray. Using a rubber spatula or your hand, smooth the foam to create a flat surface.

2. Using food dye or liquid watercolors, squeeze drops of various colors onto the shaving cream.

3. Use a toothpick to swirl the colors together to create a marbling effect.

4. Place a piece of white paper on top of the marbled colors. Press down and smooth your hands over the paper.

5. Lift the paper. Use the ruler to scrape the shaving cream off the paper.

6. Allow the paper to dry.

Levy, Joel. *Really Useful: The Origins of Everyday Things.* Richmond Hill, ON, Canada: Firefly Books, 2002.

Patrick, Bethanne, and John Milliken Thompson. *An Uncommon History of Common Things.* Washington, DC: National Geographic Books, 2009.

PERIODICALS

Trex, Ethan. "A Brief History of Shaving" *Mentalfloss Magazine* (August 11, 2009). Available online at http://mentalfloss.com/article/22490/brief-history-shaving (accessed June 25, 2015).

WEBSITES

History of Shaving Cream. http://perfectshave.com/history-of-shaving-cream-part-1-of-1/ (accessed June 29, 2015).

Skateboard and Longboard

Critical Thinking Questions

1. What are the most important differences between a skateboard and a longboard? Which board would be more useful to you? Why?

2. In the section titled "The evolving skateboard," the author describes a skateboard that does not have a deck. Do you think this is really a skateboard? Why or why not?

Skateboards and longboards are types of sports equipment made of pieces of wood with four wheels attached to the bottom. Though similar in design to skateboards, longboards are slightly longer and heavier and have larger wheels. Longboards are used mainly for racing downhill, "cruising" (riding around for fun), and getting from one place to another. Skateboards are designed mainly for doing tricks, either on the street or on specially built courses. Both skateboards and longboards are powered by the rider, who pushes one foot against the ground to move forward and to control the speed.

Surfers in California handmade the first skateboards in the 1940s or 1950s by screwing roller-skate wheels to short planks of wood. Early skateboard and longboard builders tried to recreate the experience of surfing an ocean wave on the paved streets and sidewalks of their neighborhoods. These homemade versions gained popularity, and the first mass-produced skateboards were built and sold in 1959. With specialized builders in the 1960s came a number of design improvements, most notably the use of hard rubber instead of metal to make wheels. As skateboard design improved, skateboarders were able to ride more

The Roller Derby company has been credited with making the first mass-produced skateboard around 1959. © DMITRY ZIMIN/ SHUTTERSTOCK.COM

easily and do more complicated moves, turning a relatively relaxed pastime into a new sport.

Skateboards and longboards not only provide a way to get around, but they also present a wide range of fun, recreational possibilities. Longboards are designed to be more comfortable and easier to use. Skateboards are made to be light and more flexible. Riders can flip, spin, and slide their skateboard on ramps, over obstacles, and along curbs and rails. While some skateboarders and longboarders ride competitively, boards are most often prized for how much fun they offer.

From rocker skates to skateboards

The origins of skateboarding can be traced to the mid-eighteenth century, when Belgian inventor John Joseph Merlin (1735–1803) invented "rocker skates" in London, England. Over the next century, roller-skate design improved. In 1863 American inventor James Plimpton (1828–1911) patented the "rocking" skate. Unlike previous roller-skate designs, the rocking skate included four wheels, arranged in two rows. Plimpton's skates were attached to rubber cushions, allowing the user to turn by leaning in the direction he or she wanted to go.

During the early twentieth century, a number of devices used the features of the rocking skate in new ways. In 1921 a patent was taken out for a kick scooter (also known as a push scooter). Kick scooters featured four roller-skate wheels attached to the bottom of a wooden board, which had a handle rising from the top of the board, near the front (the "nose"). Riders pushed off with their back foot to gain speed and turned the handle to change direction. Kick scooters quickly became popular, and scooter manufacturers introduced various improvements, including rubber wheels and detachable handlebars, over the next several decades. At the same time surfing was exploding in popularity in California, and surfboard technology was improving.

Inventors began to look for ways to use kick scooter and roller-skate technology to bring the experience of surfing to land. While no single inventor can be credited with building the first skateboard, surfers and children made homemade skateboards during the 1950s. Often the decks, or flat boards, were made from the scraps of old wooden boxes, and the wheels were taken from roller skates or kick scooters. Many of the first skateboards were made from 2 × 4-inch (5 × 10-centimeter) boards. However, other boards were longer and thinner—a design that more closely resembled surfboards. These longer, thinner boards were the first longboards.

Commercial skateboards began to appear in the late 1950s or early 1960s. The exact date of the first commercially available skateboards is difficult to determine because of competing claims from various builders. However, the Roller Derby company has been credited with making the first mass-produced skateboard, the Skate Board, around 1959. In the early 1960s, more skateboard manufacturers, including Hobie and Makaha, opened in Southern California. The first manufactured skateboards had decks made of flat wooden boards and either metal roller-skate wheels or wheels made of clay mixed with other materials.

Skateboarding remained popular from the late 1950s to the early 1960s, but interest in the sport suddenly dropped off around 1965. While it is hard to know exactly why, some believe it was a problem

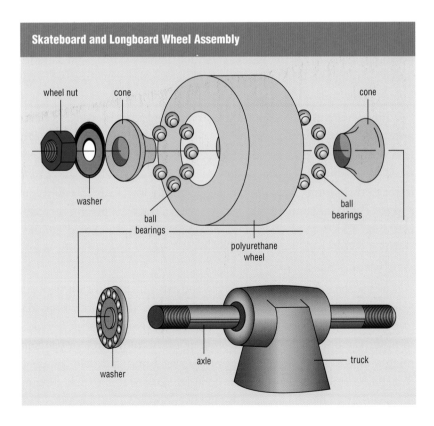

Skateboard and Longboard Wheel Assembly

wheel nut

cone

cone

washer

ball bearings

ball bearings

polyurethane wheel

washer

axle

truck

Most skateboards have wheels with a slightly smaller diameter than the wheels on a longboard. Larger wheels allow riders to travel at faster speeds. Smaller wheels are better for doing tricks. ILLUSTRATION BY LUMINA DATAMATICS LTD. © 2015 CENGAGE LEARNING

with the wheels. Metal wheels lacked grip and stability, and clay wheels tended to break and wear out. Over the next decade, mass production slowed greatly, and skateboarders returned to building their own boards at home from whatever materials were available.

Designing for new possibilities

In the early 1970s, American Frank Nasworthy (1951–) was visiting a friend who had some experimental wheels made of polyurethane, a rubberlike material. Nasworthy tried to sell these wheels to roller-skate manufacturers, but they did not catch on, in part because rubber wheels were slower than metal wheels on wooden roller rinks. He tried using the new wheels on skateboards, and he found that they offered a smoother, safer, and more controlled experience for users. Nasworthy founded the Cadillac Wheels Company in 1972 to sell his new wheels to skateboarders and manufacturers.

Over the next few years, polyurethane wheels helped skateboarding grow again in popularity. Skateboard design also improved during the 1970s. Specialized skateboard trucks (the T-shaped metal parts that connect the wheels to the deck of a skateboard) with more width offered improved range of motion. In addition, new "banana boards" made of polypropylene, a type of plastic, featured light, flexible, and colorful decks. During the 1970s skateboard designers also experimented with boards made from fiberglass, a material made of threads of glass.

Improvements in design and materials changed the way skateboards were used. For example, during a 1975 skateboarding contest in Del Mar, California, a team of skateboarders known as the Zephyr team, or the Z-Boys, introduced a new style of skateboarding. The Z-Boys rode lower to the ground, hugging the pavement the way a surfer would hug a wave. This influential style led to a new era of competitive skateboarding. Riders used drained swimming pools as skateboard courses, and skate parks were built in California, Florida, and other areas where skateboarding was popular.

As skateboarders created new styles and experimented with new places to skate, designers began to change and improve skateboards. One key improvement came after skateboarders began to "ollie"—a trick first performed around 1978 that involves popping the board into the air by slamming a foot down on the tail end of the skateboard and then jumping. Skateboarders then developed more complex versions of the trick, flipping the board, spinning the board, jumping over obstacles, and jumping onto obstacles such as railings. In response to this trend, manufacturers added curved tails to skateboards in the 1980s to allow riders to more easily pop their skateboards into the air. Since the tail of the board changes sides as the board spins, manufacturers eventually curved both ends of the deck. This led to the popularization of symmetrical (the same on both ends) decks and changed the sport of skateboarding by allowing skateboarders to perform tricks without having to worry about which end was the nose or tail. Riders could do more tricks—and more complex tricks—more easily.

While small improvements have been made since the 1980s, the basic design and materials used to make skateboards have not changed much. However, in the 1990s some skateboarders began to return to the early days of the sport, when the focus was on cruising around more than doing tricks. This led to a rise in the popularity of longboards, which feature longer, heavier, flat decks that are ideal for getting around.

Raw materials

Skateboards and longboards consist of three separate parts: the deck, the trucks, and the wheels. Decks are most often built from thin sheets of wood, usually maple, and glue. However, decks can also be made from synthetic, or artificial, materials, including fiberglass, Plexiglas, and foam. The top of the deck, where the rider stands, is covered with grip tape, which is sticky on one side and rough like sandpaper on the other side. The bottom of the deck is usually painted with a pattern. The paint is

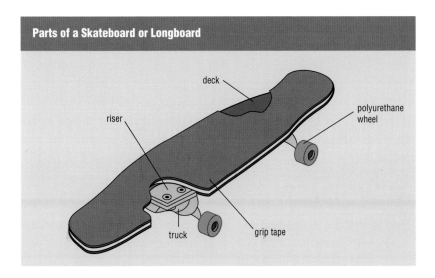

Parts of a Skateboard or Longboard

deck

polyurethane wheel

riser

truck

grip tape

Skateboards and longboards have three main parts: a deck, trucks, and wheels. A truck is a T-shaped metal part that connects the wheels to the deck.
ILLUSTRATION BY LUMINA DATAMATICS LTD. © 2015 CENGAGE LEARNING

Using a pattern representing the shape of the skateboard, a skateboard maker draws the shape on pressed boards.
© GARY OMBLER/GETTY IMAGES

typically protected with a glossy coat of polish, often a polyurethane varnish.

Skateboard trucks are made of metal. Most trucks are aluminum; others are made of steel, brass, or blends of different metals. Some advanced truck designs use nylon and other synthetic polymers to create lighter trucks that move easily when the rider moves. Wheels are almost always made from polyurethane, a material that resembles a hard rubber.

Design

The difference between skateboards and longboards lies mainly in how the three main parts (decks, trucks, and wheels) are arranged. While designers have tried using a range of materials for decks, longboard and skateboard decks are generally made of wood.

Skateboard decks are almost always made from seven thin layers of maple. These layers, or veneers, are pressed together to form a single sheet. Nearly all skateboards feature rounded noses and tails, and the nose and tail are usually curved upward. The angle of this curve depends upon the preferences of the manufacturer. The curve affects the comfort, performance, and strength of the deck. Longboard decks are made from a thicker board, which is usually bamboo, though maple or birch are also sometimes used. Longboards are usually flat, with a defined nose and tail that do not have to match each other.

The wheels of longboards and skateboards are most often made of polyurethane. On a skateboard, the wheels are attached underneath the board, on metal trucks. Longboards usually feature a narrower board and a wider truck, so that the wheels extend beyond the sides of the deck. On both longboards and skateboards, truck design varies, allowing them to be steady or flexible, depending on what the user needs.

The manufacturing process

The process of manufacturing skateboards and longboards involves making the various parts—the deck, trucks, wheels, grip tape, and paint—and then putting these elements together to make the finished product. The process varies somewhat, depending on the manufacturer and the materials used. However, boards with wooden decks and metal trucks are built with a relatively consistent method.

1 Maple is steamed using hot water for twelve to seventy-two hours to soften the wood. Within an hour of steaming, machines slice the softened wood into thin sheets known as veneers. Veneers are sent from woodshops to skateboard manufacturing facilities, where they are inspected. Veneers must be a certain temperature and have a specific moisture content to be used to make a deck.

2 Workers feed the approved veneers into a glue machine, which coats each side of each piece. The coated veneers are sorted by the direction of the wood grain. Seven veneers are needed to make each deck. Five of them—the first, second, fourth, sixth, and seventh layers—have the grain running from nose to tail of the board. Two layers—the third and fifth—have the grain running from side to side.

3 The stacked boards are put into a mold, which creates the inward curve and shape of a finished deck. A hydraulic press applies pressure and either heat or cold for minutes or hours, forcing the layers of veneer to form a single laminate board. Boards then set and cure for several days.

4 Eight holes are drilled for mounting the trucks. The board is cut in the dimensions required by the design. Cutting is done either by computerized machinery or a skilled worker using a template.

5 The deck is sanded and smoothed, then sealed with lacquer or paint.

6 Graphics are added to the bottom of the board. This is done in a variety of ways. Images and lettering are often silk-screened on, using stencils and layers of ink. Other common methods include heat printing (which involves a printed image being "ironed" onto the board) and ultraviolet printing (which applies ultraviolet light to harden traditional paint).

7 The parts of trucks—the base plate, the kingpin, the bushing, the hanger (axle), risers, washers, and lock nuts—are made from heated

Think about It!

Among the biggest improvements in the history of skateboard design was the addition of the curved tail and nose. With this small change, skateboarders were able to make much more complicated moves and do harder tricks. Can you think of another device that would not be the same without one seemingly small improvement?

WORDS TO KNOW

Fiberglass: A durable material made of threads of glass. Fiberglass is widely used in manufacturing and is often used to reinforce plastics.

Patent: An official document that gives an individual or a company exclusive rights over the use of an invention.

Polymer: A substance whose molecular structure consists of a large number of similar units bonded together.

Polyurethane: A flexible yet strong material that can be used instead of rubber and other materials.

Symmetry: The quality of having the exact same shape and features on each of an object's two sides.

Veneer: A thin piece of wood that can be a decorative covering or can be molded together with other materials to form a solid object.

metal, most often aluminum, that is poured into molds. Once the metal has hardened, the parts are removed from the molds and put together to form the truck.

8 Wheels are made from polyurethane, which is heated and mixed until it softens. Dyes are sometimes added to the polyurethane to color the wheels. The soft mixture is poured into trays with wheel-shaped molds and allowed to harden.

9 Workers add sidewalls, treads, and other features to the wheels. Machines with printing plates are used to add logos and designs.

10 The parts are put together for the finished skateboard, either by the manufacturer or by the customer. This process involves sticking grip tape to the top of the deck, bolting the trucks to the board, and using washers and nuts to join the wheels to the axle of each truck.

Quality control

The quality control process in skateboard manufacturing begins with the selection of the veneers. Inspectors carefully choose only those pieces that meet requirements for moisture, temperature, hardness, consistency, and other qualities. Once the veneers have been pressed and formed into boards, they are again inspected to make sure the layers have joined properly and that the complete deck does not have inconsistencies. During

Frank Nasworthy

Skateboarding was born and raised in Southern California. But one of its greatest figures—and greatest improvements—came from across the country. In 1970 in Annandale, Virginia, teenager Frank Nasworthy began to experiment with a new kind of wheel that would change the course of skateboarding forever.

Nasworthy had recently graduated from high school. His father was a pilot in the U.S. Navy and was stationed in Washington, D.C. One night Nasworthy went to visit a plastics factory owned by a family friend. During the visit he saw some polyurethane wheels that had been thrown away. He immediately thought they might be the right size to replace the clay wheels he and

most other skateboarders used at the time. Nasworthy took dozens of the wheels, added them to existing skateboards, and rode all over Washington.

Soon after Nasworthy moved to California and began looking for a new supply of polyurethane wheels. He found it at a company called Creative Urethanes, and in 1973 he convinced the company to make polyurethane wheels especially for skateboards. Cadillac Wheels, as he called the products, were popular, but competitors soon caught on and overtook the market. So, while his invention changed skateboarding forever by offering a smoother ride, Nasworthy moved on, eventually becoming a computer engineer.

the installation of the trucks and wheels, inspectors again test to make sure all the hardware has been properly installed.

The evolving skateboard

Skateboard and longboard design has changed very little since the mid-twentieth century. In the early twenty-first century, however, designers have begun to use computer technology to change how skateboards work. In 2015 the company Hammacher Schlemmer introduced Side-winding Circular Skates, which it bills as "The Post Modern Skateboard." This new "skateboard" does not even have a deck. Instead, it features a pair of circular electronic devices that the user steps inside, placing his or her feet on the platform inside the round "skates." As the user leans, outer rings spin, moving the rider in whichever direction he or she chooses.

For more information

BOOKS
Brooke, Michael. *The Concrete Wave: The History of Skateboarding.* Toronto: Warwick Publications, 1999.

Davis, James, and Skin Phillips. *Skateboarding Is Not a Crime: 50 Years of Street Culture.* Buffalo, NY: Firefly Books, 2004.

Hocking, Justin, Jeff Knutson, and J. Jacang Maher. *Life and Limb: Skateboarders Write from the Deep End.* Brooklyn, NY: Soft Skull Press, 2004.

Stecyk, Craig, and Glen E. Friedman. *Dogtown: The Legend of the Z-Boys.* New York: Burning Flags Press, 2000.

PERIODICALS

Davidson, J. "Sport and Modern Technology: The Rise of Skateboarding, 1963–1978." *Journal of Popular Culture* 18, no. 4 (1985): 145–57.

Weiss, Eric M. "The Reinvention of the Wheel: Annandale Teen's Idea Brought Skateboarding Back to Life." *Washington Post* (August 17, 2004). Available online at http://www.washingtonpost.com/wp-dyn/articles/A6502-2004Aug16.html (accessed July 20, 2015).

WEBSITES

International Skateboarding Federation. http://www.internationalskateboarding federation.com/ (accessed July 17, 2015).

Skateboard Science. http://www.exploratorium.edu/skateboarding/ (accessed July 17, 2015).

Transworld Skateboarding. http://skateboarding.transworld.net/ (accessed July 17, 2015).

Smartphone

Smartphones are electronic devices that combine the functions of a telephone with those of a computer. Using specially designed programs called applications, or apps, smartphones can receive and send e-mail and connect to the Internet, as well as make and receive phone calls and voice and text messages. The convenience of and ability to easily carry around smartphones has led to the introduction of many creative apps, which allow smartphones to be used as flashlights, digital recorders, music players, translators, global positioning systems (GPS), and video and still cameras, among many others.

During the 1990s many manufacturers, including Samsung, Nokia, Motorola, and Google, began developing smartphones. Though the earliest smartphones were large and clumsy, developments in technology allowed them to be smaller and easier to handle. The 2007 introduction of the Apple iPhone, with its easy-to-use touch screen, caused major

growth in the popularity of smartphones. In 2015 the Pew Research Center reported that almost two-thirds of American adults owned smartphones, while industry sources predicted that by 2018 more than 2.5 billion people, more than one-third of the world's population, will use them.

The telephone goes wireless

The telephone, a device that sends sound over electrical wires, was invented in 1876 by Alexander Graham Bell (1847–1922). Bell's telephone let users talk to each other over long distances. By 1900 almost 600,000 telephones were in use in the United States, and by 1915 calls could be made from coast to coast. Telephones made communication easier and more convenient, but their use was limited to areas where wires had been installed.

Smartphones were first introduced in the 1990s. The 2007 introduction of the Apple iPhone, with its easy-to-use touch screen, revolutionized smartphone design and caused major growth in the popularity of smartphones.
© GEORGEJMCLITTLE/
SHUTTERSTOCK.COM

Much of the early experiments with mobile phone technology was carried out by the military. During World War I (1914–1918) and World War II (1939–1945), army units used field telephones (phones that were built with protective cases and batteries so they could be carried along with the soldier) to communicate their locations and plans for battle. Although they could be carried by soldiers on the move, field telephones needed wires to work. In 1946 research company Bell Labs created a wireless telephone that used a series of towers with antennae to send and receive signals. Wireless phone transmission was available in nearly 100 American cities by 1948, but service was expensive, and the number of towers was limited. In addition, early mobile telephones used so much power that they needed a battery as large as a briefcase.

Cutting the cord

Electronic and computer technology developed during the 1960s allowed engineers to improve mobile phones, and the introduction of cellular towers made the phones more reliable. Cellular telephone service uses groups of low-voltage receiver/transmitter towers. These towers are placed in cells, six-sided arrangements that work together to pass signals from mobile phones over long distances. Cell phones are named for the arrangement of the signal towers.

Electronics company Motorola made a model of the first truly portable phone in 1973, and the first working cell tower system was built by telephone company AT&T in Chicago, Illinois, in 1978. In 1984 Motorola's DynaTAC cell phone went on the market, and by the late 1980s cell phone service was available throughout most of the United States. Early cell phones were almost as big as a shoebox, but advances in technology eventually made it possible to make smaller phones.

Blending the telephone and the computer

The first smartphone was Simon, introduced in 1993 by electronics company IBM and telephone company BellSouth. Simon worked with an IBM computer to send and receive e-mail and faxes. It also had a number of built-in apps, including an address book, a calculator, a calendar, and a notepad. Other apps could be added with a memory card. Simon cost more than $1,000, and it was around 8 inches (20 centimeters) long by 2.5 inches (6 centimeters) wide and weighed slightly more than 1 pound (0.5 kilogram). Between 1996 and 2002, electronics companies Nokia, Ericsson, and Kyocera introduced phones with greater computing capabilities and smaller, lighter designs. The Ericsson GS88, introduced in 1997, was the first to use the label "smartphone."

As some manufacturers added computing functions to the telephone, others worked to perfect a handheld device that could help users keep track of their work and personal information when they were away from their computers. These devices became known as personal digital assistants, or PDAs, and were generally used for business purposes. Early PDAs had calendars and address books, as well as a variety of other personal and business data. Although IBM produced a PDA/phone hybrid in 1994, most early PDAs, including the popular PalmPilot, introduced in 1997, did not include phones. The Treo 180, released in 2002, included a phone and ran on the Palm operating system. BlackBerry introduced a smartphone in 2003 and quickly gained popularity with professionals who wanted to keep up with e-mail and phone calls on the go.

The Apple iPhone, introduced in 2007, was a major development in user-friendly smartphones. The iPhone combined a powerful computer with an easy-to-use touch screen and could use both wireless telephone networks and Internet connections. Also in 2007 Internet company Google developed Android, a competing user-friendly operating system for smartphones. In 2008 the HTC Corporation released the Dream, the

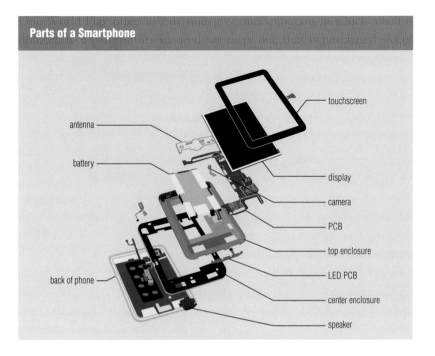

Parts of a Smartphone

- antenna
- battery
- back of phone
- touchscreen
- display
- camera
- PCB
- top enclosure
- LED PCB
- center enclosure
- speaker

Even a small smartphone is made up of many different pieces. Components such as a camera, an antenna, and a battery are made separately, then assembled to form the finished product. ILLUSTRATION BY LUMINA DATAMATICS LTD.
© 2015 CENGAGE LEARNING

first smartphone to use the Android operating system. Other manufacturers, including Nokia and Motorola, soon began producing their own versions of the Android smartphone. The convenience of a pocket-size device that combined the abilities of the telephone and the computer captured the public imagination, and smartphone sales rose quickly.

Raw materials

Though smartphones are small, as many as sixty different materials are needed to make them. Silicon, plastic, iron, aluminum, copper, and lead make up approximately 95 percent of a smartphone. Small amounts of many other elements, including zinc, nickel, barium, gold, carbon, and lithium, are needed to build the device's circuit boards, display screens, and rechargeable batteries. Some elements used in smartphone construction are very rare, including tantalum, a heavy gray metal with a very high melting point. Other elements, such as boron, arsenic, and gallium, are used in microscopic amounts. Smartphones also use small amounts of a number of "rare earth" elements such as neodymium, europium, and cerium, which have unique electronic, magnetic, and optical properties. Rare earth elements are named as such because, although common, they are hard to find in quantities large enough to mine. They also have to go through complex processes to get them into a useful form.

Design

Smartphone design is quickly changing, with manufacturers competing to create more attractive and useful products. Though early smartphone designs featured complete miniature keyboards, most smartphones in the early twenty-first century have a sleek rectangular shape with rounded edges, a solid metal or plastic housing, and a glass touch screen for entering data. Keyboards and other function buttons appear on the screen, where they can be pressed with a finger or a stylus.

The molded polycarbonate (a strong, light, flexible, petroleum-based synthetic material) or metal outer shell of a smartphone holds the circuit boards and other hardware parts that allow the phone to run applications. Many of these components are arranged on the main printed circuit board (PCB), a board on which the electrical parts are organized and connected. The PCB is usually placed in the center of the phone. Additional PCBs may be placed at the top or bottom of the phone to control the antenna that receives and sends signals when calls are made or the phone is connected to the Internet. Beneath the main PCB, the phone's rechargeable lithium battery rests on a layer of cushioning material against the back of the phone. Above the main PCB, a hard cover protects the display module, which operates the touch screen directly above it.

Other controls are placed at the top and bottom of the phone to operate various devices, such as speakers, cameras, microphones, and keypads. Charging ports and headphone jacks are placed at the edge of the phone for easy access. Because smartphones are made to be carried in a pocket or purse, synthetic (artificially made) rubber gaskets, cushions, and metal covers are carefully placed to protect delicate components from damage.

Engineers carefully study consumer trends when planning the look and feel of smartphones. Nokia was the first to offer a brightly colored smartphone, and other companies quickly followed with phones in shades of red, copper, and aqua. The surface texture of the shell is also an important factor in smartphone design. Highly polished metallic or plastic surfaces are eye-catching but may show fingerprints more easily

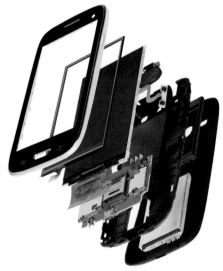

Although smartphones are thin, they are made of several layers, each with a different function.
© YOMKA/SHUTTERSTOCK.COM

than matte (non-shiny) finishes. The Nokia Asha 503 has a brightly colored polycarbonate shell with a clear coating. Some Motorola phones use the tough synthetic material Kevlar, which is also used to make bulletproof vests, to add style and strength to their phones. In 2014 the OnePlus company introduced a smartphone with a case made of powdered cashews to create a soft, skin-like texture.

Although the look of a smartphone may attract consumers, the most important design elements involve the internal features of the device. Here, too, the focus has been to balance how easy smartphones are to use with innovation in the placement of buttons, cameras, and speakers.

Safety

Doctors have noted a number of problems that are caused by frequent use of smartphones. Scrolling through text and images on tiny smartphone screens can cause computer vision syndrome, a medical condition that includes such symptoms as dizziness, blurry vision, headaches, muscle strain, and soreness in the eyes. Frequent smartphone use can also cause posture problems, spinal injuries, and carpal tunnel syndrome (numbness and weakness in the hand and wrist caused by overuse or repeated motion). In addition to these physical problems, the distraction caused by smartphone use while walking or driving can lead to serious injury.

The manufacturing process

Smartphones are mostly made by hand by workers on factory assembly lines. An assembly line is a manufacturing procedure in which workers remain in one place, performing the same task or set of tasks, while the parts of the manufactured product move past them. Many of those parts (cases, screens, circuit boards, cameras) are made in one location, then shipped to the factory where they are assembled.

1 Before assembly begins, the firmware, or permanent software that controls the phone's basic functions, is installed onto circuit boards. Workers insert circuit boards into special presses attached to computers that upload all needed firmware. These main circuit boards are called motherboards, and all of the electronic circuits in the smartphone are attached to them.

2 The programmed motherboards enter an assembly line where workers carefully solder (join together using melted metal) camera and speaker control modules.

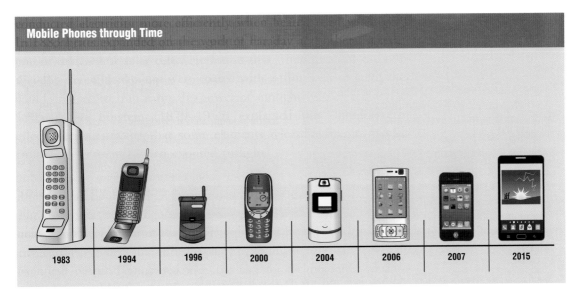

Mobile Phones through Time

1983 1994 1996 2000 2004 2006 2007 2015

Cellular phones have become much smaller and more technologically advanced since the first models were developed in the 1970s.
ILLUSTRATION BY LUMINA DATAMATICS LTD. © 2015 CENGAGE LEARNING

3 Workers on a second assembly line prepare the smartphone cases. Glass screens are checked for flaws, then cleaned with a high-pressure air nozzle before being attached to the display module.

4 The camera is installed on the back of the screen and attached to the camera module on the motherboard with thin wires.

5 Workers attach the motherboard to the shell using tiny screws. Then they install other phone components, using tweezers to handle small screws and gaskets.

6 Batteries are inserted into the completed phones, and the back and front panels of the case are snapped together. The cases are inspected, and any flaws in the plastic are polished to a smooth finish before the product is finished. A sticker is attached to each phone with information that records when and where the phone was made.

Byproducts

The process of making smartphones creates a large amount of toxic waste, much of it radioactive, meaning that it gives off harmful radiation as it decays. Environmental and health dangers have been found

Think about It!

Have you ever wondered why it is so important to recycle an old smartphone rather than just throwing it in the garbage? Many of the materials used to make smartphones are metals and metalloids (elements that have some properties of a metal and some properties of a nonmetal) that are present in the ground in limited amounts. The rapid growth of smartphone manufacturing has raised concerns that the industry may be in danger of using up Earth's supply of some important elements. These include indium, arsenic, thallium, silver, and gallium. Some elements, such as indium, which is used to make smartphone touch screens, are not replaceable by any known material. Researchers agree that more efficient smartphone recycling programs are important to save these rare resources. Now that you know how rare some of these substances are, do you think making phones is a good use for them? Why or why not?

in every aspect of smartphone manufacture. Rare earth metals used to make smartphone speakers and colorful screens are often found with radioactive elements such as thorium. Workers who mine these materials are exposed to toxic dust, and radioactive waste has leaked into nearby groundwater, affecting the health of local communities.

Many other dangerous chemicals are used to make smartphones, including polyvinyl chloride (PVC), bromine, lead, mercury, tin, cadmium, chromium, benzene, and n-hexane. Some environmentalists report that thousands of workers in Chinese smartphone factories have contracted leukemia (cancer of the blood cells), nerve damage, reproductive health issues, and liver and kidney failure due to working with chemicals on their jobs.

Quality control

At the last stage of assembly, phones are turned on to check that all main functions work correctly and that the colors shown on the screen meet design guidelines. A subscriber identity module, or SIM card, is inserted, and calls are made to test the phone's signal. Any phones that do not meet the manufacturer's standards are sent back for further work.

Once completed, smartphones go through a series of quality control tests. After each phone is turned on and retested for all functions, some phones are randomly chosen for more extensive tests. For example, chargers and headphones are put into phone jacks and removed repeatedly to test connections and durability. In another lab specially designed machines perform stress tests, opening and closing flip phones, pushing buttons, and touching screens repeatedly to discover any flaws. Phones are placed in both high-temperature and low-temperature environments to ensure that the cases do not warp or crack and that the phones continue to work properly. Other machines test seals by spraying the phones with dust. Workers drop weights onto touch screens from a height of

How Everyday Products Are Made

WORDS TO KNOW

Assembly line: A manufacturing process in which work passes from worker to worker or machine to machine until the product is put together.

Circuit board: A board on which a number of electrical connections are organized for placement in electronic devices.

Firmware: Permanent software installed in a computer device's memory.

Module: A separate unit of hardware or software that can be combined with other units.

Motherboard: The main circuit board of a computer.

Polycarbonate: A strong, light, flexible, petroleum-based synthetic material used for a variety of purposes.

Polyvinyl chloride (PVC): A common type of plastic that can be produced in both stiff and flexible forms.

Radioactive: Made of unstable atoms that give off harmful radiation as they decay.

Silicon: The second-most common element found in Earth's crust. It is often used in computers and other electronic devices.

Solder: A method of joining two pieces of metal using a bond of melted metal.

several feet and drop phones onto a metal surface to make sure they do not crack or chip.

The future of smartphones

Though they are still called smart "phones," the telephone capabilities of smartphones are perhaps the least of their achievements. In addition to connecting to the Internet, keeping track of appointments and contacts, and providing a traditional keyboard for typing, smartphone apps can turn a phone into a wide variety of useful devices, including a document scanner, a baby monitor, an alarm clock, a DVD player, a flashlight, and a tape measure. As sales grow designers continue to explore new innovations and expand the capabilities of smart devices.

However, the smartphone industry faces big challenges. Many smartphone users replace their phones every eighteen months to two years, upgrading to a newer and more advanced model. Millions of smartphones are thrown away each year, filling landfills with toxic waste and causing environmental damage. Recycling programs attempt to reuse smartphone components and educate consumers about the importance

Growing Up with Smartphones

Many people born in the twenty-first century have used or at least known about smartphones for much of their lives. While most young people have found smartphones useful for texting friends and playing games, some have been inspired to invent their own apps. Thomas Suarez (2000–) was only nine years old when he designed his first smartphone app, a daily horoscope called EarthFortune. Suarez, who was fascinated by computers, began teaching himself to program them when he was only seven. To create his app, he downloaded a software development toolkit, a program that teaches users how to design, program, and test apps.

After designing several working apps, Suarez convinced his parents to pay a fee to have his products sold through Apple's App Store. In 2011 he started an app club at his school for students who shared his interest in smartphone software development. He also started his own company, CarrotCorp, through which he continues to develop apps, as well as expanding into other areas of computer technology. He has won several awards for his work, including the 2012 Tribeca Film Festival Disruptive Innovation Award for creativity and originality.

of proper disposal of all electronic products, but the problem has yet to be solved.

For more information

BOOKS

Ahmad, Majeed. *Smartphone: Mobile Revolution at the Crossroads of Communications, Computing and Consumer Electronics.* North Charleston, SC: CreateSpace, 2011.

Woyke, Elizabeth. *The Smartphone: Anatomy of an Industry.* New York: The New Press, 2014.

PERIODICALS

Eichenwald, Kurt. "The Great Smartphone War." *Vanity Fair* (June 2014). Available online at http://www.vanityfair.com/news/business/2014/06/apple-samsung-smartphone-patent-war (accessed August 4, 2015).

WEBSITES

Smith, Aaron. "U.S. Smartphone Use in 2015." Pew Research Center. http://www.pewinternet.org/2015/04/01/us-smartphone-use-in-2015/ (accessed August 4, 2015).

"Technology Timeline." AT&T. http://www.corp.att.com/attlabs/reputation/timeline/ (accessed August 4, 2015).

Soccer Ball

A soccer ball is a spherical (round) object used in the game of soccer, or football, as the game is known outside of the United States. According to a 2006 survey by the International Federation of Football Associations (FIFA), soccer is the world's most popular sport, with approximately 265 million professional and recreational players across more than 200 countries. Although soccer balls are manufactured in a variety of sizes, colors, and materials, almost all are made up of two main parts: an inflatable inner bladder (a soft bag that is filled with air) that gives the ball its round shape and firmness and an outer covering, or casing, that protects the bladder from holes and other damage.

Early soccer balls were made of inflated animal bladders (an organ that collects urine before it passes out of the body). In the Middle Ages (c. 500–c. 1500) soccer players wrapped a hand-sewn leather covering around the inflated bladder to make the ball stronger and more long-lasting. The leather-wrapped ball was used until the mid-1900s. The modern soccer ball, which usually has a black-and-white hexagonal

The world's most popular sport, soccer only requires a soccer ball to start up a game.
© DAN THORNBERG/ SHUTTERSTOCK.COM

pattern on the outer casing, was introduced in the 1960s and is made of synthetic (artificial) leather materials such as polyurethane (PU) or polyvinyl chloride (PVC) wrapped around a natural (latex) or synthetic (butyl) rubber bladder.

Innovations in the manufacturing process, such as hidden stitching and new surface panel designs, have made modern soccer balls more aerodynamic (able to move through the air more easily), increasing players' control over the path of the ball when it is kicked or headed. Synthetic materials make balls tough and affordable, giving players in all climates and from almost any background access to equipment that is similar, if not identical, to that of the game's biggest stars. Unlike more complicated sports, in soccer only one piece of equipment—the soccer ball—is needed to start a game, and the widespread availability of balls is a major factor in the sport's popularity around the world.

The origins of soccer

While games played in ancient Asia and Central America share some similarities with what we now know as soccer, the modern form of the game began in England in the Middle Ages. As early as 700 CE, "mob football," a violent game played by large groups using an inflated pig bladder filled with dried peas, was a popular pastime. By the fourteenth century, games of mob football had become so common, and injuries to players and spectators were so frequent, that the mayor of London issued an order in 1314 banning "the striking of great footballs in the field of the public."

Gradually soccer games in England and surrounding areas became more organized. By the late fifteenth century, schools and universities in the region were forming teams and arranging competitions on grass fields used specifically for the game. The soccer ball became more sophisticated during this period, as hand-sewn leather casings were added to the inflated bladders to make them stronger. One of the oldest leather-wrapped soccer balls in existence was found among the possessions of Mary, Queen of Scots (1542–1587), who ruled Scotland from 1542 to 1567.

Standardizing the soccer ball

Leather-wrapped soccer balls remained the standard in British soccer into the twentieth century. In 1817 Benjamin Crook of Huddersfield, England, opened a tannery (a place where animal skins are tanned, or processed to become leather) that, among other things, made leather casings for soccer balls. Crook's company, Mitre, is considered one of the world's first manufacturers of soccer balls. Leather casings, however, had one huge problem: They tended to absorb water, and in England's rainy, muddy climate, leather balls could quickly soak up water and become very heavy.

One solution to the problem of waterlogged soccer balls was offered by American engineer Charles Goodyear (1800–1860), who in the 1830s developed vulcanization, a process for strengthening rubber by adding sulfur. In 1855 Goodyear designed a rubber soccer ball that consisted of eight vulcanized rubber panels glued together at the seams, looking much like what would later become the basketball. Although the vulcanized rubber balls were stronger and did not become waterlogged, leather remained the most common surface material for soccer balls because it was more readily available and easier to stitch.

Another problem with early soccer balls was that the use of natural pig bladders meant that the size and shape of soccer balls varied significantly. This problem was solved in 1862 by ball manufacturer H. J. Lindon, who developed a synthetic rubber bladder that could be inflated to a standard size and maintain its shape. Lindon's rubber bladder design quickly gained widespread use throughout the sport.

Once there was a standard soccer ball available, people began looking for ways to standardize the game itself. In 1863 representatives of several soccer clubs in London, England, formed the Football Association (FA) to establish a shared set of rules for the game they called association football. When the FA rules were revised in 1872, they included regulations on the size and shape of the ball: It must have a circumference (distance around) of 27 to 28 inches (69 to 71 centimeters) and a weight of 13 to 15 ounces (369 to 425 grams). These specifications were later adopted by the International Football Association Board (established in 1886) and have largely remained intact into the twenty-first century, with the weight specifications changed slightly in 1937 to between 14 and 16 ounces (397 to 454 grams).

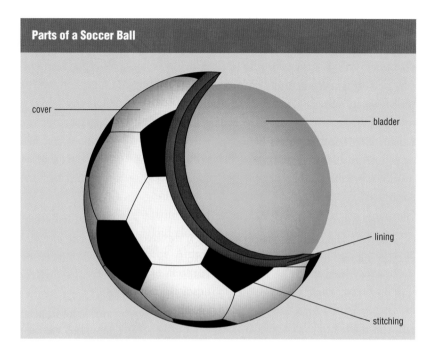

Parts of a Soccer Ball

cover

bladder

lining

stitching

The invention of the synthetic bladder allowed manufacturers to standardize the size of soccer balls. ILLUSTRATION BY LUMINA DATAMATICS LTD. © 2015 CENGAGE LEARNING

The modern ball is born

Leather soccer balls were popular until well after World War II (1939–1945), though thinner leathers and water-resistant paints were used to reduce water absorption. In 1962 Danish manufacturer Select Sport introduced a design that would influence generations of soccer balls to come. This thirty-two-panel design used twenty white hexagons and twelve black pentagons, a pattern known in geometry as a truncated icosahedron. It not only provided increased visibility for players but was also more perfectly spherical than the eighteen-panel (six interlocking sections of three rectangular leather strips) design that was previously used. This remains the most common design used for soccer balls.

The black-and-white thirty-two-panel design was used by German sporting goods manufacturer Adidas to make the official ball for the 1970 World Cup, an international soccer tournament held every four years since 1930. In 1986 Adidas made the Azteca Mexico, the first completely synthetic soccer ball to be used in World Cup competition. The Azteca included a hand-sewn polyurethane exterior, as well as three layers of synthetic materials that provided cushioning between the casing and bladder. After the 1986 World Cup, synthetic soccer balls rose in popularity, while leather casings were used less frequently. New manufacturing processes, such as the use of glue or thermal bonding (joining panels under high heat) rather than stitches to hold the panels together, were also introduced during this period.

The soccer ball goes high tech

Decades of research and testing contributed to significant changes in soccer ball design in the early twenty-first century. In 2006 Adidas made a fourteen-panel design for use in that year's World Cup competition in Germany. In 2010 the company further reduced the number of panels on its World Cup ball to eight. Players did not care for the new designs, however, and complained that the balls had unpredictable flight patterns. Further study showed that balls with fewer panels were prone to the "knuckling effect." When a smooth ball flies through the air without much spin, its seams can cause the air to flow around it at different speeds, making the ball suddenly change direction (an effect known as knuckling). Adidas responded to the criticism by developing its 2014 World Cup ball, which had just six panels, with a rougher texture than earlier balls, which greatly reduced the occurrence of knuckling.

Innovations in soccer ball design have also occurred outside of official World Cup play. Beginning in the 1980s, for example, a number of companies made balls that included sensors to notify referees when the ball crossed the goal line. One version of this type of "goal-line technology" was the Adidas Smart Ball used in the 2005 World Under-17 Championship in Peru. The Smart Ball concept was later applied to the miCoach Smart Ball, which features a built-in microchip that can track shot speed, trajectory (the path of the ball), spin, and other types of data for use in training. Another example of an innovative modern soccer ball is the Soccket, first developed by students at Harvard University in 2008, which captures the kinetic (motion) energy of the ball during play and can power an LED lightbulb for up to three hours after just thirty minutes of use.

Raw materials

The outer casing of a soccer ball is made from polyvinyl chloride (PVC) or polyurethane (PU). PVC is cheaper, does not last as long as PU, and is more commonly found in decorative or replica soccer balls. PU is softer and feels more like natural leather, making it the material of choice for

A man sews panels for a soccer ball in Sialkot, Punjab, Pakistan. Hand stitching can take up to three hours to complete. © ASAD
ZAIDI/BLOOMBERG/GETTY IMAGES

most soccer balls used in competition. The stitching that holds the panels of the outer casing together is waxed five-ply twisted polyester cord. The lining between the outer casing and the inner bladder is made of multiple layers of thin polyester, cotton, or nylon, with some manufacturers including a layer of polyurethane foam for increased softness. The bladder is made from either butyl rubber, which holds air for long periods but is prone to losing its shape over time, or natural latex, which offers a softer feel and better response to contact but loses air faster than butyl rubber. The air valve is almost always made of butyl rubber due to its ability to hold in the air.

Design

Despite the advances in soccer ball design since the turn of the twenty-first century, the thirty-two-panel design introduced by Select Sport in

the 1960s is still the most popular. The interlocking pattern of hexagons and pentagons has
several benefits, such as creating a (mostly) round
surface that is easily visible to players and spectators when contrasting colors are used. Another
benefit of the thirty-two-panel design is that it has
a longer total seam length than balls with fewer
panels. Seams help the air cling more closely to the
ball when it is struck or thrown at moderate to
high speeds, reducing the amount of turbulence,
or aerodynamic drag, the slowing that is caused
by the air as the ball moves through it. Less drag
means the ball will fly faster, farther, and straighter
than it would if more drag was present.

Think about It!

How can the soccer ball help to unite communities in conflict or bring hope to groups living
in poverty? Could inventions such as the
Soccket, which captures and stores energy
while in use and can later be used to power
lightbulbs or charge cell phones, or the indestructible One World Futbol make a difference
in the life of a young person in need?

The manufacturing process

Before 1997 (when Chinese manufacturer Top Ball Corporation
developed a method for stitching soccer balls by machine) all soccer
balls were stitched by hand, and as many as 90 percent of them were
made in Pakistan. As of 2014 Pakistan still exported around 30 million
soccer balls per year, accounting for 70 percent of all hand-stitched
balls and 40 percent of soccer balls of any kind produced in the world.
Balls are also made in China, India, and Thailand. The following
represents the typical manufacturing process for a traditional thirty-
two-panel soccer ball.

1 Layers of polyester or cotton lining are glued to the back of large
strips of the casing material (PVC or PU). Less expensive soccer balls
use a single layer of lining. More expensive balls have four or more layers
and may use many different types of materials to get the desired level of
softness and padding.

2 The lined casing material is fed into a hydraulic die-cutting machine,
which cuts the material into the hexagons and pentagons used to give
the casing its shape and pattern. The machine also punches holes on the
outer edge of each panel to make stitching easier. One panel receives an
extra hole for access to the bladder's air valve.

3 The panels are individually painted with patterns, logos, and other
text using a screen-printing device in which ink is passed through a
template made of fine mesh.

4 The bladder is made by feeding heated butyl rubber or latex into a balloon-shaped mold. When the rubber cools and hardens, an air valve is attached using a strong adhesive, and a small amount of air is injected into the bladder to check its ability to hold air and to give the ball a round shape.

5 A worker stitches the individual panels together either by hand or using a sewing machine. The panels are sewn together inside out so that the stitches and seams do not stand out over the ball's surface. Before making the final stitches, the worker turns the casing right-side out and inserts the bladder through the opening, lining up the air valve with the precut hole. The final stitches are the most difficult because they must be made without poking a hole in the bladder and with the stitch holes tucked inside the ball. Overall, hand stitching can take up to three hours to complete, and the last set of stitches can take as long as fifteen minutes.

Quality control

Because there are strict regulations for the size and weight of soccer balls used in competition, and because the balls will have to stand up to as many as two thousand kicks per game, manufacturers use a number of tests to make sure their products are ready for shipment. After the panels are cut, they are checked for flaws and to ensure a uniform shape. They are also

Try This!

Kickin' it

Professional soccer has very strict regulations for the size, weight, air pressure, and materials used to construct a soccer ball. This is because small adjustments can make a huge difference in the way the ball reacts to being kicked. How might overinflating or underinflating a ball change its performance?

To experiment, try a few kicks with a ball that is inflated a normal amount (the ball itself may have a recommended air pressure printed on the casing), and notice how far the ball flies and how high it bounces. Next, inflate the ball until it is difficult to bend the surface with your thumb, being careful not to pop the bladder inside, and note the difference in the way the ball reacts to being kicked. Finally, deflate the ball to the point where it is still round but can be easily dented, and pay attention to the changes in its performance. If possible, use an air pressure gauge to record the pressure inside the ball in pounds per square inch (PSI) each time you inflate or deflate. A ball with a higher PSI should fly farther and bounce higher than a ball with a lower PSI. Can you imagine why the International Football Association Board would require balls to be inflated between 8.5 and 15.6 PSI?

weighed to confirm the finished casing will not be too light or too heavy. The finished and inflated ball is weighed and measured to make certain it meets official size and weight requirements, and it may be stored for a period of time to see if it loses air. Balls manufactured for professional use may also be tested by outside groups. FIFA, for example, tests officially licensed balls for weight, circumference, roundness, bounce, water absorption, pressure retention, and size and shape retention.

The global game

More than 70 million soccer balls are sold worldwide every year. Because soccer is played around the world, many people believe that they can use the game to help break down political, cultural, ethnic, and economic barriers and contribute to a more peaceful world. This idea has led to the development of a number of projects designed to provide affordable, or even free, soccer balls to children in developing countries, where violent conflict and extreme poverty are common.

One such project, One World Play, began in 2006 with the invention of a nearly indestructible soccer ball made out of a highly durable foam, allowing players to organize games on rocky or bumpy ground.

One World Play offers a "buy one, give one" program in which a ball is donated to a community in need for every one that is purchased. As of 2014 more than 850,000 One World Futbols had been distributed across 165 countries, and auto manufacturer Chevrolet had agreed to distribute another 1.5 million balls to areas affected by war and poverty.

For more information

BOOKS

Chetwynd, Josh. *The Secret History of Balls: The Stories behind the Things We Love to Catch, Whack, Throw, Kick, Bounce, and Bat.* New York: Perigee Trade, 2011.

Goldblatt, David. *The Ball Is Round: A Global History of Soccer.* New York: Riverhead Books, 2008.

PERIODICALS

Della Cava, Marco. "Change Agents: Matthews' Soccket Lights Up Lives." *USA Today* (May 27, 2014). Available online at http://www.usatoday.com/story/tech/2014/05/27/change-agents-jessica-matthews-soccket-ball/9013529/ (accessed August 19, 2015).

DeSantis, Alicia, Mika Gröndahl, Josh Keller, Graham Roberts, and Bedel Saget. "The World's Ball." *New York Times* (June 13, 2014). Available online at http://www.nytimes.com/interactive/2014/06/13/sports/worldcup/world-cup-balls.html (accessed August 19, 2015).

WEBSITES

N. V. "Difference Engine: A Ball Fit for Brazil." *Economist.* http://www.economist.com/blogs/babbage/2014/06/difference-engine-0 (accessed August 19, 2015).

One World Play Project. http://www.oneworldplayproject.com/ (accessed August 19, 2015).

"Soccer Ball Construction and Design." Soccer Ball World. http://www.soccerballworld.com/Soccer_Ball_Construction.htm (accessed August 19, 2015).

Yirka, Bob. "Physicists Test Aerodynamics of Soccer Ball Types Prior to World Cup." Phys.org. http://phys.org/news/2014-06-physicists-aerodynamics-soccer-ball-prior.html (accessed August 19, 2015).

Solar Cell

A solar cell is a device designed to change sunlight into electric power. Solar cells may be small, such as those used to power handheld calculators, or they may be combined to create larger panels, such as those that supply electricity for homes, businesses, or even space stations. Solar cells are sometimes described as "photovoltaic" (PV), a term created by combining the Greek word for light (*phos*) with "voltaic," which refers to the production of electricity. Solar cells are constructed of semiconductors. A semiconductor conducts electricity at high temperatures and resists it at lower temperatures.

The first solar cells were produced in the 1800s during the Industrial Revolution, a period marked by major advances in invention and mechanization. During this time scientists such as Michael Faraday (1791–1867) and Charles Fritts (1850–1903) learned a great deal about the properties of semiconductors and how they could be used to transform light into electric energy. It was not until 1954, however, when the growth of the computer industry led to the practical use of the element silicon, that the first modern solar cell was introduced. In the decades that followed, scientists and engineers worked to increase the efficiency of and uses for the technology.

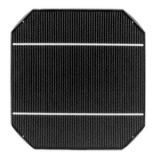

Solar cells, which change sunlight into electric power, are small. They are generally no more than 16 square inches (97 square centimeters). © NEIJIA/ SHUTTERSTOCK.COM

In the late twentieth and early twenty-first centuries, concern over decreasing fuel resources and the damaging environmental effects of coal, oil, and nuclear power led to a growing interest in solar power. This, in turn, led to increased use of solar cells in a wide range of applications, from heating and lighting homes to powering aircraft. Many experts believe that solar cell technology may be a key to sustainable energy resources in the future. Sustainable energy resources are those that do not completely use up or destroy natural resources. Because solar cells do not require complex infrastructures to work, PV technology has been useful in distant locations such as isolated towns, lighthouses, oil rigs, space stations, and satellites.

Power for an industrialized society

Even before the age of technology, early civilizations attempted to harness solar power. Ancient Romans and Native Americans, for example, constructed buildings designed to take advantage of the sun's heating and lighting power. Early thinkers were also fascinated by the natural power of electricity. As long ago as 600 BCE, the Greek philosopher Thales (c. 624–c. 546 BCE) noted that when amber, a fossilized substance, was rubbed, it would attract light materials such as feathers or hair. This is one of the earliest observations of the properties of static electricity.

During the Industrial Revolution, scientists experimented with ways to create and control electric power. In the 1740s Dutch scientist Peter van Musschenbroek (1692–1761) invented the Leyden jar. This device, which was made of glass, water, and brass, could store static electricity. In 1794 Alessandro Volta (1745–1827), an Italian chemist, created an early form of battery using copper, zinc, paper, and salt water. This "voltaic pile," as it was called, produced the first continuous electrical current.

Almost as soon as practical uses for the powerful force of electricity were discovered, scientists and inventors began exploring the connections between sunlight and electrical energy. In 1833 Faraday made one of the earliest observations of the properties of semiconductors when he discovered that silver sulfide crystals conducted electricity more efficiently when heated than when cold. In 1883 Fritts expanded on the work of Faraday and others to create one of the earliest solar cells. He found that when disks of the non-metallic element selenium were coated with a thin layer of gold, they could be used to transform the power of sunlight into electricity. In 1905 Albert Einstein (1879–1955) explained this "photoelectric effect," demonstrating that some elements release a stream of electrons (or electricity) when exposed to light.

Solar energy and the dawn of the computer age

The early solar cell designed by Fritts was very inefficient, converting only around 1 percent of the sunlight absorbed by the cell into electricity. Advancements came with the growing technological resources of the twentieth century, combined with the race for technological advancement prompted by World War II (1939–1945).

The growth of the computer industry led to the development of transistors in 1947. First introduced by Bell Laboratories, transistors use semiconductor technology to regulate current in computers and other electronic devices. In 1954 Bell Labs made an important improvement to the transistor. Using silicon, a semiconductor, scientists invented a solar cell capable of producing useful amounts of electric energy from sunlight. In an early test, Bell's solar cell provided power for the small rural community of Americus, Georgia. By the early 1960s, Hoffman Electronics had improved the efficiency of solar cells to 14 percent. Solar power provided electricity for U.S. space projects, including the first communications satellite, Telstar, in 1962. In 1977 U.S. president Jimmy Carter (1924–) installed solar panels on the White House in an effort to promote alternative energy.

The solar cell becomes part of modern life

Because solar energy promises to be profitable as well as beneficial to society, many business and research companies have worked to improve the solar cell. In the early 1990s, photoelectrochemical cells and dye-sensitized cells were introduced. These cells use complex chemical reactions to increase efficiency in converting sunlight to electricity. By 1999 more than 1 billion watts of power worldwide were produced by the installation of solar cells.

In 2008 the National Renewable Energy Laboratory of the U.S. Department of Energy announced that it had produced a cell that could convert a record 40.8 percent of incoming solar energy into electricity. Most commercial solar cells work at an efficiency rate of about 20 percent. As oil, gas, and coal prices climbed in the early twenty-first century and as scientists expressed growing concern over the environmental damage caused by retrieving and burning these fuels, solar energy became an increasingly popular choice. Production and sales of solar cells rose greatly, and innovation continued to result in more efficient, reliable, and affordable solar cells.

Raw materials

The main material used in solar cells is silicon. Silicon is the second-most plentiful element on Earth (only oxygen is more common), making up almost a quarter of Earth's crust. Silicon is a metalloid, which means that it has some properties of a metal and some properties of a nonmetal. This is shown by silicon's ability to conduct electricity. When heated (by exposure to sunlight, for example), silicon is an excellent conductor, much like a metal, but when it cools, its ability to conduct electricity decreases.

In addition to its role in the construction of solar cells, silicon has many industrial uses. It is important in the production of such things as computer chips, glass, lubricants, and insulators. Silicon is one of the

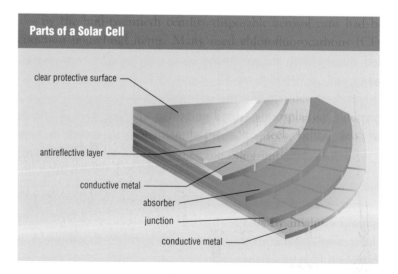

Parts of a Solar Cell

clear protective surface

antireflective layer

conductive metal

absorber

junction

conductive metal

Solar cells consist of several very thin layers of different materials, including metal that helps collect and send the electricity produced within the cell. ILLUSTRATION BY LUMINA DATAMATICS LTD. © 2015 CENGAGE LEARNING

How Everyday Products Are Made

main ingredients of sand and is usually obtained by superheating (heating liquid past the boiling point without bubbles of vapor forming) clean sand with carbon. Some solar cells also use other semiconductor materials, such as gallium arsenide or indium phosphide.

Design

Solar cells are small. They are generally no more than 16 square inches (97 square centimeters), the same as a square with 4-inch (26-centimeter) sides. Cells used to power handheld devices, such as calculators and mobile phone chargers, may be even smaller. Solar cells are often grouped together to form panels, and many panels may be placed together to create a large group (called an array), such as those used on space stations or power plants.

Solar cells have several very thin layers of different materials. Each layer plays a specific role. A clear protective surface, usually glass or plastic, covers an antireflective layer that captures as much light as possible and funnels it to the layers below. This antireflective layer is made of a material that does not reflect light, such as silicon oxide or titanium oxide. Below the antireflective layer is a grid of very thin metal wire. This helps collect and transmit (send) the electricity produced within the cell. In order to transmit electrical power successfully, solar cells must form a complete circuit. In other words, the electrons that produce electric current must flow in an unbroken loop from the solar cell to the device receiving the power and back to the cell. To make this possible, the bottom layer of the cell is made of a material that conducts electricity well, typically metal.

Between the two layers of conductive metal are several layers in which the conversion of sunlight into electricity takes place. These consist of an absorber and one or two junction layers. The absorber is made of a semiconductive material, usually silicon, and the junction layers may consist of another semiconductor or of silicon combined with another element. Because silicon atoms have a fairly stable structure, with an even number of electrons, they must be contaminated, or "doped," with other substances, such as phosphorus or boron, in order to perform their function of releasing electrons. Phosphorus and boron atoms have an odd number of electrons. When one of these atoms bonds with a stable silicon atom, its extra electron remains "free," or unbonded. Doped silicon produces millions of these free electrons, and when silicon receives sunlight, it conducts the electrons as an electrical current. In many solar cell designs, a thin layer of silicon doped with phosphorus is placed over a thicker layer of silicon doped with boron.

There are many variations on this basic design, which use different elements and compounds in the absorber and junction layers. As the use of solar power grows, scientists and engineers continue to improve the design of solar cells. In 2013 physicists at North Carolina State University discovered they could improve the efficiency of solar cells by adding a microscopically thin junction layer of the compound gallium arsenide. In 2014 engineers at the University of Utah added a specially designed layer of glass to a solar cell to increase its ability to gather light. Some researchers have even begun to add color to solar cells in order to make them more visually appealing.

Safety

Solar cells are generally considered safe and effective generators of electric power. They do, however, contain some toxic chemicals that may make disposal of discarded cells dangerous to the environment. Therefore, although solar cells are harmless when used as intended, they should not be taken apart by nonprofessionals, and they should not be disposed of in the regular trash.

The manufacturing process

By 2015 most solar cells were manufactured in China, although there were also producers in both the United States and Canada. No matter where solar cells are made, however, the manufacturing process is similar.

1 The first step in the manufacture of solar cells is the creation of a pure form of silicon. Metallurgical-grade silicon is produced by heating purified sand with carbon. This is then refined in another high-heat process to form polysilicon rock.

2 Once the pure polysilicon rock is obtained, it is ready for doping. This is done by placing the polysilicon in a melting pot with a silicon disk containing a tiny amount of boron or another material. This combination is then placed into a furnace, where it is heated to 2,500 degrees Fahrenheit (1,370 degrees Celsius), causing the polysilicon and boron to melt together.

3 To help the melted silicon form one large crystal, a smaller crystal of silicon, known as a seed crystal, is lowered into the liquid. As

Solar cells are often grouped together to form panels. Most industry analysts believe that solar power will become increasingly important in the future. © HOUGHTON MIFFLIN HARCOURT/SHUTTERSTOCK.COM

the melting pot and the seed crystal are rotated in different directions, the cooling liquid begins to crystallize in a shape identical to the seed crystal. Because of the rotation of the melting pot, the crystal that forms is shaped like a cylinder, making it easier to cut and shape.

4 The next step of the process is called wafering. Precision industrial saws, which have thin wires coated with microscopic diamonds rather than blades, are used to trim the ends and sides of the crystals to make them into regularly shaped cylinders. Called ingots, the cylinders are approximately 2.0 feet (0.6 meters) long. The ingots are placed into another wire cutter, which slices them into thin wafers less than 0.02 inch (0.5 millimeter) thick. These wafers are often in the shape of small squares with rounded corners, but other shapes may be cut in order to use the raw materials more efficiently and to provide flexibility in assembling the finished solar cells into panels.

Think about It!

"Sustainability" describes an action that can be maintained in an ongoing way. Solar power is considered a sustainable energy source because it uses the sunlight that surrounds Earth every day rather than using up fuels that are available in only a limited supply. Like using solar energy, recycling, water conservation, and carpooling promote environmental sustainability. Can you think of ways that you practice sustainability in your daily life? Are there changes you can make at home or at school to promote sustainability?

5 The doped silicon wafers are put through a variety of treatments to improve their ability to capture light. First, they are given a chemical wash to roughen their exterior. This helps to provide more surface area to absorb light. Next, the wafers are placed in a sealed chamber with phosphorus gas, causing phosphorus molecules to be deposited on their surfaces in a thin layer. This is the junction layer that will help release the silica's electrons and guide them into an electric current.

6 The wafers are then moved into a vacuum chamber, where they are coated with an anti-reflective chemical, such as silicon nitride, to prevent loss of light within the cell. Sodium nitride gives solar cells their distinctive dark blue color.

7 Metal conductors must be attached to each solar cell in order to transmit the stream of free electrons as electricity. Though the back of the cell may simply be covered with a thin layer of metal, the top must be as open to light as possible. Therefore, a thin grid of metal is applied to the top of each wafer, in a process similar to silk screening. During this process most of the wafer is covered with a thin layer of wax, leaving only fine lines for the conductive metal "paint" to adhere.

8 Once construction is complete, cells are generally wired together with metal contacts and placed between two layers of specially strengthened glass or plastic, sealed with resin, and placed in aluminum frames.

Byproducts

Although solar power is widely considered an environmentally friendly form of energy, the manufacture of solar cells produces some toxic byproducts. The most significant of these is silicon dust, which is created in large quantities when silicon crystals are cut into ingots and wafers. This dust poses an environmental problem when it enters the air and water. It is especially dangerous to workers in manufacturing plants, who may develop the lung condition silicosis from inhaling dust.

Other chemicals involved in the purification of polysilicon rock and the formation of silicon crystals, including silane gas, hydrochloric acid,

WORDS TO KNOW

Doping: The addition of impure chemicals to a pure semiconductor to change its electrical properties.

Metalloid: An element that has some properties of a metal and some properties of a nonmetal.

Semiconductor: A substance that exhibits special properties when exposed to electricity, conducting it at high temperatures and resisting it at lower temperatures.

Silicon: The second-most common element found in Earth's crust. It is often used in computers and other electronic devices.

Silk screening: A printing process in which ink is applied to a surface through a piece of mesh cloth. Also known as screen printing.

Superheat: To heat liquid past the boiling point without bubbles of vapor forming.

Transistor: A device that regulates and controls electric current through the use of semiconductors.

and copper, may also pose considerable health risks if allowed to escape into the environment.

Quality control

Manufacturers must pay strict attention to quality control in order to produce effective solar cells. The International Electrotechnical Commission established quality guidelines for solar technology during the 1980s, but most manufacturers recognize that new standards of quality should be developed as the industry grows.

Even before manufacturing begins, strict testing procedures need to be carried out on the silicon and other materials used in production to make sure the materials are pure. High-powered computerized microscopes have been introduced, capable of measuring wafer flatness, surface roughness, and the ability to absorb light. Similar technology is used to inspect the diamond-wire saws used to cut the silicon wafers to guarantee that each wafer is cut evenly and exactly.

Manufacturers often advertise their high standards of quality control, which include attention to design details, sample inspection of materials at each stage of production, and "peel tests," in which cells are taken apart to confirm that the electrical connectors are unbroken and that the metal joints between cells are stable. In addition, manufacturers regularly perform tests to make sure their products work well after they are installed.

Many Uses for Solar Power

Solar energy has many practical uses, including powering homes and businesses. Designers and inventors have also found other creative uses for solar energy that can make life easier. Solar radios and alarm clocks have become favorites for campers. Wearable solar cells in everything from backpacks and jackets to bikinis allow wearers to use the power of the sun to charge cell phones and other gadgets on the go. Solar energy has been used to cook food, power computer keyboards, and light up walkways and gardens.

Other designs are less practical but a lot of fun. Solar cells have been used in jewelry design, allowing wearers to illuminate small LED lights on necklaces. They have been incorporated into sculptures, including "Sonic Boom," a collection of giant flowers by artist Dan Corson (1970–) on display at the Pacific Science Center in Seattle, Washington. Solar cells have also been used to power small toys such as cars and robots. People have even used solar lights to light up their Jack-o'-lanterns at Halloween.

The future of the solar cell

Improvements in the design and construction of solar cells have continued into the early twenty-first century. Newcomers to the field, such as perovskite, a mineral compound with photovoltaic qualities, challenged the common silicon solar cell and made it possible for cells to become smaller and used for more purposes. Ultra-thin perovskite cells can even be painted in layers onto plastic film. Some solar engineers have suggested that these painted cells could be placed on umbrellas, tents, and clothing to provide a portable power source.

Although solar cells have not yet reached the level of fossil fuels in terms of power production, most industry experts agree that solar power will become increasingly important in the future. As prices have decreased, solar options have become more accessible to individuals and to businesses. National and local governments around the world have encouraged solar power use by offering tax breaks and other incentives for those who install solar technology.

For more information

BOOKS

Bearce, Stephanie. *How to Harness Solar Power for Your Home (and Who's Already Doing It).* Hockessin, DE: Mitchell Lane Publishers, 2010.

Sobey, Ed. *Solar Cell and Renewable Energy Experiments.* Melrose Park, IL: Lake Book Manufacturers, 2011.

PERIODICALS

Perlin, John. "The Invention of the Solar Cell." *Popular Science* (April 22, 2014). Available online at http://www.popsci.com/article/science/invention-solar-cell (accessed May 28, 2015).

WEBSITES

"How Do Solar Cells Work?" Physics.org: Your Guide to Physics on the Web. http://www.physics.org/article-questions.asp?id=51 (accessed May 28, 2015).

Solar Cell Central. http://solarcellcentral.com/ (accessed May 28, 2015).

Sports Drink

> ## *Critical Thinking Questions*
>
> 1. What is one situation in which it would be better to drink a sports drink than to drink water? What is one situation in which it would be better to drink water than a sports drink? Why?
>
> 2. Based on information in the entry, how do you think sports drinks will change in the future? What evidence from the passage supports your answer?

Sports drinks are noncarbonated (non-fizzy) beverages designed to increase energy and hydrate (add water to) a body during intense exercise or athletic activity. Available in a variety of colors and flavors, sports drinks such as Gatorade and Powerade are made mostly from water, carbohydrates (substances that provide the body with energy), and electrolytes (substances in body fluids that process waste and absorb vitamins and minerals). Together these ingredients help people maintain energy and replace the basic fluids they lose through sweat. Water best rehydrates, or restores the bodily fluids of, athletes who have exercised for an hour or less, while sports drinks are useful for athletes completing longer workouts.

Sports drinks first became popular with the 1965 invention of Gatorade. Researcher and professor Robert Cade (1927–2007) developed the beverage for the University of Florida football players during hot summer practices, who needed a way to rehydrate and replace the electrolytes they lost by sweating in the hot and humid Florida summers. The drink, named Gatorade, quickly became a must-have on the Florida

Sports drinks such as Powerade and Gatorade have become a popular drink for athletes during exercise.
© PHOTOMAIMAI/ SHUTTERSTOCK.COM

Gators sideline. Gatorade gradually gained popularity among college and professional athletes throughout the 1970s. In 1983, ads starring professional basketball player Michael Jordan (1963–) helped sell $100 million worth of the drink. In the early twenty-first century, Gatorade remains the best-selling sports drink in an industry that includes many competitors, especially Powerade, a hydrating, electrolyte-filled beverage that debuted in 1990.

Sports drinks help athletes by replacing the carbohydrates and electrolytes lost during exercise. Restoring carbohydrates increases the athlete's energy levels, and replenishing electrolytes helps the body's muscles communicate with the brain. Sports drinks also keep athletes hydrated and help prevent heat stroke during intense workouts. Athletes who drink too many sports drinks during one workout, however, might get muscle cramps. Some Americans consume sports drinks as a snack, which floods bodies with so many calories and so much sugar that it could result in weight gain if not combined with exercise.

It's getting hot in here

The development of sports drinks began when Dwayne Douglas, assistant football coach at the University of Florida, tried to understand why heat was wearing down so many of his players. To solve the problem, the university called on Robert Cade, researcher and professor at the university. In the summer of 1965, along with fellow researchers Dana Shires (1932–), H. James Free, and Alejandro de Quesada, Cade began studying how heat affects the human body.

Soon Cade and his team realized that, when the players were sweating during exercise, they were burning large amounts of carbohydrates and losing electrolytes such as sodium and potassium, which are minerals in blood that affect its acidity. They were also losing muscle function and water. Their study confirmed that football practices were leaving the players' electrolytes out of balance and their blood volume and blood sugar alarmingly low.

Although players were using up electrolytes and carbohydrates during intense practices, they were not taking any steps to replace them. Cade decided to create a beverage that combined the rehydrating properties of water, enough salt to replace the carbohydrates and electrolytes lost through sweat, and plenty of sugar to maintain normal blood sugar levels.

Onward to the Orange Bowl

After several bad-tasting batches, the researchers finally perfected their formula when Cade's wife recommended adding lemon juice. The beverage was tested during a practice game between the Florida Gators B team and its freshmen, who came back to beat the B team after drinking the beverage at halftime. The next day, with Cade's drink in their coolers, the Gators defeated Louisiana State in 102 degree Fahrenheit (39 degree Celsius) heat. The Gators continued using Cade's drink throughout the 1965 season, finishing the season with a winning record of seven wins and four losses.

The beverage was named Gatorade in honor of the team, and the following year it was available to the players on the sidelines at every game. After ending the 1966 season with nine wins and just two losses, the Gators won their first-ever Orange Bowl victory. Numerous colleges and universities, starting with the University of Richmond in Virginia and Miami University in Ohio, began ordering Gatorade for their own football teams. Gatorade is now the official sports drink of intercollegiate sports teams at more than seventy Division I colleges.

From campus to the pros

In 1969 Ray Graves (1918–2015), the Gators' head coach, recommended Gatorade to the Kansas City Chiefs of the National Football League (NFL) during a particularly hot summer. The beverage kept the Chiefs hydrated for what turned out to be a remarkable season that ended with a Super Bowl victory over the Minnesota Vikings.

Soon other NFL teams were supplying their players with Gatorade, which was named the league's official sports drink in 1983. Three years later the New York Giants celebrated seventeen straight victories by pouring a cooler of Gatorade over Coach Bill Parcells (1941–), thus beginning a tradition after a major win—a custom nicknamed the "Gatorade shower." Many other professional sports leagues, including the National Basketball Association (NBA) and Major League Baseball (MLB), have made Gatorade their official sports drink.

A nationwide industry

Gatorade soon became a go-to beverage for all athletes, whether they were professional players or beginners. In 1967 Stokely-Van Camp,

An automated machine fills up bottles with a sports drink in China. At some plants, more than 1,000 bottles are filled every minute. © 06PHOTO/ SHUTTERSTOCK.COM

a beverage manufacturer in Indianapolis, was given the rights to manufacture and distribute Gatorade nationwide. Due to the company's marketing campaign, hundreds of thousands of gallons of Gatorade were sold each year. Those numbers increased in 1983 when Quaker Oats bought Stokely-Van Camp and, due in part to the Michael Jordan ad campaign, sold $100 million worth of product. By 2001, when PepsiCo purchased Quaker Oats, Gatorade was earning $2.2 billion a year.

Several other brands, including Powerade, which was introduced by Coca-Cola in 1990, now compete for the lead in the sports drink market, but Gatorade remains the most popular brand. In addition to its signature beverage, the Gatorade brand now includes energy bars, nutrition shakes, and more. Between 1973 and 2015, the University of Florida earned more than $80 million from Gatorade sales, which the school used to create on-campus research institutes and laboratories. The company even founded its own lab, Gatorade Sports Science Institute, where visiting athletes such as professional women's soccer player Mia Hamm (1972–) and NBA player Vince Carter (1977–) are observed by scientists who study people's biochemical (relating to chemical reactions in living beings) and physiological (relating to a body's normal functions) reactions to exercise and the foods they eat.

Raw materials

The three main ingredients in sports drinks are water, carbohydrates, and electrolytes. Most sports drinks are made up of between 4 percent and 8 percent carbohydrates, and the average 8-ounce (227-gram) sports drink serving includes 0.004 ounce (100 milligrams) of sodium to replace electrolytes following physical activity.

Since the 1960s Gatorade's formula has changed very little. The sugars sucrose, glucose, and fructose are its primary carbohydrates, and potassium and sodium are its main electrolytes. A mixture of natural and artificial flavorings creates its variety of fruity flavors.

Powerade, which is designed to replace electrolytes instead of carbohydrates, relies on salt, magnesium chloride, calcium chloride, and monopotassium phosphate as its main electrolyte sources. The beverage also includes a small amount of vitamins (including B3, B6, and B12), high-fructose corn syrup for flavor, and the chemical compound calcium disodium EDTA to give the beverage its bright color.

Design

There are three categories of sports drinks: isotonic, hypertonic, and hypotonic. Isotonic drinks are designed to quickly replace the fluids a body loses when it sweats. They also provide a significant amount of carbohydrates. Isotonic drinks are generally meant for athletes undergoing daily training, as well as runners racing relatively long distances. Powerade and Gatorade are examples of isotonic drinks.

Hypertonic drinks are intended to increase the amount of carbohydrates an athlete gets. Therefore, they contain the most carbohydrates of any type of sports drink. Because they help bodies store energy, hypertonic drinks are best for athletes participating in long-distance events such as marathons. If consumed along with isotonic drinks, hypertonic beverages can also be useful during an average workout. Fruit juices and Red Bull are examples of hypertonic drinks.

Hypotonic drinks are also made to quickly replace fluids lost by sweating, but they contain far fewer carbohydrates than isotonic and hypertonic beverages. That makes them popular among athletes such as horseracing jockeys and gymnasts, who need to replace fluids but not add carbohydrates, as well as among athletes at the end of a workout looking to avoid dehydration without adding a lot of carbohydrates. Water and unsweetened tea are examples of hypotonic drinks.

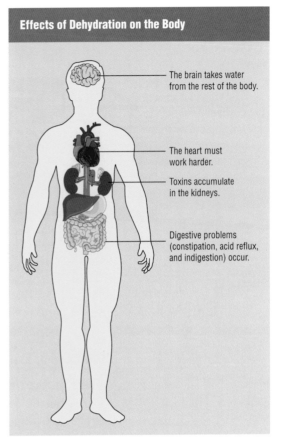

Effects of Dehydration on the Body

The brain takes water from the rest of the body.

The heart must work harder.

Toxins accumulate in the kidneys.

Digestive problems (constipation, acid reflux, and indigestion) occur.

Sports drinks are designed to help athletes avoid the health dangers associated with dehydration. ILLUSTRATION BY LUMINA DATAMATICS LTD. © 2015 CENGAGE LEARNING

Think about It!

Part of the reason the University of Florida asked Robert Cade (1927–2007) to invent a rehydrating formula for its players might seem strange: athletes in the 1960s were told not to drink water because coaches worried it would cause nausea or stomach cramps. In the early twenty-first century, however, athletes drink water for rehydration and to keep electrolytes balanced. For workouts lasting sixty minutes or less, most exercise experts suggest drinking water instead of a sports drink. If an athlete wanted to exercise longer but not drink a sports drink, what snacks could he or she pair with water that would replace the carbohydrates and electrolytes lost by working out?

The manufacturing process

The manufacturing process for sports drinks varies depending on the recipe being used. For example, Gatorade uses a formula that is different from Powerade, although the recipes are similar. For the most part, every sports drink company follows the same steps.

1 Each beverage starts with water (an average bottle of Powerade, for instance, includes 32 ounces [907 grams] of water). Sugars and salts are added to the water. These vary depending on the drink. In Gatorade, for example, the sugars include sucrose and dextrose, and salts include sodium and potassium. This mixture is then blended until the sugars and salts completely dissolve.

2 The remaining ingredients, including natural and artificial flavorings, as well as any vitamins, are added to the mixture.

3 After all the ingredients have been stirred together, the mixture is refrigerated.

4 Once the drink has been chilled, quality control workers test each batch to make sure it meets company standards.

5 Automated machines fill up bottles with the sports drink. At Gatorade's plant in Pryor, Oklahoma, nearly 1,200 bottles are filled every minute.

6 The bottles are capped, labeled, and shipped to distributors.

Quality control

Every batch of sports drink is tested between mixing and bottling. Among other things, these steps help make sure that all ingredients (each one approved by the U.S. Food and Drug Administration, or FDA) have been properly mixed and that the beverage's taste meets the company's standards.

In addition to checking the drink itself, sports drink companies make sure their product reaches customers in clean, safe bottles. The process is different from company to company. Some use steam and jet streams to get rid of any dirt on the bottles. Others use an air rinser,

WORDS TO KNOW

Biochemical: Relating to chemical reactions in living beings.

Blood sugar: A measure of the amount of sugar in the blood.

Blood volume: A measure of the amount of blood in a human body. Blood volume is affected by the amount of water and sodium taken in and lost through urine and sweat.

Carbohydrate: A substance made of carbon, hydrogen, and oxygen that is found in food and provides the body with energy.

Electrolyte: A substance that conducts electricity. In the body, electrolytes regulate nutrients into and waste out of cells.

Fructose: A very sweet sugar found in fruit and honey.

Glucose: A sugar found in plants and fruits.

Hydrate: To add water to something.

Petition: A written request with many signatures sent to a person or an organization to do or change something.

which removes any harmful matter still attached to the plastic with ionized, or purified, air.

A healthier road ahead

Sports drinks are a multibillion-dollar industry, but Gatorade and Powerade have been criticized for being unhealthy. Studies have examined everything from whether sports drinks cause tooth decay (a study at the 2009 International Association for Dental Research said yes, though a similar study by Ohio State University said no) to whether sports drinks help stimulate the brain. Gatorade and Powerade have taken steps toward improving their products. In addition to removing some harmful ingredients that could cause nerve disorders or memory loss if consumed in high doses, both companies released low-calorie versions of their drinks—G2 in 2007 and Powerade Zero in 2008.

For more information

BOOKS

Benjamin, Holly J. "Sports Drinks." In *Encyclopedia of Sports Medicine.* Edited by Lyle J. Micheli. Vol. 4. Thousand Oaks, CA: SAGE Publications, 2011.

Perritano, John V. "Sports Drinks and Energy Bars." In *The Truth about Physical Fitness and Nutrition.* Edited by Robert N. Golden and Fred L. Peterson. New York: Facts On File, 2011.

A Teen's Fight against BVO

Tired and thirsty after playing with her younger brother one afternoon in November 2012, high school student Sarah Kavanagh of Hattiesburg, Mississippi, reached for a Gatorade. Before taking her first sip, however, the fifteen-year-old vegan (a person who does not eat animals or animal products) checked the ingredients list to make sure Gatorade was safe for her to drink. That is how she found out about the food additive brominated vegetable oil (BVO), which, she later learned from an article in *Scientific American*, is banned in Japan and the European Union. Though the U.S. Food and Drug Administration (FDA) reported that small doses of BVO in Coca-Cola and Pepsi products are not harmful, *Scientific American* highlighted the cases of patients who developed skin lesions, which are abnormal (unusual) growths that appear on the skin, and had memory loss after drinking too much soda and therefore consuming too much BVO.

Kavanagh began a petition on the website change.org to remove BVO from Gatorade. In eighteen months she collected more than 200,000 signatures, helping to inspire PepsiCo, the makers of Gatorade, to stop using BVO. Kavanagh followed this with another petition, this one directed at the makers of Powerade, which had the same results. Kavanagh was proud to play a role in making sports drinks healthier for consumers, and she was especially happy to prove that teen voices matter to big corporations. In 2014 she told *People* magazine, "I believe that everybody who sees something in a product they don't like should feel empowered to do something about it."

"Sports Drinks." In *Fast Food and Junk Food: An Encyclopedia of What We Love to Eat.* Edited by Andrew F. Smith. Vol. 2. Santa Barbara, CA: Greenwood Press, 2012.

PERIODICALS

Breuer, Howard. "Small-Town Teen Gets Gatorade and Powerade to Drop Ingredient." *People* (May 15, 2014). Available online at http://www.people.com/article/teen-gatorade-powerade-ingredient-petition (accessed June 24, 2015).

Kays, Joe, and Arline Phillips-Han. "Gatorade: The Idea that Launched an Industry." *Explore* (Spring 2003). Available online at http://www.research.ufl.edu/publications/explore/v08n1/gatorade.html (accessed June 24, 2015).

WEBSITES

"Heritage." Gatorade. http://www.gatorade.com/company/heritage (accessed June 20, 2015).

"Make Your Own Sports Drink." BBC Sport. http://news.bbc.co.uk/sport2/hi/health_and_fitness/4289704.stm (accessed June 22, 2015).

Spray String

1. Based on information in the entry, could spray string be made without a propellant? Why or why not?

2. Can you think of a practical use for spray string other than those described in the entry?

Spray string is a liquid plastic resin that is placed into a pressurized spray can. When the nozzle on the can is pressed, the resin is released in a thin stream of foam that hardens in midair. The resulting long, thin, rubbery ribbon sticks for a short time to whatever surface gets in its way.

Best known under the brand name Silly String, spray string is also sold under other names, including Party String and Goofy String. It was introduced in 1972 by the toy company Wham-O. Spray string cans are able to shoot string in a variety of colors at a distance of 10 to 12 feet (3 to 3.5 meters), making the product popular at parades and parties. Although cleanup is a problem, especially when the string is sprayed on rough surfaces such as brick and concrete, most people enjoy watching the can's liquid contents change into a solid string.

During the 1990s and early 2000s, the U.S. military found a more serious use for the product. American soldiers serving in wars overseas found that they could use spray string to reveal trip wires, or hidden wires used to set off bombs. These trip wires, which were hidden along roads by enemy troops, were often so fine that they were almost invisible. Although a heavy touch would cause the bomb to explode, a light ribbon of spray string could safely land on the wire. Before entering an area, soldiers could spray the air with string. If the string fell to the ground, they knew there were no trip wires. If the string became caught on a wire, they knew a bomb was nearby.

The first aerosol sprays

Inventors began experimenting with the idea of using pressurized containers to dispense (give or provide) liquids as early as the eighteenth century. The earliest devices used carbon dioxide as a propellant. Propellants are substances used to force liquid out of a pressurized container. In 1813 British inventor Charles Plinth patented the Regency Portable Fountain, which used pressurized carbon dioxide to dispense flavored soda water. By the end of the nineteenth century, the first basic aerosol cans were introduced. The cans used the gases ethyl chloride and methyl chloride as propellants to produce a fine spray. However, these early aerosol containers were too clumsy and heavy for everyday use.

In 1929 Norwegian inventor Erik Rotheim (1898–1938) produced the first practical aerosol spray can. The cans used hydrocarbon gases (compounds containing only hydrogen and carbon) as propellants. They could dispense a variety of liquids, such as insect spray. The first widespread use of aerosol sprays occurred during World War II (1939–1945). American soldiers fighting in tropical areas used the cans to spray insecticide (a chemical used to kill insects).

By the mid-twentieth century disposable aerosol cans had become common household items. Many used chlorofluorocarbons (CFCs) as propellants. CFCs are gaseous compounds made up of carbon, chlorine, fluorine, and sometimes hydrogen. By the mid-1970s, however, scientists and environmentalists began to worry that widespread use of CFCs in aerosol cans might be damaging Earth's atmosphere. Concerned citizens pressured aerosol manufacturers to seek other, less harmful propellants.

An accidental invention

Spray string was created in the early 1970s by inventors Leonard A. Fish and Robert P. Cox, who were trying to develop an aerosol-based material that could be used as a spray-on cast for broken bones.

Spray string is sold in pressurized spray cans. When the nozzle on the can is pressed, a thin stream of foam is released, and the foam solidifies into "string" in midair.
© THOMAS RIGGS & COMPANY

How Everyday Products Are Made

They successfully created a plastic casting material but had a hard time finding the right aerosol can. As they tested dozens of spray valves, they found one that dispensed the liquid resin in a long, thin stream. As the stream traveled through the air, it solidified into a long, sticky string.

Because the invention had no medical uses, Fish and Cox decided to sell it as a children's toy named Squibbly. They patented the product in 1972 as a "foamable resinous composition" and licensed it to Wham-O, which made other popular toys such as the Frisbee, Slip 'N Slide, and Super Ball. Wham-O changed the name of the product to Silly String, and its popularity quickly grew. Spray string soon became a common item at parties and other celebrations, where it replaced traditional streamers and confetti. In 1997 Wham-O sold the Silly String product line to Just for Kicks, a division of the Car-Freshner Corporation. Other manufacturers began to produce similar products

Military applications

As spray string brands focused on the fun, playful side of the product, members of the armed forces discovered an important practical use for spray string. The lightweight foam string, which could be sprayed 10 feet (3 meters) ahead of the person using it, could land on a hidden trigger wire and expose the location of a bomb without setting it off. One of the earliest uses of spray string to uncover bombs happened during the Bosnian War (1992–1995), a conflict in eastern Europe that involved U.S. troops as part of a peacekeeping mission. The use of spray string continued during the U.S. wars with Iraq and Afghanistan, a series of military invasions that began in the years following the September 11 terrorist attacks on New York and Washington, D.C. In 2006 a New Jersey woman named Marcelle Shriver collected 80,000 cans of the product and shipped them to Iraq after her son told her how useful spray string was in finding bombs.

Raw materials

Although modern manufacturers of spray string keep their formulas secret, the major ingredients include plastic resins such as poly(isobutyl methacrylate), a synthetic polymer used to make acrylic plastic, and solvents, which are generally made of a compound of carbon and fluorine.

Inside a Spray String Can

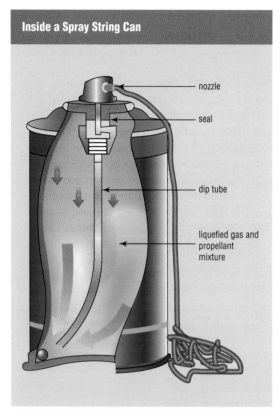

nozzle

seal

dip tube

liquefied gas and propellant mixture

The mixture inside a spray string can is made up mostly of resin, surfactant, propellant, and dyes. Spray string cans have a spray valve that dispenses the mixture in a long thin stream. ILLUSTRATION BY LUMINA DATAMATICS LTD. © 2015 CENGAGE LEARNING

Sorbitan trioleate, a compound created from vegetables, is commonly used as a surfactant, or a substance that gives liquids a foamy texture.

Another important material used in the construction of spray string is the propellant, which pushes the foamed ingredients through the spray nozzle. Early versions of the product used the propellant dichlorodifluoromethane, a CFC gas often found in refrigerators. Since the negative environmental effects of CFCs were discovered, however, manufacturers have begun to use less damaging propellants such as dimethyl ether, butane, and propane.

The composition of spray string is about 15 percent resin, 5 percent surfactant, 75 percent propellant, and 5 percent other ingredients, such as dyes. Plastic and aluminum are used to make the aerosol can and spray mechanism.

Design

Spray string is packaged in a cylindrical aluminum can approximately 8 inches (20 centimeters) tall and 2 inches (5 centimeters) in diameter. The can is designed to withstand high pressure. A plastic insert with a long tube and valve to control the flow of liquid is attached to the top of the can. A rubber gasket creates an airtight seal. The valve is activated when the user pushes the nozzle on top of the can. The nozzle releases the fluid through a small hole.

The fluid inside the can is created by blending a synthetic resin with a solvent. The solvent keeps the fluid in a liquid state. The fluid is then combined with a surfactant, which creates a foam. The remainder of the can is filled with propellant. When the nozzle is pushed, the liquid mixture is forced through the hole in the nozzle by the propellant in a long, thin stream. The solvent disappears quickly when it comes in contact with air, which causes the thin stream of liquid to solidify into a lightweight, rubbery, slightly sticky plastic string.

Because almost all spray string products are sold as toys, their cans are decorated with brightly colored lids. The lids show the color of the string inside. Some manufacturers have produced special devices to hold and shoot spray string, such as toy machine guns and action figures.

Safety

The use of silly string can pose some dangers. As the string is dispensed, the quick evaporation of solvent can cause the can to become very cold. In some cases this can cause skin damage from frostbite. In addition, many of the compounds used as propellants are highly flammable and may present a fire hazard. The plastic in the string can easily set on fire and should not be used near heaters or open fires. Direct contact with spray string may cause skin irritation in some people, and the string may damage surfaces such as vinyl upholstery and wallpaper.

Spray string has become a popular part of many celebrations. © THOMAS RIGGS & COMPANY

The manufacturing process

The cans that contain and dispense spray spring liquid are stamped from thick disks of aluminum, which are cut from a large sheet. The disks are placed into molds, and a metal punch is used to strike the disks. The force of the impact pushes the aluminum up the sides of the mold, creating a cylinder with a bottom and sides. After the cans are cleaned and prepared for painting or labeling, the top is trimmed and shaped with a rolled edge so that the aerosol spray mechanism can be sealed inside. The cans are then shipped to the spray string manufacturer for filling.

1 Synthetic resin is mixed with a chemical solvent and combined with a surfactant. The mixture is placed in large tanks with nozzles.

2 The premade cans are placed on a conveyor belt, which passes under the nozzles. The nozzles dispense a specific amount of liquid (usually about 3 ounces [89 milliliters]).

3 Workers place a spray mechanism consisting of a long plastic tube topped by a valve in each can as it moves past on the conveyor.

4 The cans are taken to another machine that seals the spray mechanism to the rolled top of the can.

5 Pressurized propellant is added through the top of the sprayer valve. The propellant is forced down the spray tube to the bottom of the

Think about It!

Although spray string received positive media coverage during the early twenty-first century as an aid to soldiers searching for hidden explosives, it also has become a public annoyance. During the 1990s a Connecticut town outlawed spray string after pranksters sprayed a police officer. The widespread use of spray string on Halloween became so troublesome in Hollywood, California, that in 2004 the city council passed a law forbidding anyone to carry the spray in the area from the morning of October 31 until noon on November 1. Can you think of the advantages and disadvantages of using spray string during public celebrations?

can. When the pressure inside the can is equal to the pressure of the propellant entering the can, the flow stops.

6 Another machine attaches a push-button nozzle, called an actuator, onto the top of the spray mechanism of each can.

7 The filled cans are moved to other machines where they are labeled and capped.

Byproducts

The most significant byproduct of spray string manufacturing is the propellant that enters the atmosphere when the string is dispensed. Because CFCs are made up of very stable molecules that do not dissolve in water, they are not washed away by rain. Instead, they rise into the atmosphere, where the sun's rays break them down into the elements of carbon, chlorine, and fluorine. The chlorine breaks down the molecules of ozone, an unstable form of oxygen that protects Earth's atmosphere. In spite of restrictions on the use of CFCs in aerosols, these destructive propellants were found in cans of spray string as recently as 2002.

Discarded plastic string is another byproduct. A number of towns and cities have banned the use of spray string at festivals and celebrations due to the difficulty of cleaning up large piles of sticky plastic debris. Because spray string is not biodegradable, it contributes to landfills.

Quality control

Manufacturers of spray string perform a number of quality control procedures at each stage of production. Before the aerosol cans are filled, they are tested with a high-pressure air spray to make sure that there are no tiny holes through which gas can escape. The raw materials in the spray are inspected for purity and proper measurement before mixing. After the cans are filled, they are tested with air pressure gauges to guarantee that each has the proper amount of propellant. At the end of production, the cans are weighed to confirm that they contain the correct amount of ingredients. The cans are then inspected for flaws as they are packed in boxes for shipping.

WORDS TO KNOW

Acrylic: A type of synthetic material used to make plastics and resins.

Actuator: A mechanical device that produces movement or action.

Aerosol: A substance kept under pressure in a container, often a can, and released as a spray.

Biodegradable: Able to be broken down naturally with the help of living things.

Chlorofluorocarbon: A compound of carbon, chlorine, fluorine, and sometimes hydrogen, often used in refrigerators and aerosol cans.

Ozone layer: The layer of the stratosphere that absorbs UV radiation from the sun. The ozone layer shields Earth from the harmful effects of this radiation.

Patent: An official document that gives an individual or a company exclusive rights over the use of an invention.

Polymer: A substance whose molecular structure consists of a large number of similar units bonded together.

Propellant: A substance or device that causes something to move forward with force.

Resin: A substance obtained from tree gum or sap (or created synthetically) that is commonly used in the manufacture of plastics and varnishes.

Surfactant: A substance that reduces surface tension of water, promoting foaming.

Synthetic: Artificially made.

Fun, creative, and surprisingly useful

Manufacturers of various brands of spray string sell millions of dollars' worth of their product each year. Some creative consumers have used spray string as a "weapon" in mock battles, as a garland on Christmas trees, or to create sticky "spider webs" for Halloween. Others have used different colors of string to create removable outdoor art projects. Its life-saving role in several armed conflicts around the world also increased public awareness of spray string.

For more information

BOOKS

Fisher, Michael, Martin Abbott, and Kalle Lyytinen. *The Power of Customer Misbehavior: Drive Growth and Innovation by Learning from Your Customers.* New York: Palgrave Macmillan, 2014.

Green, Joey. *Last-Minute Survival Secrets: 128 Ingenious Tips to Endure the Coming Apocalypse and Other Inconveniences.* Chicago: Chicago Review Press, 2015.

Try This!

Make your own spray string

You can experiment with the chemical principles behind spray string using just a few simple ingredients.

You will need:

- rubber gloves
- protective goggles
- hydrogen peroxide (30 percent solution)
- food coloring
- plastic squeeze bottle
- yeast

Directions:

Note: Because 30 percent hydrogen peroxide solution is very strong, you should avoid contact with your eyes or skin.

1. Before beginning your experiment, put on old clothes, rubber gloves, and protective goggles. Work outside in an area you can wash down with a hose when you are finished.

2. Fill the bottle with peroxide and add your choice of food coloring. Keep the bottle cap close to you. Make sure the hole at the top of the cap is open.

3. Add 1 teaspoon of yeast to the colored peroxide and place the cap on the bottle quickly. Cover the hole on the top of the cap with a gloved finger, and shake the bottle to mix the ingredients. Release your finger. Do not point the bottle at any person or objects.

4. As the ingredients mix, strings of foam will shoot out, propelled by the interaction of the peroxide and the yeast.

PERIODICALS

Aspan, Maria. "Novelty Maker Benefits as Silly String Goes to War." *New York Times* (October 22, 2007). Available online at http://www.nytimes.com/2007/10/22/business/22silly.html?_r=0 (accessed August 19, 2015).

Drahl, Carmen. "Silly String: It's a Party for Polymer Chemistry, All in a Can." *Chemical and Engineering News* (October 26, 2009). Available online at http://cen.acs.org/articles/87/i43/Silly-String.html (accessed August 19, 2015).

Santana, Rebecca. "N.J. Woman Collects Silly String for Serious Use." *NBC News* (December 6, 2006). Available online at http://www.nbcnews.com/id/16079446/#.VdUz2Zfw9x5 (accessed August 19, 2015).

WEBSITES

"Products." Silly String. http://www.silly-string.com/silly-products/index.cfm (accessed August 19, 2015).

Sticky Note

Critical Thinking Questions

1. How would the manufacturing process change if sticky note pads were cut before step 4? Would the result be the same? Why or why not?

2. Engineers at 3M had to work backward to find a product that fit their new technology. What was one time in your life when you had to work backward to achieve a goal or solve a problem?

3. Which would be more useful to you in your daily life, a traditional sticky note or a digital one? Why?

Sticky notes, or self-adhesive notes, have become important school and work supplies for millions of people worldwide since they were introduced in 1980. Sold in blocks, each small, removable note paper has a strip of sticky adhesive on the back that can be stuck to a surface and then removed and stuck to a new surface. Sticky notes make it easy to physically move information from one thing to another: for example, from a notebook to a computer, from a calendar to a refrigerator, or from one person to another.

The adhesive used on sticky notes was first developed by the Minnesota Mining & Manufacturing Company (3M) in the 1960s. The company first sold its Post-it® sticky notes in a lined yellow design. As Post-it notes became popular among consumers, they were available in a wide range of colors and sizes. Since 1980 sticky notes have been everyday items in schools, offices, and homes. They have even been used in art.

Sticky notes are uniquely useful in two main ways. First, the adhesive strip on the back of the notes allows for multiple uses. A note might be attached to a folder, then moved to a document, before being attached to a computer monitor. Because they are "restuck" so many times, sticky notes are made to be quite durable, even though they are eventually thrown away. Second, the small size and eye-catching color of most notes make them useful for note-taking and as memory aids. People use them to leave notes and reminders throughout the home or office. Other shapes of sticky notes, such as thin, rectangular sticky flags, can be used to mark information in books or other documents without writing on the paper.

An adhesive without an application

Sticky notes were the result of the 3M "Polymers for Adhesives" research program. The company makes a number of commonly used adhesive and office products, including many kinds of tape. In the mid-1960s, 3M purchased the rights to a family of polymers (substances whose molecular structure consists of a large number of similar units bonded together) from Archer Daniels Midland (ADM). Chemical engineer Spencer Silver (1941–) conducted creative—and sometimes unusual—tests on these materials, first as part of a search for a powerful, super-strong adhesive that could be used to build planes in the aerospace industry. However, his experiments led him to the discovery of an adhesive that was quite weak.

Silver's new adhesive, a polymer compound, was called acrylate copolymer microspheres (ACM). He produced it by introducing a catalyst (a substance that speeds up a chemical reaction without undergoing a permanent chemical change itself) to the ADM-family monomers (single molecules that may bind chemically to other molecules to form a polymer). This caused a chemical reaction that polymerized the substance. The resulting polymer adhesive was weak, not very sticky, able to stick by using a bit of pressure, and completely reusable.

During a pro-democracy movement in Hong Kong in October 2014, people used sticky notes in a government office to express their views. © LEWIS TSE PUI LUNG/SHUTTERSTOCK.COM

ACM adhesive is made up of tiny spheres. The spheres cannot be easily broken, melted, or dissolved and are practically indestructible. Although they stick strongly to one another, the spheres adhere only lightly to flat surfaces because each is only partly and indirectly in contact with the surface to which it is stuck. Because none of the spheres are stuck down at more than one point, the adhesive can be easily peeled away, and the note does not lose all of its adhesiveness. This makes it almost endlessly "restickable."

Working backward

For five years 3M looked for a practical use for ACM adhesive, with little success. Silver called the adhesive a "solution without a problem." In 1973 he approached 3M products laboratory manager Geoff Nicholson (1938–) with his discovery. Nicholson had an open-use policy that encouraged employees to experiment with products still in development. One early idea was to spray the adhesive over the surface of bulletin boards, which would allow notes to be put up without using tape or pins. However, the boards were clunky and did not greatly improve on existing bulletin board designs.

The turning point came in 1974, when Silver's coworker Arthur Fry (1931–), a 3M product development engineer with a chemical engineering background, came up with the idea of putting a small amount of the adhesive on the back of a bookmark. He could then stick it to the page to mark the exact spot, without worrying about the bookmark slipping or falling out. He could also remove and restick it as needed without damaging the book. Through Fry's innovation, 3M realized the potential for notes that were sticky themselves. When Fry attached a piece of one of his adhesive bookmarks to the cover of a report and sent it to his supervisor, the "sticky note" became a development priority.

Even though management knew the idea for sticky notes was a good one, 3M faced challenges in bringing the idea to market. One of these was controlling the stickiness of the adhesive, which clings more to itself than it does to other objects. Because of this the adhesive sometimes came apart from the note when a note was peeled off the block of notes. The company worked to fix this problem, putting a strip on the back of each note to hold the adhesive permanently without letting it peel off on other surfaces.

Manufacturing the new product also presented some challenges for 3M. Up to that point the company had mostly made products sold in spools and rolls, but Post-it notes required different machining approaches. The first machine for Post-it note block production, built by Fry in his home basement, was so large after all the necessary adjustments that entire walls had to be knocked down in order to remove it from his house.

Marketing memos

Post-it notes were given a preliminary trial in 1977, with blocks of notes being given to a selection of secretarial and office workers to test their usefulness in the real world. The notes, first branded "Press 'n Peel," were a hit with these initial testers, but it took time and a lot of work to develop a commercial market. The first formal test

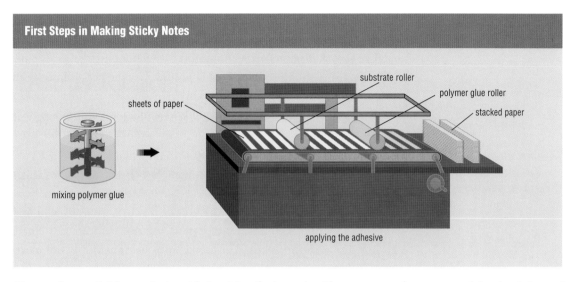

First Steps in Making Sticky Notes

substrate roller
polymer glue roller
sheets of paper
stacked paper
mixing polymer glue
applying the adhesive

The manufacture of sticky notes begins with the mixing of polymer glue. The paper moves along a conveyor belt, where it is coated with the glue and stacked into pads. ILLUSTRATION BY LUMINA DATAMATICS LTD. © 2015 CENGAGE LEARNING

markets—in Denver, Colorado; Tulsa, Oklahoma; Tampa, Florida; and Richmond, Virginia—in 1977 were weak, and many people thought there was no future for the Post-it note.

Nicholson and other members of 3M management were convinced that Post-it notes could sell if they were advertised and demonstrated properly. People who had never used Post-it notes struggled to see their usefulness, whereas those who had used them were enthusiastic, giving support to Nicholson's view. In 1978 3M launched a new effort, focused this time in the city of Boise, Idaho. It called the campaign the "Boise Blitz" and gave away huge quantities of free samples to city workers and residents. The company also planned widespread personal demonstrations of its product's usefulness. The strategy paid off, and 90 percent of the Boise Blitz sample testers placed orders for more of the self-adhesive notes.

Post-it notes went on sale throughout the United States in 1980, rebranded under their current name. The lined, canary-yellow notes were sold in blocks of two sizes: 1.5 × 2 inches (3.8 × 5.0 centimeters) and 3 × 5 inches (7.6 × 12.7 centimeters). Within four years Post-it notes had become one of 3M's most popular products, and soon they were being manufactured in a variety of shapes and colors. By 1995

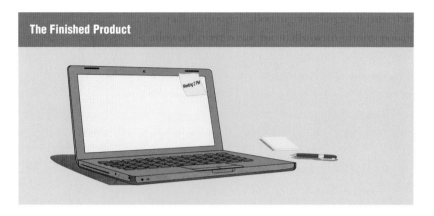

The Finished Product

Post-it notes were one of the top five best-selling office products in the world, with estimated sales of $500 million.

Continuing development

3M held the patent (an official document protecting the rights of an invention) on Silver's polymer adhesive exclusively until 1997. Until then Post-it notes were only produced at the company's plant in Cynthiana, Kentucky. Even after the patent expired, 3M retained a tight hold on the sticky note market, and Post-it notes are still made in the United States. In 2003 a "super sticky" version of the classic Post-it note debuted, with a revised adhesive formula that held a better grip on vertical surfaces.

Raw materials

Sticky notes are made of two key ingredients: paper and adhesive. Sheets of paper are coated with a strip of the patented polymer adhesive ACM. The adhesive helps the paper stick together into the blocks in which they are sold and also provides them with their restickable quality. Some sticky notes are made from post-consumer waste recycled paper, an environmentally friendly alternative.

Design

Most sticky notes are made and stacked with only a thin strip of adhesive at the top of each note. Full-adhesive-backed versions are also available. Sticky notes come in a variety of sizes and colors but are mostly rectangular in shape and relatively small. Yellow paper was used for the original Post-it notes and is still sold as the standard design. The reason the first notes were yellow was that the lab next door to the one in which they were machined had a surplus of yellow scrap paper, which was repurposed as note material. Some sticky notes are printed with patterns, lines, or phrases.

The manufacturing process

Sticky notes are assembled and cut by machines. The materials are produced in bulk, then combined, stacked, and cut to the desired proportions before packaging. Because the notes are manufactured mechanically, many blocks can be assembled and cut quickly and efficiently, making them easy to mass-produce.

Think about It!

What are some ways in which you could use sticky notes to help with studying? Maybe you could use them to storyboard writing projects so you can quickly and easily rearrange points and restructure your thinking. Or you could make a sticky-note flipbook. Another idea is to use sticky notes to mark your progress with schoolwork, marking the beginning and end for assignments so you know exactly how much you have left to do. Use sticky notes to study smarter too: write information you are learning on sticky notes, and remove them as you master each idea, leaving a clear visualization of what you have left to learn.

1 First, the polymer adhesive is mixed. A chemical reaction using a catalyst creates a sticky "un-glue." This adhesive is then placed into a machine, where it will be applied to large sheets of paper.

2 Preprinted or blank paper is fed in sheets into the machine through continuous rollers. The paper first passes through a device that primes the sheets with a substrate, or base, that helps the adhesive bond with the paper.

3 The polymer adhesive is applied on top of the substrate, where it quickly dries.

4 After being coated with adhesive, sheets of paper are stacked by a second machine until they form thick pads. At regular intervals, sheets printed with the product and brand name are inserted. These will be the bottom of the blocks and are not intended for use as notes.

5 The pads are cut into standard sizes, which can range from 1.5×2 inches (3.8×5.0 centimeters) to full 8.5×11-inch (21.6×27.9-centimeter) sheets. Special cutting dies can create pads in different shapes.

6 The finished pads are wrapped in plastic packaging and then shipped to distributors and vendors in bulk.

WORDS TO KNOW

Adhesive (noun): A substance used to stick objects together.

Adhesive (adjective): Capable of being used to stick objects together; sticky.

Catalyst: A substance that speeds up a chemical reaction without undergoing a physical change itself.

Chemical reaction: The process through which the structure of a substance is transformed.

Monomer: A single molecule that may bind chemically to other molecules to form a polymer.

Patent: An official document that gives an individual or a company exclusive rights over the use of an invention.

Polymer: A substance whose molecular structure consists of a large number of similar units bonded together.

Substrate: A base.

Byproducts

The process of making the polymer adhesive produces some chemical byproducts. It also requires the use of mercury and carbon dioxide, which must be correctly disposed of. The excess paper trimmed off the pads is saved and recycled.

Quality control

Finished blocks of notes are inspected before shipment, and the adhesive and substrate mixtures are tested for quality before being used in notepad manufacture.

The digital frontier

Sticky notes have proved to have an enduring appeal. They are used in many aspects of daily life across the globe. Teachers use them in classrooms to help their students develop note-taking skills or to comment on student work. They are also commonly used in business and office environments. New uses for sticky notes are being discovered all the time.

As the world continues to move from written to digital information, sticky notes have adapted. "Desktop notes" apps create graphic reproductions of the familiar sticky-note design, allowing users to virtually "stick" notes on digital documents. 3M offers its own official computerized "Post-it Brand Software Notes," and both Macintosh and PC operating systems come with "Sticky" applications.

Try This!

Sticky notes from scratch

Although sticky notes are made with a special adhesive, you can make your own version out of easy-to-find materials.

You will need:

- ruler
- scissors or paper cutter
- pen or pencil
- scrap paper
- repositionable glue sticks
- scrap cardboard

Directions:

1. Decide what size and shape you want your sticky notes to be, and measure and cut rectangles out of scrap paper. Your notes will be more uniform in size if you cut several notes at the same time.

2. Run the glue stick along the top of one of the cut notes. Match the top of another cut note over the strip of glue, and press them together. Run the glue stick along the top of that note, and stick another note on top. Repeat this step until you have formed a pad.

3. Create a backing for your pad of notes by sticking the bottom sheet to a piece of cardboard trimmed to the same size.

The Evernote app works with the camera on a smartphone or tablet to transfer physical sticky notes to digital environments. Evernote can capture standard 3 × 3-inch (7.6 × 7.6-centimeter) notes and 11 × 11-inch (27.9 × 27.9-centimeter) notes. The digitized notes reproduce color and handwriting. They can be organized into digital notebooks, tagged, and used to set reminders.

For more information

BOOKS

Gershman, Michael. *Getting It Right the Second Time.* New York: Addison-Wesley, 1990.

Nayak, P. Ranganath, and John M. Ketteringham. *Breakthroughs!* New York: Pfeiffer, 1994.

Petroski, Henry. *The Evolution of Useful Things.* New York: Alfred A. Knopf, 1992.

PERIODICALS

Fry, Art, and Spencer Silver. "First Person: 'We Invented the Post-it Note.'" *FT Magazine* (December 3, 2010). Available online at http://www.ft.com/intl/cms/s/2/f08e8a9a-fcd7-11df-ae2d-00144feab49a.html#axzz18hyDnyKX/ (accessed June 20, 2015).

Newman, Andrew Adam. "Turning 30, an Office Product Works at Home." *New York Times* (July 27, 2010). Available online at http://www.nytimes.com/2010/07/28/business/media/28adco.html/ (accessed June 20, 2015).

WEBSITES

"Post-it Note Notes." Post-it Brand: The Official Site of Post-its. http://www.post-it.com/wps/portal/3M/en_US/PostItNA/Home/Support/About/ (accessed June 20, 2015).

Evernote Market. https://www.evernote.com/market/feature/3m (accessed June 20, 2015).

Sunglasses

Sunglasses are a form of protective eyewear with shaded lenses designed to absorb or reflect light. Sunglasses increase comfort in bright sunshine and protect eyes from ultraviolet light, or UV light, an invisible form of sunlight that can cause serious damage to the eye. Sunglass lenses can be made in many different colors or coated with chemicals that make them shatter-resistant, scratchproof, reflective, or corrective. In addition to protecting eyes from damaging light, sunglasses are a popular fashion accessory.

Glasses with shaded lenses were used in twelfth-century China, although modern sunglasses did not appear until the 1500s. In the early 1900s, sunglasses were an expensive specialty item mostly worn by movie stars. American entrepreneur Sam Foster (1879–1966) created the first affordable and easy-to-manufacture sunglasses in 1929, selling them on the boardwalk in Atlantic City, New Jersey, and beginning a worldwide trend.

Sunglasses are an important invention because they protect the human eye, which can be easily damaged by bright light and naturally

Sunglasses protect eyes from harmful ultraviolet light, as well as dust and debris. They also reduce glare, making it easier and safer to drive, bike, or ski. © JAKKAPAN/ SHUTTERSTOCK.COM

weakens with age. Sunglasses have also become a significant element in culture. The styles of sunglasses worn by public figures and celebrities often grow into fashion trends.

The origin of sunglasses

The practice of wearing shaded eyewear began in prehistoric times. To protect their eyes from the glare of the sun reflecting off the snow, the Inuit people, who lived in the Arctic region, made goggles out of flattened walrus ivory. These goggles covered the entire eye except for a very thin slit, which the wearer looked through while hunting or fishing. According to historical accounts, Roman emperor Nero (37–68 CE) watched gruesome gladiator battles, in which men fought against animals or other men, through the green tint of polished emeralds. Judges in twelfth-century China wore glasses fitted with lenses made of thin smoky quartz, which concealed their eyes and masked any emotion from those on trial.

The first modern sunglasses—those that completely shield the eyes from the sun's glare—appeared in Italy around 1430. In the 1600s people began to recognize the health benefits of wearing protective eyewear, especially for older people, who commonly have fading vision and are sensitive to light. The first experiments with the corrective powers of colored lenses began in the eighteenth century, when optician James Ayscough (d. 1759) developed glasses with blue- and green-tinted lenses, believing that they could correct certain visual problems. In the nineteenth and twentieth centuries, yellow- or brown-tinted glasses were prescribed for people with medical conditions that caused them to have painful sensitivity to light.

Just like a movie star

Early sunglasses were an expensive specialty item worn only by very wealthy people and those with poor or problematic vision. The widespread popularity of sunglasses came about mainly because of the influence of American movie stars of the 1920s and 1930s, who wore them to protect their eyes against blinding arc lamps used in the production of silent films. The glasses also helped protect actors' eyes from camera flashes and, off the red carpet, helped them avoid being recognized by

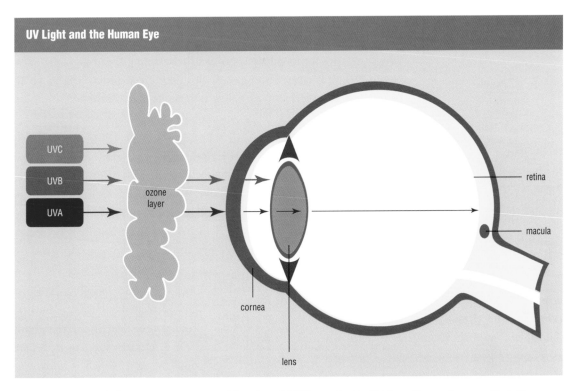

UV Light and the Human Eye

Without sunglasses, the human eye is not protected from harmful UV rays. A pair of high-quality sunglasses can block 99 percent of UVA and UVB rays. ILLUSTRATION BY LUMINA DATAMATICS LTD. © 2015 CENGAGE LEARNING

their fans. Many people wanted to imitate the styles worn by their favorite celebrities, but sunglasses were not yet manufactured cheaply or in large quantities, so they remained available only to wealthy people.

In the summer of 1929, American entrepreneur Sam Foster developed inexpensive, mass-produced sunglasses. Foster sold his sunglasses from a boardwalk booth in Atlantic City, New Jersey, a popular seaside vacation spot. Sales were excellent, and in the following years, sunglasses became a must-have accessory that nearly anyone could afford. By 1937 news articles called sunglasses a wildly popular fashion accessory, estimating that Americans bought 20 million pairs in that year alone.

Changing trends and technology

Since Foster's first design, new technologies, discoveries, and needs have brought about drastic changes in the style and usefulness of sunglasses. In the 1930s the U.S. Army Air Corps hired Bausch & Lomb, a company that made monocles, glasses, and other vision products, to produce specialty sunglasses for its pilots to protect them from glare in high altitudes. Bausch & Lomb created sunglasses with dark-green-tinted lenses, which filtered out a larger part of the visible light spectrum than ordinary sunglasses.

In 1936 inventor Edward H. Land (1909–1991) applied his patented Polaroid camera lens technology to sunglass design. These "polarized" lenses blocked vertical light bouncing off of irregular surfaces such as roadways or shimmering water, protecting the wearer's eyes from glare. In 1936 Ray-Ban, a division of Bausch & Lomb, started producing polarized aviator-style sunglasses, which featured unusually long lenses that dipped far below the wearer's eye to protect pilots against glare on their plane's instrument panel. Aviator-style sunglasses were worn by pilots in World War II (1939–1945) and eventually became a popular style for general wear.

Sunglass design has developed as a result of medical discoveries about the effects of certain kinds of light on the eye. Modern sunglass lenses are specifically designed to protect eyes from UV light, which is known to cause cataracts, a condition in which the lens, or front part of the eye, becomes cloudy, making vision difficult. They also help prevent eye cancer and other health conditions. UV light is commonly designated as either UVA or UVB depending on the wavelength.

Studies also suggest that high-energy visible light, HEV, found within the blue and violet bands of the visible light spectrum, can injure the retina, a light-sensitive area near the back of the eye, and lead to early vision loss. To protect against HEV, manufacturers make sunglasses with amber or brown lenses, which are also called blue-blocking lenses for their ability to filter out blue and violet light. As researchers discover more about eye health and the effects of sunlight, sunglass and lens design continues to change.

Cool shades

In a word, sunglasses are cool. After Foster began manufacturing affordable sunglasses, other designers started offering their own cutting-edge styles, which covered the eyes of America's coolest celebrities, including actors Marlon Brando (1924–2004) and James Dean (1931–1955), in the 1930s and 1940s. Although most sunglasses were affordable, high-end fashion designers continued to make their own expensive styles, which they sold to the wealthy. In the following decades, designers produced a variety of new styles: the iconic "cat eye" frames made famous by actress Marilyn Monroe (1926–1962) in the 1950s, the large plastic frames worn by First Lady Jacqueline Kennedy Onassis (1929–1994) in the 1960s, the blue lenses worn by musician John Lennon (1940–1980) in the 1970s, and the classic Ray-Ban Wayfarer made popular by musician Bob Dylan (1941–) in the 1960s and 1970s.

Sunglasses remain popular across the world, worn by people in all social and economic classes. The quality and sales price of sunglasses covers a wide range. Consumers can buy a flimsy pair of plastic sunglasses for $2 at a gas station or spend hundreds of dollars for designer styles.

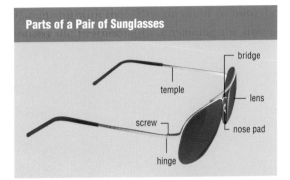

Parts of a Pair of Sunglasses

bridge
temple
lens
screw
nose pad
hinge

Although there are many styles of sunglasses, most include the same basic components.
ILLUSTRATION BY LUMINA DATAMATICS LTD. © 2015 CENGAGE LEARNING

Raw materials

All sunglasses consist of two light-filtering lenses held in place by a frame, although the materials used to make these elements depend on the specific model's quality and price. Inexpensive sunglasses typically have frames and lenses made of plastic, such as polycarbonate. More expensive frames are likely made of metal, such as nickel and stainless steel, or carbon-fiber-reinforced plastic, which is stronger and lighter in weight than other forms of plastic. Higher-quality sunglasses often have ground glass lenses that are "optically perfect," meaning that they do not distort shapes or lines in the wearer's field of vision. Dyes and pigments are added to frames and lenses in order to shade or color them. Many manufacturers are increasingly producing sunglasses made from recycled materials and wood.

Design

The particular design of each style of sunglasses is determined based on fashion trends, comfort, level of protection from harmful light, and the intended use. Although appearance varies widely, all sunglasses are made of the same general structural parts: lenses and frames.

Sunglass lenses differ in color, shape, material, and the level of protection they provide. Lenses can be tinted any color, and each color has

A worker in Massachusetts assembles aviator-style sunglasses. © VICTOR J. BLUE/BLOOMBERG/GETTY IMAGES

a unique effect on the wearer's sight. Brown lenses increase contrast but cause some color distortion. Amber or yellow lenses provide sharp definition in snow or haze and are effective at blocking harmful HEV rays. Gray or green lenses cause the least amount of color distortion. Sunglass lenses can also be gradated, or change shade from top to bottom; polarized; or mirrored on the outer surface. Lens shape varies according to intended function. There are sunglasses designed for many specific groups of people, including pilots, skiers, doctors, windsurfers, elderly people, and individuals who work long hours at the computer. While most sunglasses have two lenses, one to cover each eye, some sunglasses designed for athletes feature a single large lens, or shield.

Sunglass frames are designed to hold the protective lenses in front of the wearer's eyes. The length of the frame between the lenses is called the bridge; this is where the frame sits on the wearer's nose. The frame is held in place by two stems, also called temples or arms, which are attached to the frame with a hinge and rest on top of the wearer's ears. Most stems are designed to curve slightly down around the back of the ear, providing a secure fit. Sunglass frames come in a wide variety of shapes, colors, and patterns, including star-shaped and heart-shaped. Frames and stems can be made from all sorts of materials, though sports models tend to be made of lightweight and durable plastic or nylon. Stems are typically narrow, although some designs feature thick stems that protect the eyes from "stray light," or light that enters through the space around the lenses and frame.

Safety

To prevent serious injury in the case of an accident, sunglass lenses are designed to be shatterproof. Plastic lenses are naturally shatterproof, while glass lenses must be treated to make them shatterproof.

The manufacturing process

Sunglasses are made using automated and highly precise machines. The process varies for each unique design element, including lens material, frame material, lens properties and coatings, lens prescriptions, and overall quality. The lenses and frames are built separately, then fitted to each other near the end of the process.

1 Glass and plastic lenses are formed when the raw materials are brought to a very high temperature and liquefied. Color can be added to the lenses at this point or later in the process. If the manufacturer shades the lenses during this step, dyes and pigments are added to the liquefied plastic, while liquefied glass is combined with metal particles. Once the desired color and shade have been reached, the plastic or glass is cooled and formed into rough lens shapes, also called pucks or blanks.

2 Workers select a blank that has the desired shape, color, and thickness. This blank is placed into a lensometer, a machine that detects the optical center, or center point where no distortion takes place. The

Think about It!

Most people think of outer space as an extraordinarily dark place. In fact, the light in outer space is far more intense and damaging than the light that reaches Earth's surface. Without the protection of Earth's atmosphere, which filters and reflects sunlight, astronauts are forced to wear sunglasses inside and outside of the spacecraft. Astronauts' specially designed sunglasses are very dark, have a thin coating of gold on the outside for extra protection, and are designed to stay on in zero-gravity conditions. Look around: Can you think of other everyday objects that would need to be redesigned to function well in outer space?

WORDS TO KNOW

Distortion: The condition of something being altered from its normal or original condition or shape.

High-energy visible (HEV) light: The blue and violet bands of the visible light spectrum, which have been shown to have damaging effects on the human eye.

Lensometer (also lensmeter): An instrument used to detect the prescription of a lens.

Ozone layer: The layer of the stratosphere that absorbs UV radiation from the sun. The ozone layer shields Earth from the harmful effects of this radiation.

Polarized lens: A lens that has been treated with a protective chemical coating that blocks reflective glare and reduces the effects of UV light on the eye.

Ultraviolet (UV) light: An invisible form of light produced by the sun. It can cause serious damage to the human eye.

blanks are then placed into a curve generator, which uses a cone-shaped grinder on the back of the lens to achieve the required curvature, thickness, and any necessary prescription. An edge grinder is used to form the outer edge of the lens to the proper shape and cut the edge so that it will easily fit into the frame.

3 The lenses are placed into a machine that cleans and etches them to ensure that any coatings stick to the surface. The lenses are treated with coatings and chemicals to provide color, UV and HEV protection, reflective properties, and protection from scratches. Coatings are applied using a vacuum-coating method, during which all of the air is removed from the chamber and the lenses are continuously rotated as gaseous chemicals are released, evenly coating the surface.

4 Metal and plastic frames are created in the same way as the lenses: using molds. The raw material is heated until liquefied, and any desired dyes or additives are mixed into the liquid. The liquid is poured into a computer-generated mold, a hollow container in the exact pattern of the frame design. The mold is cooled with water, and the newly made frames are polished and cleaned.

5 In the case of plastic frames, the lenses are pushed through the front of the frame, which stretches slightly to allow the lenses to click into place. In the case of metal frames, which bend easily and do not hold lenses well, the lenses are mounted with small screws. The stems are attached to the frames with small metal hinges.

Shady Eyedeas

In 2013 eighteen-year-old New Jersey native Matthew Sheffield (1995–) was shopping online for sunglasses but could not find the exact color combination he wanted. Instead of settling for an existing color, Sheffield redesigned sunglasses altogether. He envisioned a new style of sunglasses with completely interchangeable lenses, frames, and stems. Rather than continuing to buy expensive sunglasses as styles and tastes changed, people could create dozens of unique looks by mixing colored components. Three pairs of sunglasses could be mixed and matched to create eighty-one unique combinations.

To make this idea a reality, the young entrepreneur invented a mechanism to replace the hinge that usually attaches the stem to the glasses frame. With this new invention, Sheffield's sunglasses could be taken apart, mixed, matched, and put back together in a matter of minutes without any tools. After winning an entrepreneurship competition and raising $25,000 on crowd-funding website Indie-GoGo, Sheffield was able to manufacture and sell the world's first completely interchangeable sunglasses, which he called Shady Eyedeas.

6 Once the sunglasses are completely assembled, they are inspected for imperfections and packaged for sale.

Quality control

The U.S. Food and Drug Administration (FDA) sets strict safety standards to control the quality of sunglasses sold in the United States. The FDA sets standards for the durability of frames and shatterproof lenses, as well as for the light-blocking qualities of the lenses. The ANSI Z80.3 blocking requirements state that lenses must block at least 99 percent of all UVB and UVA light. Many sunglasses exceed these requirements. There are no standards for lens perfection, and low-quality lenses often contain vision-distorting imperfections.

A bright future

Sunglasses remain a beloved fashion accessory, a cultural symbol, and a vital tool for protecting eyes. Researchers are always learning about the ways in which different kinds of light affect eyes and bodies, and medical experts suggest that people wear sunglasses whenever they are outside, particularly young people whose eyes are still developing. Sunglasses will likely continue to play an important role in studying the harmful effects of the deterioration of Earth's ozone layer, which reflects and filters harmful forms of light.

For more information

BOOKS

Brown, Vanessa. *Cool Shades: The History and Meaning of Sunglasses.* London: Bloomsbury Academic, 2015.

PERIODICALS

Hill, Simon. "Does Staring at Screens All Day Really Damage Your Eyes? We Asked an Expert." *Digital Trends* (February 7, 2015). Available online at http://www.digitaltrends.com/mobile/does-your-phone-damage-your-eyes-an-experts-advice/ (accessed July 12, 2015).

Sikes, Scott. "How Digital Devices Are Affecting Your Vision." *Optometry Times* (September 2014): 24.

WEBSITES

"History of Sunglasses." Optical. http://optical.com/sunglasses/history-of-sunglasses/ (accessed June 15, 2015).

Tennis Racket

Critical Thinking Questions

1. The section titled "Wooden rackets" explains how the rules of tennis changed over time. Why is it important to have a uniform set of rules for the game?

2. Do you think high-tech rackets such as the Babolat Play should be allowed in competitions? Why or why not?

A tennis racket is a type of sports equipment used in the game of tennis. It consists of a handle connected to an oblong and open frame, called the head of the racket. Across the frame, strings are tightly stretched in a grid pattern. Players hold the racket by the handle and hit the ball with the grid of strings, which is known as the hitting surface. Tennis rackets come in a variety of shapes, styles, weights, and colors, depending on the age, grip, playing style, and preferences of the players. However, per the International Tennis Federation (ITF), the international governing body of the sport, racket size cannot exceed 29 inches (73.7 centimeters) long or 12.5 inches (31.8 centimeters) wide. The hitting surface cannot be more than 15.5 inches (39.4 centimeters) long or 11.5 inches (29.2 centimeters) wide.

Modern tennis rackets date to the mid-1870s, when a British army officer received a patent for a kit containing the rules and equipment for tennis, including a wooden racket. Racket design remained much the same until 1967, the year Wilson Sporting Goods began producing metal rackets. By the 1980s graphite and other composites (something made up of different parts) replaced metal as the material of choice for rackets. Lighter and stronger composite rackets led to significant changes

Tennis rackets are designed for the needs of the player. Graphite frames, which are stiff, are more powerful, while aluminum frames, which are more flexible, are better for beginners. © C-YOU/ SHUTTERSTOCK.COM

in racket design, allowing for larger heads that allowed players to hit balls with more power than was previously possible.

Tennis is one of the world's most popular sports, and it cannot be played without a racket. The specific design of each racket allows players to emphasize their strength, whether it is power, accuracy, or spin on the court.

Wooden rackets

Historical evidence suggests that the first tennis club was established in the English town of Leamington in 1872. A year later Major Walter Clopton Wingfield (1833–1912), a British army officer who was interested in racket games such as court tennis (also known as real tennis) and rackets, which were played indoors, published a booklet titled "Sphairistiké, or Lawn Tennis." (*Sphairistiké* is Greek for "ball game.") Wingfield's book described the rules of lawn tennis, as the game was then known. According to his rules, tennis should be played outside, on grass, on an hourglass-shaped court. In 1874 Wingfield patented the game and developed a set of equipment for playing it. His kit included a net, poles, court markers, balls, instructions, and wooden rackets.

The game took off, and in 1877 the All England Croquet and Lawn Tennis Club in the London suburb of Wimbledon organized a tennis tournament. In organizing the tournament, the club changed and refined some of Wingfield's rules, creating the framework for the modern game in the process. According to these changes, tennis matches would be played on a rectangular court 27 feet (8.2 meters) wide and 78 feet (23.8 meters) long.

Over the next several decades, tennis grew internationally, becoming popular among both men and women. As interest in the game spread, the rules of tennis were refined and formalized, but the size, shape, and materials used to make rackets were not regulated. It was not until 1979 that the ITF limited racket size to 29 inches (73.7 centimeters) long and 12.5 inches (31.8 centimeters) wide for professional play. In 2000 the regulations were extended to nonprofessional play as well.

Although there were some early experiments with metal frames and other innovations, wooden rackets with relatively small and round heads became standard. The design changed very little between the 1870s and the 1960s.

Metal and composite rackets

The first major change in racket design came in 1967, when Wilson released its T2000 model. The T2000 featured a frame made of steel instead of wood. It also had a long neck and a rounded head. With these features, the T2000 was lighter and stronger than other rackets, allowing players to move the racket more swiftly and with more agility. As a result, the T2000 caught on quickly. Among its most famous proponents was the American tennis star Jimmy Connors (1952–), who used it throughout his career.

During the 1970s racket designers and manufacturers made more innovations, releasing lighter rackets made of aluminum and rackets with much larger heads. The expansion of the racket's hitting surface made it easier to hit a ball with accuracy and power. But as racket heads grew bigger and players were able to hit balls harder, aluminum, steel, wood, and other materials for making frames were not strong enough to withstand the increased force. The frames often twisted or bent during play, sending shots off target.

As designers looked for a material that would add strength without adding weight, they mixed plastic resin with carbon fiber, a composite that gave the plastic greater strength. The combination was known as graphite. Although cheap rackets continued to be made of aluminum, most high-end rackets had graphite frames by the 1980s.

Between the 1980s and the 2000s, manufacturers and designers experimented with composite materials to create increasingly strong and light frames. Fiberglass, titanium, and Kevlar were among the materials mixed with plastic resin to make rackets. Designers also experimented with increasing the depth of the frames, adding material to strengthen the frame upon impact with the ball. As a result, modern rackets are more durable, lighter, more powerful, and more accurate than earlier designs. This has helped make the sport easier for beginners, while also increasing the quality of play among competitive tennis players.

Raw materials

The raw materials used to make modern tennis rackets vary. Wooden rackets are generally no longer produced, and nearly all rackets have a

Parts of a Tennis Racket

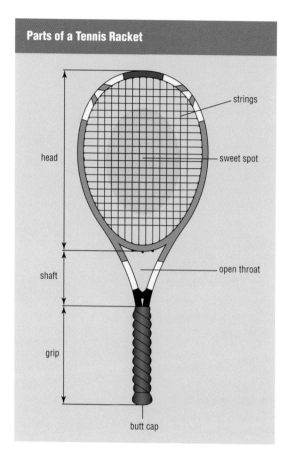

When a ball hits a tennis racket's sweet spot, the player feels less vibration.
ILLUSTRATION BY LUMINA DATAMATICS LTD. © 2015 CENGAGE LEARNING

frame made of some synthetic material or a composite of various synthetic materials. Graphite, aluminum, boron, titanium, fiberglass, and Kevlar are among the most common materials used, in various combinations, to make tennis racket frames.

In addition to the frame, tennis rackets include a grip and strings. Grips can be made of leather, rubber, or synthetic leather, such as neoprene. Most new strings are made of synthetic materials, most often nylon or polyester. However, most professional tennis players continue to use strings made from a part of cattle intestine called the serosa.

Design

The design of a tennis racket is determined by tennis players, who seek light, powerful, and accurate tools for hitting the ball past their opponents. The frame material is one of the most important factors in determining how a racket plays. For example, graphite frames are stiffer than other materials, making them better for players who hope to emphasize the power of their shot. Aluminum frames, on the other hand, are more flexible, making them more forgiving and, thus, better for beginners.

Another important factor in racket design is the size. Although rackets have size limits, they are available in many sizes that fall below the ITF's range. So-called "oversize" rackets have hitting surfaces greater than 100 square inches (645.2 square centimeters). Midsize rackets have a surface between 85 square inches (548.4 square centimeters) and 100 square inches (645.2 square centimeters). Standard rackets have a hitting surface between 80 square inches (516.1 square centimeters) and 85 square inches (548.4 square centimeters). Larger heads give players more power with their shot and make it easier to make contact with the ball, but they also are less accurate. Smaller rackets have a smaller "sweet spot," but they offer a cleaner shot when a player connects correctly with the ball. Longer rackets give players greater reach and power, but they are harder to control.

Nearly all modern rackets feature a so-called "open throat" design in the neck of the racket. An open throat is a triangular hole in the racket's shaft, below the head and above the grip. This design gives the racket greater stability and improves shot accuracy. Rackets feature five grip sizes, ranging from 4.0 inches (10.1 centimeters) to 4.6 inches (11.7 centimeters). The grip is the surface where the player holds the racket. Players select their grip size depending on the size of their hand.

Strings are important factors in tennis racket design. Players determine what kind of strings to use, choosing from nylon, polyester, or animal intestine. They also select how tightly the strings are strung. Higher tension means more control, whereas lower tension means more power.

The manufacturing process

Most tennis racket manufacturers are located in Japan, China, and elsewhere in East Asia. Most store-bought rackets come with the strings already strung, but higher-end rackets do not. Although some racket frames are made of a single material, such as aluminum, most are composites of various substances. The steps below describe the manufacturing process for a composite racket with strings.

1 The first step is known as prepreg, which refers to the process of pre-impregnating sheets of composite fibers—most often graphite, plus some combination of Kevlar, titanium, fiberglass, and tungsten—with resin that has only partially hardened.

2 The large sheets of prepreg are cut into smaller pieces. Multiple sheets of prepreg are laminated together in a way that strengthens each individual sheet. The combined sheets are folded and formed around a plastic tube.

3 The composite material, with the plastic tube running through it, is pressed into a mold in the shape of the racket frame. A second mold of the frame is placed on top of the material, enclosing it.

A factory worker makes Kunnan tennis rackets. Based in Taiwan, Kunnan has been one of the world's largest producers of tennis rackets.
© PIERRE VAUTHEY/SYGMA/ CORBIS

Think about It!

As technology for sports equipment continues to advance, some observers have begun to argue that these changes make things too easy on the players and change the nature of the games being played. For example, critics have argued that metal bats, which allow players to hit baseballs with greater power, distort the game of baseball. As a result, Major League Baseball does not allow metal bats, requiring players to use wooden bats instead. If you were going to put one limitation on the technology used in your favorite sport, what would it be? Why?

4 The mold is heated to 300 degrees Fahrenheit (149 degrees Celsius). While the heat is applied, air is pumped into the plastic tube running through the composite material, adding pressure from the inside while the heat bears down from the outside.

5 The frame is removed from the mold and sanded until it is smooth. Holes are drilled around the head of the racket. Frames are painted with manufacturers' logos and other designs.

6 A butt cap is added at the bottom of the handle. Double-sided tape is wrapped around the handle. Grip tape is wrapped around the double-sided tape.

7 A strip of material (typically plastic), known as a grommet strip, is placed in the groove that circles the head of the frame. The grommet includes holes. These holes are lined up with the holes that have been drilled around the head.

8 Workers then string each racket individually using a stringing machine. The machine holds the racket horizontally and helps pull the nylon or polyester string through the holes in the grommet and the frame. The worker guides the string through the holes and adjusts the strings to make sure the tension is correct.

Quality control

Rackets go through a series of inspections during the manufacturing process. They are tested for hardness, stiffness, and balance to make sure the finished products have no flaws that will weaken their durability or playability. In addition, the strings are continually checked for the proper tension. Before packaging, workers visually inspect rackets from the grip to the head, looking for scratches and other imperfections.

Next generation of rackets

Over the course of tennis's history, the fundamentals of tennis racket design have changed only slightly. At the same time, however, the metals and composites used to construct frames have made rackets more

WORDS TO KNOW

Composite: Something made up of different parts.

Fiberglass: A durable material made of threads of glass. Fiberglass is widely used in manufacturing and is often used to reinforce plastics.

Graphite: A composite made of plastic resin and a carbon filler.

Grommet: A ring (usually made of plastic or metal) that is used to strengthen a hole in leather or cloth.

Neoprene: A synthetic rubber commonly used in the manufacture of sporting gloves and grips.

Patent: An official document that gives an individual or a company exclusive rights over the use of an invention.

Resin: A substance obtained from tree gum or sap (or created synthetically) that is commonly used in the manufacture of plastics and varnishes.

accurate, more powerful, and easier to use. These improvements have helped tennis grow as a worldwide sport, making it easier for beginners to play and improving the quality of professional matches.

At the beginning of the twenty-first century, tennis manufacturers looked to computer technology to create the next generation of rackets. In 2012 the French company Babolat introduced the Babolat Play, a racket that has equipment inside the handle that can record and store data about how a player is hitting, including information about power, stroke, and endurance. The Play transfers this information, either through a USB or wireless connection, to a computer or smartphone. With this data in hand, players can adjust and improve their game. The ITF initially banned the Play from competition, but in 2014 computer-enhanced rackets were approved for match play, with one condition: players cannot consult the data being collected until after the match.

For more information

BOOKS

Brody, Howard, Rodney Cross, and Crawford Lindsey. *The Physics and Technology of Tennis.* Solana Beach, CA: Racquet Tech Pub., 2002.

Cross, Rod, and Lindsey Crawford. *Technical Tennis: Racquets, Strings, Balls, Courts, Spin, and Bounce.* Vista, CA: Racquet Tech Pub., 2005.

Parsons, John, and Henry Wancke. *The Tennis Book: The Illustrated Encyclopedia of World Tennis.* London: Carlton, 2012.

Walter Wingfield

The inventor of tennis, Walter Clopton Wingfield (1833–1912), was born in Wales, England, on October 16, 1833. At the time his father, a captain in the British army, was serving in Canada, and Wingfield was living with his grandfather. Both of Wingfield's parents had died by the time he turned thirteen, and Wingfield was raised by an uncle, a great-uncle, and other relatives.

After completing school, Wingfield was admitted to an impressive cavalry regiment in the British army, the 1st King's Dragoon Guards. With the army, Wingfield traveled the world, heading first to India, which was then a British colony. While there he met his future wife, Alice Lydia Cleveland, the daughter of a general. From there he traveled to China before returning to Britain in 1861, living first in Wales and then in London.

It was in London that Wingfield pursued his interest in racket sports and, in 1874, received his patent for lawn tennis. Wingfield later developed a new design for a bicycle, which he called the Butterfly, and he created methods for riding bicycles in patterns set to music. Wingfield also became interested in cooking and served as the vice president of England's Universal Cookery and Food Association. He died on April 18, 1912.

PERIODICALS

Gandu, Gurvinder Singh. "The Evolution of the Tennis Racket." *Complex* (August 28, 2012). http://www.complex.com/sneakers/2012/08/the-evolution-of-the-tennis-racket (accessed July 8, 2015).

Goodall, Jason. "Pulling All the Strings." *Wall Street Journal* (November 23, 2010). Available online at http://www.wsj.com/articles/SB10001424052748703805704575594390443262092 (accessed July 8, 2015).

Miller, Stuart. "Modern Tennis Rackets, Balls, and Surfaces." *British Journal of Sports Medicine* 40, no. 5 (May 2006). Available online at http://www.ncbi.nlm.nih.gov/pmc/articles/PMC2577483/ (accessed July 8, 2015).

Oidemizu, Takayuki. "The Quest for the Perfect Racket: Advances in Tennis Racket Design." *Illumin* 5, no. 1 (Fall 2003). Available online at https://illumin.usc.edu/50/the-quest-for-the-perfect-racket-advances-in-tennis-racket-design/ (accessed July 8, 2015).

WEBSITES

"Illustrated History of the Tennis Racket." *Sports Illustrated.* http://www.si.com/tennis/photos/2013/06/25/evolution-tennis-racket/start (accessed July 8, 2015).

International Tennis Federation. http://www.itftennis.com/technical/rackets-and-strings/other/manufacture.aspx (accessed July 8, 2015).

Toothpaste

Critical Thinking Questions

1. How did Washington Wentworth Sheffield influence the development of modern toothpaste? What evidence from the entry supports your answer?

2. Based on information in the section "The manufacturing process," does it matter what order the ingredients are added to the toothpaste mixture? Why or why not?

Toothpaste is used to clean teeth, prevent cavities and tooth decay, freshen bad breath, and keep teeth white. The rough, abrasive texture of toothpaste helps to remove food and dental plaque, a sticky deposit that builds up on teeth and causes bacteria. The motion of toothbrush bristles against the teeth is what does most of the cleaning, but toothpaste also contains ingredients such as fluoride, a chemical commonly added to toothpaste and drinking water to help keep teeth healthy. Toothpaste is usually sold in squeezable tubes and is often white or blue in color.

Throughout history abrasive toothpastes or tooth powders have been used to clean teeth. Many common household products, including salt and baking soda, can help keep teeth clean and prevent decay. First sold in the nineteenth century, modern toothpastes contain active ingredients such as fluoride, tooth whiteners, and mint flavoring that freshens breath. They are also designed to remove food and plaque without rubbing off tooth enamel, the tooth's protective outer layer.

Toothpaste can be found in one form or another in nearly every home worldwide. Along with toothbrushes, dental floss, and other oral hygiene

products, toothpaste is something people begin using as children and continue to use their entire life. The foamy, sudsy texture of toothpaste helps clean teeth more thoroughly than a brush alone, and toothpaste has also provided an easy way to deliver fluoride and other substances to aid in healthy teeth. The average person in the United States uses more than 350 tubes of toothpaste during his or her lifetime.

Oral history

Dentistry was difficult and dangerous in the ancient world, and keeping teeth clean was known to be an important part of preventing tooth decay. Toothpastes or powders were applied to the teeth with rags or with peeled twigs. In ancient Greece and Rome, powdered bones or shells were rubbed on teeth to clean them. "Tooth powders" like these are still sold, especially in developing countries. Before the Middle Ages (c. 500–c. 1500), people in the Middle East used fine-grained sand or stones to clean their teeth.

First sold in the nineteenth century, toothpaste contains active ingredients such as fluoride, tooth whiteners, and mint flavoring that freshens breath. © GEPARDU/ SHUTTERSTOCK.COM

The oldest known pastes for cleaning teeth were made in ancient Egypt and contained incense and green lead, which now is considered toxic when consumed. One of the most popular toothpaste recipes in the ninth century came from Iraq, supposedly created by the musician Ziryab (789–857). Many early toothpaste recipes contained unusual ingredients such as gunpowder or, in the case of a recipe from the colonial United States, ground-up burned bread. Whether because they contained toxic ingredients or because they were so harsh that they wore away at tooth enamel, many early tooth-cleaning methods were actually harmful to oral health.

Modern toothpaste can be credited to the nineteenth-century American dental surgeon Washington Wentworth Sheffield (1827–1897). Sheffield began experimenting with tooth-cleaning creams in his private dental practice. He saw such good results from their use that he decided to sell his formula as a commercial product. Sheffield began selling his "Creme Dentrifrice" in 1850.

Sheffield's toothpaste quickly became popular, and he set up a factory to produce it on a large scale. The "cream" was originally packaged in small glass jars. Sheffield's son Lucius (1849–1919) came up with the idea of packaging toothpaste in tubes. Lucius had noticed the neatness and efficiency of tube packaging while looking at paints, which at the time were sold in collapsible lead tubes. Adapting the technique, he filed a patent in 1892 for collapsible toothpaste tubes. The first toothpaste to use the tube design was the Colgate-Palmolive Company's 1896 toothpaste "Colgate Ribbon Dental Creme." Collapsible plastic tubes, still made much the same way, are the preferred packaging for toothpaste in the early twenty-first century.

Toothpaste grins

Toothpaste became increasingly common in the early twentieth century. As several toothpaste brands became popular, advertising campaigns emphasized the importance of brushing with toothpaste at least once a day. Because of these ad campaigns, dental care started to become a part of people's everyday bathroom routines. Commercial toothpaste became a fixture in most homes in Europe and the United States.

Toothpaste companies also influenced popular culture. Toothpaste ads contained endorsements (public approval and support) from dentists and other medical experts, and celebrity spokespeople campaigned for toothpaste brands. By the mid-twentieth century, toothpaste ads connected the glamour of the popular celebrity culture with tooth cleaning. By highlighting the beauty of celebrities' white smiles, the ads encouraged people to care for the health and appearance of their own teeth.

Businessman and advertising expert Claude C. Hopkins (1866–1932), who started managing ad campaigns for the Pepsodent Company in Chicago in 1915, created a famous animated neon sign for Pepsodent toothpaste that featured a girl on a swing. An iconic part of New York City's Times Square during the 1930s, the sign is so famous that it has been recreated for movies such as *King Kong* (2005). Pepsodent also sponsored a popular radio program, *The Pepsodent Show Starring Bob Hope* that was broadcast by NBC for more than ten years, beginning in 1938.

New and improved!

In the 1940s researchers discovered that treating teeth with fluoride helps prevent tooth decay by strengthening the teeth's protective outer layer of enamel. Developers realized that toothpaste was an easy, convenient way for people to get the recommended fluoride. Toothpastes with fluoride as an active ingredient began to be sold in the 1950s.

Not everyone believed that fluoride was effective or necessary, but in the early twenty-first century the scientific community firmly believes in the usefulness of fluoride treatments. In 1960 the American Dental Association (ADA) stated that fluoride toothpastes worked as anticavity treatments, and additional studies have confirmed its conclusion.

Toothpaste formulas have continued to change as more is discovered about tooth care and oral health. In the 1980s active ingredients were added to many toothpastes to help control the buildup of plaque (tartar, or dental calculus) on teeth. Tartar formation can cause staining and can make it difficult to clean the teeth effectively. Bicarbonate soda (baking soda) started to be added to many toothpastes in the 1990s, also mainly to control tartar. Toothpaste designed for sensitive teeth began appearing in the 1990s as well.

Scientists continue to develop new kinds of toothpastes. One of the most exciting recent advances in toothpaste is the use of the synthetic

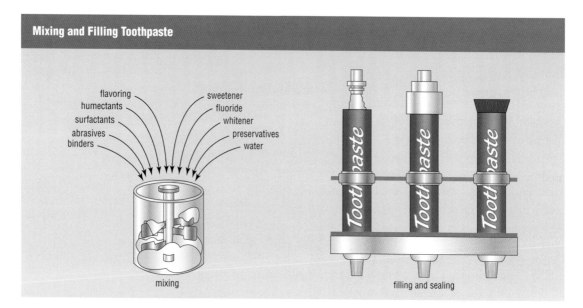

Mixing and Filling Toothpaste

flavoring
humectants
surfactants
abrasives
binders

sweetener
fluoride
whitener
preservatives
water

mixing

filling and sealing

All of the ingredients used to make toothpaste are mixed together under carefully controlled temperature and humidity. Tubes are capped and sanitized, then filled with toothpaste before the bottoms of the tubes are sealed. ILLUSTRATION BY LUMINA DATAMATICS LTD. © 2015 CENGAGE LEARNING

Workers on an assembly line for Tom's of Maine, a toothpaste owned by Colgate-Palmolive Company, in Maine in 2006. © JOE RAEDLE/GETTY IMAGES

(artificially made) compound hydroxylapatite, pioneered by the European company BioRepair in 2006. Hydroxylapatite is substituted for fluoride. Instead of strengthening existing enamel the way fluoride does, hydroxylapatite creates an entirely new layer of synthetic tooth enamel each time it is used, repairing damage and wear.

Raw materials

Modern toothpastes are all made out of the same basic ingredients: a rough abrasive to scrub the teeth, fluorides and tooth whiteners, binders and humectants to form the paste, a surfactant to make the toothpaste foamy, sweeteners and other flavors, some form of preservative, and water.

An abrasive is the most basic active ingredient in toothpaste. It scrubs the outside of the teeth and loosens food and plaque. An overly

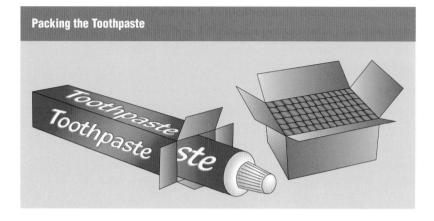

Packing the Toothpaste

After each tube of toothpaste is packed in a box, the individual boxes are packed into cartons for shipping. ILLUSTRATION BY LUMINA DATAMATICS LTD. © 2015 CENGAGE LEARNING

harsh abrasive can damage tooth enamel. Different abrasives can change a toothpaste's texture, consistency (thickness), opacity (how transparent it is or is not), and taste. Abrasives commonly used in modern toothpastes include hydrated silica (softened silica dioxide), calcium carbonate (also known as chalk), sodium bicarbonate (baking soda), dibasic calcium phosphate, calcium sulfate, tricalcium phosphate, and sodium metaphosphate hydrated alumina.

Fluorides and tooth whiteners are other active ingredients that improve dental health or appearance. Fluorides increase the strength of tooth enamel. Sodium fluoride is the most common type of fluoride in commercial toothpastes. A frequently used tooth-whitening additive is sodium perborate, which works by bleaching the teeth.

In addition to active ingredients, toothpastes need binders to hold the paste together and humectants, or moisturizers, to keep it from drying out. Binders, such as karaya gum, bentonite, sodium alginate, methylcellulose, carrageenan, and magnesium aluminum silicate, keep the liquid and solid components of the toothpaste from separating over time. They also thicken the toothpaste and can affect appearance, taste, foaminess, and rinsability. Humectants, such as sorbitol, glycerin, and propylene glycol, work to hold in moisture. The humectants in toothpaste help make it feel pleasantly cooling to the mouth.

Surfactants, also called foaming agents or sudsers, give toothpaste its foamy quality by lowering the surface tension of water, creating lots of tiny bubbles. The resulting foam helps remove finer particles from the surface of teeth. Surfactants include sodium lauryl sulfate, sodium lauryl sulfoacetate, dioctyl sodium sulfosuccinate, sulfolaurate, sodium lauryl sarcosinate, sodium stearyl fumarate, and sodium stearyl lactate.

Sweeteners and other flavors make toothpaste taste better. Sugar cannot be used as a sweetener because it causes tooth decay, but alternative sweeteners such as saccharin, ammoniated diglyzzherizins, and aspartame are sometimes included in toothpastes. The most traditional and common flavor of toothpaste is mint. Mint oils (usually spearmint, wintergreen, or peppermint) make the mouth feel cool and fresh. Cinnamon is another common toothpaste flavor. Some children's toothpastes use a sweet bubblegum flavor. Other spices or flavors are also used.

The most commonly used preservative in modern toothpastes is p-hydroxybenzoate. This extends the paste's shelf life. Other ingredients added to some toothpastes include artificial colors.

Think about It!

How much toothpaste do you use when you brush your teeth in the morning, after eating, or before bed? Most toothpaste ads show large amounts of toothpaste being squeezed onto the bristles of the brush, displaying the paste in a thick ribbon. In reality, you do not need to use nearly that much. The American Dental Association recommends a pea-size dab of toothpaste for each application. Why do you think ads show so much more toothpaste per use than is really needed?

Design

Toothpastes are often colored, either brightly, when made for children, or in a way that suggests cleanliness or freshness. Some toothpastes are multicolored, creating a ribbon effect when squeezed from the tube.

Toothpastes have been sold in tubes since the early twentieth century. The tubes were originally made of metallic lead but are now most frequently made of plastic. Beginning in the 1980s, a stand-up pump design for toothpaste was also marketed. Both upright and collapsible tubes remain available to consumers.

Safety

Although the widespread use of toothpastes has produced noticeably good results, improving dental and oral health by preventing cavities, maintaining whiteness, and freshening breath, controversies have come up over active and additive ingredients. Some people still argue the effectiveness of fluoride. Others have brought up concerns

WORDS TO KNOW

Abrasive: A substance that is used to scrape or rub away at something in order to make it smooth.

Fluoride: A chemical commonly added to toothpaste and drinking water to promote dental health.

Foaming agent: A material used to aid in the formation of foam.

Humectant: A substance that helps prevent the loss of moisture.

Hydroxylapatite: A synthetic compound substituted for fluoride.

Surfactant: A substance that reduces surface tension of water, promoting foaming.

Viscosity: The state of being thick, sticky, and semifluid.

about potential fluoride toxicity, although testing has convinced scientists that fluoride is safe for oral use. However, fluoride should not be swallowed in large quantities, which is one of the reasons why it is important to spit toothpaste out after brushing rather than swallowing it.

The manufacturing process

Toothpaste is manufactured in factories, and most of the steps in the manufacturing process are performed mechanically. Ingredients are combined in large factory-grade mixers. The finished paste is then inserted into tubes, which are sealed and boxed.

1 The raw materials are carefully weighed and measured. All ingredients are combined in a monitored mixing vat. Often, the first ingredients to be mixed are glycerin (a humectant) and water.

2 Blowers and vacuum cleaners remove any contaminants from the mixed paste.

3 The tubes are prepared with caps screwed on but with the bottom end left open. This is where the toothpaste will be inserted.

4 A descending pump injects toothpaste into the tubes, which are then crimped closed and sealed.

5 The finished tubes of toothpaste are prepared for shipping and delivery. After being individually packaged, the final products are boxed and sent to distributors.

Try This!

Make your own toothpaste
Whip up a batch of homemade toothpaste using just a few common household ingredients.

You will need:

- ⅔ cup baking soda
- 1 to 2 teaspoons peppermint extract or 10 to 15 drops peppermint essential oil, or any other flavor you want to try
- 1 teaspoon fine sea salt (optional)
- filtered water
- small storage container with lid

Directions:

1. Mix the baking soda, peppermint, and sea salt (if desired) in a bowl. The minerals in salt can be beneficial for teeth, but baking soda is the most effective ingredient in your toothpaste, so leave out the salt if you do not like the taste of it.

2. Add water a little at a time, stirring until the paste reaches the desired consistency.

3. Each batch will yield the equivalent of one 5-ounce (148-milliliter) tube of toothpaste. Store the paste in a glass jar or other small storage container with a tight-fitting lid.

4. When you are ready to start brushing, scoop the toothpaste onto your brush and brush as usual to enjoy the feeling of clean teeth.

Quality control

Toothpaste standards date back to 1934, when the American Dental Association Council on Dental Therapeutics began categorizing products as "Accepted," "Provisionally Accepted," or "Unaccepted." Modern toothpastes are all stamped with a code showing the date of manufacture. Each batch of manufactured toothpaste is closely inspected by testing labs, often by hand, before being boxed up and shipped to distributors.

The future's so bright

For more than a hundred years, toothpaste has been an important part of public health around the world. Preventive tooth care saves the general public money by reducing the need for expensive oral surgeries or other dental procedures, and it also promotes general well-being by keeping people free from pain or other unpleasant consequences of tooth decay. Toothpastes and toothbrushes make it easy to maintain healthy teeth at home. It is also important to have professional dental cleanings at standard intervals, but regular toothpaste use helps to cut down on plaque, tartar, and bacterial buildups in between appointments. Toothpastes in the early twenty-first century are cosmetic as well as health products. Whitening toothpastes help consumers maintain white smiles and fresh, minty breath.

While the formulation and appearance of toothpastes is likely to continue to change, toothpastes themselves are likely here to stay. Toothpaste is the easiest, most cost-effective way for people to take care of their own oral and dental health and hygiene on a daily basis.

For more information

BOOKS

Darby, Michele Leonardi, and Margaret Walsh. *Dental Hygiene: Theory and Practice.* St. Louis: Elsevier Health Sciences, 2014.

Duhigg, Charles. *The Power of Habit: Why We Do What We Do in Life and Business.* New York: Random House, 2012.

Stone, Tanya Lee. *Toothpaste: From Start to Finish.* New York: Blackbirch Press, 2001.

Van Loveren, C., ed. *Toothpastes.* Basel, Switzerland: Karger, 2013.

PERIODICALS

Petersen, Poul Erik, et al. "School-Based Intervention for Improving the Oral Health of Children in Southern Thailand." *Community Dental Health* 32, no.1 (2015): 44–50.

Sohn, Emily. "Spit Power." *ScienceNews for Students* (January 23, 2006). Available online at https://student.societyforscience.org/article/spit-power (accessed July 24, 2015).

WEBSITES

American Dental Association. http://www.ada.org/en/science-research/ada-seal-of-acceptance/product-category-information/toothpaste (accessed June 28, 2015).

Pleis, Donna. "Historical Facts about Toothpaste." Colgate. http://www.colgate.com/en/us/oc/oral-health/basics/selecting-dental-products/article/sw-281474979354594 (accessed July 25, 2015).

Vinyl Record

Critical Thinking Questions

1. Based on information in the entry, why are master copies an important part of the vinyl record manufacturing process? Do you think you can play a master copy? Why or why not?

2. Vinyl records are an older product that are enjoying new popularity. Can you think of any other once outdated technology that is popular again?

Vinyl records are round, grooved discs made of plastic resin that record and store sounds. Commonly known as "vinyl" or "records," vinyl records require a record player, or turntable, to be played. The record player turns the record so that a needle runs through the record's grooves, which have the shape of sound waves. The needle reads the sound waves, which are then played through speakers or headphones.

The first full-length vinyl records were available for purchase in 1931, but the format really became popular in 1948, when record companies began advertising heavily. Vinyl records fell out of fashion in the late twentieth century, as consumers turned first to cassettes, then to compact discs, and finally to computer-based formats for their music.

Vinyl records are valued for their high-quality sound. Many listeners consider vinyl records to offer a clearer sound than newer digital formats. Vinyl records are also valued by disc jockeys, or DJs, who play and change music for an audience, because they can be moved by hand using a technique known as scratching to produce new sounds. As a result, vinyl records have grown in popularity in the early twenty-first century.

Full-length records are made of vinyl and rotate thirty-three and one-third times per minute. © DAVORANA/ SHUTTERSTOCK.COM

Early records

The origins of the vinyl record can be traced to the late nineteenth century, when American inventor Thomas Edison (1847–1931) began the first successful experiments in recording and playing sounds with a mechanical device known as a phonograph. Edison's first phonograph, which he completed in 1877, was a simple machine. It required the user to turn a crank to spin a cylinder wrapped in tinfoil. The foil was grooved, and the phonograph was equipped with a stylus, a pointed piece of metal, and a horn to amplify the sound waves, or make them louder. As the stylus ran through the cylinder's grooves, it vibrated. The vibrations made sounds, which played through the horn.

Over the next decade, Edison and others worked to improve upon the phonograph's design. In 1888 two competing models were released for sale to the public. Both relied on the same basic design but used wax cylinders instead of tinfoil to record and play sounds. These cylinders, which were known as records, offered better fidelity, or sound quality, than tinfoil, but could only hold about two minutes of music or sound.

The next major development in sound recording and reproduction came in the mid-1890s, with the invention of the flat, disc-shaped record. These records were made of zinc and wax and were played on a machine called a gramophone. Discs were spun at seventy-eight revolutions per minute, giving them the nickname "78s." Flat discs were easier to make and featured a louder sound than wax cylinders. Over time shellac became the preferred material for making flat discs. While this new technology grew in popularity, it did not replace wax cylinders entirely. In the early twentieth century, both kinds of records—flat discs and cylinders—competed for listeners.

Longer plays and better sound

In the 1920s and 1930s, many changes were made in the recording and storage of sound. One of the most important was the use of electricity to record sound using microphones, vacuum tubes, and electromagnetic disc cutters. These tools let engineers capture a more accurate and "full" sound. Soon the electric process for recording sound replaced earlier methods, and record companies looked for new ways of storing sound on discs.

In 1930 record company RCA Victor made the first full-length, 12-inch (30-centimeter) record. Compared to earlier discs, it had finer grooves and turned at a slower rate of thirty-three and one-third revolutions per minute, allowing more sound to be stored on the record. In another change, records were made of vinyl, a flexible plastic.

Grooves creating sound are cut into a vinyl disc. © YAKUB88/ SHUTTERSTOCK.COM

Over the next two decades, the design of the vinyl record improved while keeping the same basic form. The result, in 1948, was the release of the modern long-playing, or LP, vinyl record by Columbia Records. Soon after RCA Victor introduced a 7-inch (18-centimeter) vinyl record. Seven-inch records turn slightly faster than LPs, spinning at forty-five revolutions per minute. This shorter format was known as an EP, or extended play. LPs could hold around thirty minutes of music on each side, while EPs held about four minutes per side. Because of the difference in length, LPs became the format for albums, while single songs were released as EPs.

Vinyl records soon became the most popular means for storing and listening to music. Because of the popularity of vinyl, shellac records were no longer made by the early 1960s. In the late 1950s, improvements were made to the recording process, most notably with the adoption of stereophonic sound in 1957. Stereo, as it is commonly known, allowed for two or more independent channels of audio to be stored and played back on a single record. Using two or more channels gave sound greater depth and fullness. Since the introduction of stereo sound, vinyl record design has changed very little.

Raw materials

The main ingredient for making vinyl records is polyvinyl chloride, or PVC. In hard form, PVC is used to make pipes and other durable materials. To make the flexible vinyl used in records, PVC is combined with additives known as plasticizers. Occasionally color is added to the vinyl. Colored vinyl records are typically produced in small batches because colored vinyl is more expensive to make than standard black vinyl. Vinyl

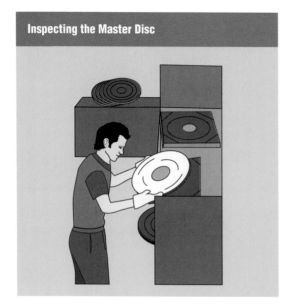

Inspecting the Master Disc

Workers carefully inspect the master disc. Once it passes inspection, the master disc is used to create a stamping record from which other records will be made. ILLUSTRATION BY LUMINA DATAMATICS LTD. © 2015 CENGAGE LEARNING

records also commonly include labels, made of paper and applied with glue, which indicate the name of the artist as well as other information about the recording.

Design

The design of vinyl records is highly standardized, meaning all records of the same type are designed in the same way. In order to be played on a turntable, a record must include some very specific and basic features. It must be round and feature a groove that begins near the outside edge of the record and spirals toward the center. The width of the groove has to meet certain specifications, which are slightly different for records produced in stereophonic (multichannel) and monophonic (single channel) sound. Grooves of stereophonic records are slightly wider than grooves in monophonic records. Vinyl records must also include a center hole with a diameter of 0.286 inches (0.726 centimeters). The diameter of most vinyl records is either 7 or 12 inches (18 or 30 centimeters). However, some less common sizes, such as 10-inch (25-centimeter) records, are also sometimes produced for material of unusual length.

The weight and thickness of vinyl records varies somewhat. While a standard LP weighs 4 ounces (120 grams) and is approximately 0.1 inch (0.2 centimeter) thick, thicker and heavier records are sometimes produced. Much of the inventiveness in vinyl record design comes not from the vinyl itself but from its packaging. Record companies and artists have produced a wide variety of record sleeves (the thin, inner covering of the vinyl record) and record jackets (the thicker, outermost covering). These designs are meant to reflect the artistic vision of the recorded music and to be attractive to consumers.

The manufacturing process

A factory where records are manufactured is commonly known as a pressing plant. At the height of the popularity of vinyl records during the twentieth century, pressing plants were massive facilities that churned out millions of records a year. But when compact discs, or CDs, began to overtake vinyl records as the most common format for playing recorded music in the

1980s, production at pressing plants slowed almost to a stop. The last new pressing plant was built in 1982.

However, as demand for records has grown in the early twenty-first century, some existing pressing plants have increased production. In addition, several new plants have opened. Some of these are small operations that press only tens of thousands of records a year. Others put out millions of new vinyl records annually. The process of making a vinyl record has changed little since the 1960s.

1 A recording is made. This process typically begins with the use of microphones, which change sounds into electrical signals. The electrical signals are transferred through cords either to a computer or to a magnetic tape recorder.

2 Once the recording is complete, it is transferred to an aluminum disc coated in lacquer, a liquid substance that hardens when dried. This is known as the master disc.

3 During the making of the master disc, a mastering engineer determines how wide to make the record's grooves. The engineer makes this decision based on the quality of the original recording and his or her preferences about how the completed record should sound.

4 The engineer uses a special machine known as a record lathe to cut the grooves. The lathe includes an electronically guided stylus, or needle, to cut grooves that correspond to the sound waves of the original recording. It also features a small vacuum tube, which sucks up the leftover lacquer that is cut out of the groove.

5 The finished master disc, which is slightly larger than the vinyl records it will be used to produce, is coated with a thin layer of silver. Once this happens, the master disc is known as the metal master. A mold is made of the metal master. Liquid nickel is poured into the mold. Once the mold hardens, it forms a negative impression of the final record. The metal negative is sprayed with atomized silver and coated with a layer of copper and a thin layer of a sturdier metal, such as steel, to prevent scratching.

6 The mold is removed. The metal negative that is left over is known as a "matrix." The matrix is used to press grooves into a sheet of metal. This impression is known as the "mother."

Mass Record Production

Vinyl records are mass-produced and packaged for sale to consumers. ILLUSTRATION BY LUMINA DATAMATICS LTD. © 2015 CENGAGE LEARNING

Think about It!

Get into the groove

The grooves of vinyl records contain their sounds. These grooves hold the shape of sound waves. When a needle passes through them, the needle vibrates, creating an electric pulse that is made louder through speakers or headphones. Instruments feature their own means of creating vibrations and amplifying them for listeners. For example, guitar strings vibrate when strummed or plucked; the vibrations echo within, and project from, the guitar's hollow body. If you were going to design an instrument, what would vibrate? How would these vibrations be made louder?

7 From the mother, a new negative is made. This negative is known as the "stamper," because it will be used to stamp grooves into blank vinyl records.

8 Raw vinyl, which comes to the pressing plant in tiny chunks, is heated and mixed into a thick, gooey substance. The softened vinyl is fed through rollers, which flatten it into sheets with the desired thickness. When the flattened vinyl cools, it forms flexible sheets.

9 Machines cut round discs, known as biscuits, from the sheets. Each biscuit has approximately half the diameter of, and is about three times as thick as, a finished record.

10 The biscuit is placed in the press, and steam is applied to soften the vinyl. The press smashes the biscuit with the stampers, squeezing the vinyl into the right shape and imprinting the correct grooves on each side of the disc. The disc is placed into cool water, where it hardens.

11 Labels, which are printed with ink and baked in special ovens to eliminate moisture, are stuck to the center of each side of each disc with glue. A blade trims the vinyl so that each disc has a neat, rounded edge.

12 Finished discs are checked for defects and, if they pass inspection, are placed into paper sleeves.

Quality control

Each record undergoes a quick visual inspection after it is pressed and before it is packaged. In addition, workers listen to a small sample of albums from each pressing, or run, to ensure the audio is correct and of high quality. If a problem is found, the pressing is halted while engineers work to identify and correct the issue.

A growth in popularity

In the late twentieth century, as new formats were developed for recorded music, vinyl records seemed destined to become a thing of the past. First

WORDS TO KNOW

Lacquer: A liquid substance, commonly used as a coating, that hardens when dried.

Master: An original creation from which all others are made.

Monophonic sound: A recording featuring a single channel of audio.

Resin: A substance obtained from tree gum or sap (or created synthetically) that is commonly used in the manufacture of plastics and varnishes.

Shellac: A naturally occurring resin.

Stereophonic sound: An innovation in recording that allows for two or more independent channels of audio on a single recording.

came CDs, which were smaller, easier to store, and more portable than records. CDs also could store more material and, according to some, offered higher sound quality. Next came computer-based formats for storing and playing music, such as MP3s. These formats kept audio in digital files that lacked any physical presence, could be easily shared, and could be stored and played on portable devices such as MP3 players, laptops, tablets, and smartphones.

As a result of these new formats, vinyl sales nearly stopped during the 1980s and 1990s. However, they have begun to recover in the early twenty-first century. In 2014, after a long period of growth, vinyl sales in the United States reached $9.2 million, a level not seen since 1996. While the reasons for the growth are unclear, most observers think that vinyl's popularity is because of a growing consumer desire for physical objects in a world filled with digital media. Instead of simply streaming digital files on a computer, vinyl listeners get to flip through artwork, build a collection of records, and spend time with other people in record shops, searching the bins for albums. Another draw is the sound. Vinyl, many record lovers argue, offers a warm, rich tone that no computer file or CD can replicate.

For more information

BOOKS

Edmunds, Alice, and John Freeman, eds. *Who Puts the Grooves in the Record?* New York: Random House, 1976.

Milner, Greg. *Perfecting Sound Forever: An Aural History of Recorded Music.* New York: Faber and Faber, 2009.

Osborne, Richard. *Vinyl: A History of the Analogue Record.* Farnham, UK: Ashgate Publishing, 2012.

A Change of Orientation

Many observers credit the recent popularity of vinyl records to listeners' love of the look and feel of this otherwise old-fashioned format for listening to music. Gramovox, a Chicago-based company, is hoping to take advantage of this preference by turning traditional turntable design upside-down—or rather, on its side.

In 2015 Gramovox revealed a design for what it is calling the Floating Record, a turntable that plays records vertically instead of horizontally. While the Floating Record has a visually striking design, it operates much like a traditional record player. The base is made of wood, either maple or walnut, and includes a built-in amplifier, built-in speakers, and outputs that will connect the turntable to a stereo system. From the base, an arm with a cartridge and needles reaches up into the air. An acrylic platter is also mounted vertically. Records are attached to the platter, and a belt drive system turns the platter at either thirty-three and one-third or forty-five revolutions per minute, depending on the format of the record being played. The Floating Record features a clamp that keeps the record mounted upright and has a spring in the cartridge to keep the needle pressed against the grooves with the right amount of pressure.

The Floating Record does not offer any improvement in the sound of vinyl records, but it does allow for a big change in how turntables look. Instead of having a turntable just sitting on a shelf, the Floating Record allows listeners to watch their vinyl as it plays.

PERIODICALS

Kehe, John. "Vinyl Spins On … and On." *Christian Science Monitor* (June 9, 2015). Available online at http://www.csmonitor.com/The-Culture/Music/2015/0609/Vinyl-spins-on-and-on (accessed June 30, 2015).

Kozinn, Allan. "Weaned on CDs, They're Reaching for Vinyl." *New York Times* (June 9, 2013). Available online at http://www.nytimes.com/2013/06/10/arts/music/vinyl-records-are-making-a-comeback.html (accessed June 30, 2015).

Oliphant, Joel. "Wax and Wane: The Tough Realities behind Vinyl's Comeback." *Pitchfork* (July 28, 2014). Available online at http://pitchfork.com/features/articles/9467-wax-and-wane-the-tough-realities-behind-vinyls-comeback/ (accessed June 30, 2015).

WEBSITES

Analog Planet. http://www.analogplanet.com/ (accessed July 1, 2015).

Gramovox. http://www.gramovox.com/ (accessed July 1, 2015).

The Record Collectors Guild. http://recordcollectorsguild.org/ (accessed June 30, 2015).

Wireless Video Game Controller

Critical Thinking Questions

1. How did the rise of cell phones and cell phone technology influence video game controller design? How would controllers be different if there were no cell phones?

2. How will the process of manufacturing wireless video controllers have to change to include the improvements described in the entry?

Wireless video game controllers are handheld devices that give players more freedom of movement by getting rid of the cords that traditionally attached controllers to the game console. Controllers have buttons, pads, and joysticks (handles that move in all directions to control game movement) that allow the player to control game play. They vary somewhat in size and design depending on the brand and what types of games the controller is used for.

Wireless technology for video game controllers was developed to meet players' wishes to move more freely and away from the game console. However, early wireless controllers were big and clumsy, had batteries that did not last long, and often responded to commands more slowly than wired controllers. As technology has advanced, however, wireless controllers have become smaller, sleeker, and easier to handle. In addition, batteries last longer or are rechargeable, and response time is quicker and more accurate. More than one player can even play at a time. Some wireless controllers are also motion-sensitive, meaning the controller can sense the gamer's movements, providing a higher level of interaction between the gamer and the game.

Wireless video game controllers have changed the nature of video game play. Controllers that were tied to consoles limited how much a gamer could move without the cord getting in the way or multiple gamers getting tangled in each other's wires. As wireless controllers have changed so have video games, which are now more interactive and allow more players to play at the same time. Wireless technology has also led to the development of games that help players improve their hand and eye coordination and problem-solving skills.

Video game controllers have buttons, pads, and joysticks to control a player's movements and other elements of the game.
© SAMSONOVS/
SHUTTERSTOCK.COM

Early radio frequency technology

The first technology used for wireless controllers was radio frequency (RF) technology, which allowed gamers to move about 20 to 30 feet (6 to 9 meters) from game consoles. This was an improvement over controllers with attached wires, which were usually about 3 to 8 feet (1 to 2.5 meters) long. Before RF was used by video game makers, it was used for radios, walkie-talkies, and automatic garage door openers. It uses electromagnetic radio waves (a type of radiation that moves at the speed of light) to send information through the air.

In 1982 the Atari 2600 became the first game console to use radio waves to free players from corded controllers. The controllers looked like Atari's traditional joysticks, but they had a bigger base to hold batteries. Many players found the bulky joysticks awkward to use. They also complained that they used up batteries quickly and were slower to respond to players' commands than traditional controllers. Because of this, they were not very popular.

Infrared technology

The next technology used for wireless controllers was infrared (IR) technology. IR technology is sometimes called invisible radiant energy because its wavelengths (the distance between the tops of two waves) are longer than visible light, so the human eye cannot see them. IR was commonly used to operate remote controls for televisions before it was adapted for wireless controllers beginning in the late 1980s. Console manufacturers such as Nintendo and Sega, as

How Everyday Products Are Made

well as some video game accessory manufacturers, produced wireless IR controllers.

IR technology improved on RF technology by allowing for smaller controllers that required less frequent battery changes. However, like television remote controls, IR video game controllers had to be pointed directly at the console to work. If someone walked between the player and the console, the game would be interrupted.

Despite their limitations, IR controllers were common until a newer generation of game consoles and games came on the market that required sending large amounts of data between the controller and the console. IR controllers could not handle the increased data load. Also, because IR controllers allowed for only one-way communication between the controller and the console, they could not be used for games featuring rumble, or "force feedback," features, in which the controller reacts to what is happening on the screen. For example, if an on-screen character crashes into something, the controller vibrates.

One problem with early video game controllers was that players had to sit or stand close to the console in order to play.
© STEFANO TINTI/
SHUTTERSTOCK.COM

A return to RF technology

While game makers were experimenting with IR technology in the early 1990s, RF technology came into wider use for cordless phones and cell phones. The phones needed higher frequencies (shorter wavelengths) to send more information than earlier RF devices. Using these higher frequencies meant more data could be sent at a faster pace than with IR technology, so the makers of video game controllers went back to using RF. Manufacturers of accessories for the Super Nintendo Entertainment System (NES), released in 1990, and the Sony PlayStation, introduced in 1994, produced some of the first examples of these second-generation RF wireless controllers. The controller did not need to point directly at the sensor, and more than one controller could be used during a game.

Around the turn of the twenty-first century, a new group of high-powered wireless devices, such as the WiFi (wireless fidelity) Internet signal router, were designed to operate at a higher frequency (2.4

gigahertz, or 2.4 billion wave cycles per second) than cordless phones (900 megahertz, or 900 million wave cycles per second). This new high-frequency signal range was quickly used by video game console and accessory manufacturers.

Controllers for the Sony PlayStation 2 (released in 2000) and the Nintendo GameCube (released in 2001), as well as controllers for the Microsoft Xbox 360 (released in 2005), took advantage of the 2.4 gigahertz (GHz) radio signal range. With 2.4 GHz controllers, gamers could still be about the same distance from the console, about 30 feet (9 meters), but the response time between the wireless controller and the game console was much quicker than older versions. Use of the 2.4 GHz range also allowed up to four controllers to connect to consoles at the same time and required less frequent battery changes. The biggest problem for users of 2.4 GHz controllers was that other computers or systems using the same frequency (such as WiFi routers) could interrupt or slow down the game.

Bluetooth technology and motion sensitivity

In response to the interference problems of 2.4 GHz controllers, some manufacturers began to use Bluetooth, an RF technology specifically designed for communication between electronic devices and the Internet. Bluetooth did not interfere with other devices because it transmitted at slightly different frequencies, from 300 MHz to 3 GHz. Bluetooth also let users play with up to seven controllers at once and had a longer battery life. Gamers could move a maximum of 32 feet (9.75 meters) away from the console. The PlayStation 3, released in 2006, was one of the first consoles to include a Bluetooth controller. The Xbox One, released in 2013, took advantage of a new WiFi technology, WiFi Direct, which offered a more stable 2.4 GHz connection to the console. It also allowed for more information to be shared between the controller and the console than could be exchanged over a Bluetooth connection.

Motion-sensitive technology for wireless controllers have also greatly changed how games are played. Motion-sensitive controllers, such as those included in the Nintendo Wii, released in 2006, determine the speed and movement of players' controllers through sensors known as accelerometers. When combined with IR technology, motion-sensing controllers for the Wii and the Xbox Kinect, released in 2010, reflect the user's movement on the screen. For example, if a person playing a boxing game punches her opponent with her right hand, the on-screen character's right hand moves the same way. This motion-sensitive technology, combined with the power of Bluetooth or high-speed WiFi, has led to more sophisticated interactive games.

Raw materials

The standard components of a wireless game controller are the internal circuit board, buttons, thumb pads or joysticks, and an external case. The circuit board, also known as a printed circuit board, or PCB, is made of many copper connections set in a material such as glass epoxy laminate, a substance made from woven glass fabric and epoxy resin (a sticky plastic that hardens into a solid). The copper wiring on the PCB forms a number of loops, or circuits, that send electrical signals to an antenna. The antenna communicates the signal to the game console. The controller's buttons are made from plastic and are lined with copper on the bottom. When the button is pushed, this copper comes into contact with the copper connections of the PCB, completing an electrical circuit and sending an electrical signal to the antenna.

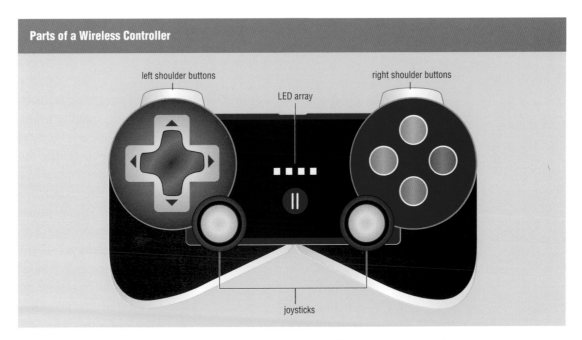

Parts of a Wireless Controller

left shoulder buttons

right shoulder buttons

LED array

joysticks

Video game controllers have evolved to include multiple buttons that allow players to use complex combination moves. ILLUSTRATION BY LUMINA DATAMATICS LTD. © 2015 CENGAGE LEARNING

The joysticks are made of plastic posts that are covered with silicone, a synthetic rubber, for increased comfort and grip. The posts are connected to two adjustable resistors, which react to the forward, backward, and side-to-side movements of the joystick and send electrical signals to the PCB that reflect these movements. The controller's external case is made of molded plastics such as polypropylene that are shaped to rest comfortably in the user's hands and provide easy access to the buttons and joysticks.

Design

Wireless video game controllers are designed to be easy to use and to allow for interactive gaming. Some controllers are designed mainly with comfort and handling in mind. Others focus on game features. In addition to the plastic base, wireless controllers have some combination of buttons, triggers, joysticks, and lights. Buttons and triggers can be in the front, back, or sides of the controller. Some controllers are designed to look and react like steering wheels, guitars, wands, paddles, bats, or guns. Others are pads that are placed on the floor, allowing the player's feet to control the game. Some controllers are motion-sensitive gloves that fit over the player's hand or are a hat or glasses that are worn.

Safety

In 2008, Greenpeace, an organization that works to protect the environment, released a report noting that many of the materials used in manufacturing game consoles and controllers are toxic. The bottom layer of PCBs, for example, typically contain bromine, a compound that can cause skin sores and liver or kidney damage. The plastic exterior may also contain phthalates, chemicals used to soften plastics that have been shown to slow down sexual development. Many console manufacturers have limited their use of such chemicals by using bromine-free PCBs or plastics with reduced levels of phthalates. Although these substances are not dangerous if the equipment is used properly, Greenpeace pointed out that they may pose a danger to the environment if the controllers are thrown away improperly.

People who frequently use wireless video game controllers are at risk of developing a repetitive stress injury (RSI). An RSI happens when a person repeats a certain motion many times. Symptoms of these injuries can include pain, swelling, numbness, and weakness of the thumbs, wrists, hands, or other parts of the body. People who experience RSI can experience tendon, nerve, and other soft tissue damage. A type of RSI of the thumb is so common among video game players that it is sometimes called "gamer's thumb," "Nintendonitis," or "Nintendo thumb." Gamer's thumb is a painful swelling of the thumb. Other fingers and the wrist can also be affected.

Wireless controllers that use RF technology release electromagnetic fields. Some scientists and medical professionals believe that exposure to electromagnetic fields for long periods of time may be damaging to children's health. However, the American Academy of Pediatrics has stated that no such link has been found. Various consumer groups promote the idea that video game controllers and other RF devices such as cell phones may cause cancerous tumors, but the American Cancer Society has stated that research on health effects from cell phones is inconclusive, meaning that no link has been proven.

Manufacturing process

The manufacturing process begins with construction of the PCB. Then the buttons, joysticks, and exterior casing are made. Finally, all of the components are assembled.

1 Engineers design the circuit pattern using specialized computer software. The design is sent to a precise cutting and drilling machine.

2 The machine cuts the glass epoxy material, or substrate, based on the engineer's design and adds the copper lining for the electrical circuits.

3 When the PCB is complete, workers solder (join together using heat) connectors onto the PCB where components such as the adjustable resistors (potentiometers), accelerometers, and buttons will come into contact with the PCB. They also add an antenna that will send signals to the console.

4 The buttons and joystick posts are made by injecting heated liquid acrylic resin into shaped molds. As the resin cools, it hardens into solid plastic in the shape of the mold.

5 The tops of the plastic joysticks are dipped into liquid silicone that hardens when exposed to air, forming a soft, nonslip cushion.

6 The potentiometers, accelerometers, buttons, and joysticks are connected to the PCB.

Think about It!

Video games often get a bad rap for encouraging unhealthy habits in gamers of all ages, but certain games take advantage of wireless controller and motion-sensing technologies to help users get more exercise. The Nintendo Wii, Xbox Kinect, and PlayStation Move offer many sports and workout games, as well as accessories such as wireless footpads and weighted controllers, which study users' movements and calculate the number of steps taken, calories burned, or weight lost. Are fitness-related video games a good way of encouraging people to stay in shape? Or are they yet another distraction that keep users from taking part in healthy activities in the real world?

7 The external case is formed by injecting plastic into two molds, one for the top half of the controller and one for the bottom half. The molds leave holes where the buttons and joysticks will be.

8 The finished case is assembled around the PCB using small screws.

Quality control

Because the PCB must send signals to the console, it is tested at several stages during the manufacturing process. The boards are inspected by workers and by machines during the cutting process to make sure that there are no flaws in the size or shape of the board and that the holes and the circuit pathways are smooth and in the right place. Once the connectors have been attached to the board and the buttons and joysticks have been added, the PCB is tested to make sure it correctly transmits electronic signals. After the controller receives its plastic case, workers inspect it visually and test it again to make sure it performs properly.

Costs, compatibility, and creativity

In the early twenty-first century, wireless video game controllers and video games became increasingly complex and expensive. To keep prices down, developers began to design controllers that could work with a variety of games and consoles. Some controllers were designed to have a main body that could be easily changed to work with different systems, including computers, tablets, and smartphones, by adding different accessories. Some manufacturers also produced accessories that allowed smartphones to be used as wireless controllers through downloadable apps or special cases.

New and creative designs for wireless controllers have helped gamers feel more immersed in the game. The WiiU, for example, includes a video screen in the controller that allows users to video chat during game play or see features of the game not shown on the main screen. Camera accessories such as the PlayStation Camera and the Xbox One Kinect

WORDS TO KNOW

Bluetooth: A technology designed to allow communication between electronic devices and the Internet.

Circuit board: A board on which a number of electrical connections are organized for placement in electronic devices.

Frequency: A unit of measurement for a wavelength. The higher the frequency, the shorter the wavelength.

Infrared (IR): An invisible electromagnetic wave that is shorter than a radio wave and carries less

information. Also known as invisible radiant energy.

Radio frequency (RF): A way of sending large amounts of information using invisible electromagnetic waves.

Wavelength: The distance between the crest, or top, points on an electromagnetic wave.

WiFi: Wireless fidelity; a local area wireless computer network.

camera read players' facial expressions and voice commands, offering users a new, hands-free way of controlling games. Virtual-reality headsets, such as the Oculus Rift, promise an even more immersive gaming experience in which users interact with lifelike 3D environments. With each advancement in wireless controller technology, the boundaries between controller, user, and game continues to blur.

For more information

BOOKS

Murphy, Sheila C. "Controllers." In *The Routledge Companion to Video Game Studies.* Edited by Mark J. P. Wolf and Bernard Perron. New York: Routledge, 2014.

Zackariasson, Peter, and Timothy L. Wilson, eds. *The Video Game Industry: Formation, Present State, and Future.* New York: Routledge, 2012.

PERIODICALS

Mlot, Stephanie. "Game Controller Can Read Players' Emotions." *PC Magazine* (April 8, 2014). Available online at http://www.pcmag.com/article2/0,2817, 2456191,00.asp (accessed August 24, 2015).

"Oculus' Virtual-Reality Headset to Simulate Touch, Gestures." *New York Times* (June 11, 2015). Available online at http://www.nytimes.com/ aponline/2015/06/11/business/ap-us-oculus.html (accessed July 11, 2015).

Stein, Scott. "Game Change: iOS 7 Welcoming Game Controllers Is a Big Deal." *CNET* (June 13, 2013). Available online at http://www.cnet.com/news/game-change-ios-7-welcoming-game-controllers-is-a-big-deal/ (accessed July 11, 2015).

Engineering Student Corry McCall Taps into the Brain

In 2013 Corry McCall, a doctoral student at Stanford University in California, began experimenting with a new kind of wireless video game controller that could keep track of changes in the body. The controller could read changes in body temperature, heart rate, or breathing, all of which are connected to different emotions. Measuring these signals can provide information about what is happening in the unconscious (not aware) part of a person's brain, also known as autonomic activity.

McCall conducted a study in which he put tiny metal sensors on the back of an Xbox 360 controller to measure a user's autonomic activity. As the user's measurements were recorded, special software measured what was happening in the game. This allowed scientists to track the relationship between what was going on in the game with how the user was feeling.

The point of McCall's study was to find a way for video games to react to what the sensors are recording. For example, if a user becomes frustrated and stressed, the game could slow down or even pause and ask if the user wants to take a break. If the person is bored, the game might introduce more challenging tasks. The study attracted significant attention from video game developers and controller manufacturers looking to match the gaming experience with the user's state of mind.

WEBSITES

"History of the Game Controller." Video Game Console Library. http://www.videogameconsolelibrary.com/art-controller.htm#page=motion (accessed July 11, 2015).

"Microwaves, Radio Waves, and Other Types of Radiofrequency Radiation." American Cancer Society. http://www.cancer.org/cancer/cancercauses/radiationexposureandcancer/radiofrequency-radiation (accessed August 25, 2015).

"Playing Dirty: Analysis of Hazardous Chemicals and Materials in Games Console Components." Greenpeace. http://www.greenpeace.org/international/Global/international/planet-2/report/2008/5/playing-dirty.pdf (accessed August 20, 2015).

Seppala, Timothy. "A Look at the Evolution of Modern Video Game Controllers." Engadget, August 1, 2015. Available online at http://www.engadget.com/2015/08/01/a-look-at-the-evolution-of-modern-video-game-controllers/ (accessed August 25, 2015).

Research and Activity Ideas

The following research and activity ideas complement classroom work on studies related to the manufacture, history, and use of everyday products. These suggestions enhance learning and provide cross-disciplinary projects for classroom, library, and Internet use.

Activity 1: Factory tour

Relates to all entries.

Schedule a tour of a factory in your area. Before you go, research the company whose factory you will be visiting. Find out how long the company has been in business, what it makes, and, if possible, a little bit about the machinery and processes it uses. Prepare a list of questions to ask your guide if you have an opportunity, and put your questions in a notebook or an electronic device, such as a smartphone or tablet. During the tour take notes about what you see. Ask your questions and record your answers.

After the tour think about what you have seen and heard. Were the factory and manufacturing processes what you imagined before the tour? In what ways? Did it change your understanding of the products manufactured at the factory? Write a brief summary of what you observed and learned during the tour.

Where to learn more

WEBSITES

"Factory Tours." Explore All 50. http://exploreall50.com/tag/factory-tours (accessed August 27, 2015).

Factory Tours USA. http://factorytoursusa.com (accessed August 27, 2015).

Activity 2: Manufacturing debate

Relates to all entries.

This activity can be done in pairs or small groups.

Many of the entries in this book discuss where products are manufactured. The lava lamp company Matmos chooses to manufacture its products in the same English town where they have always been made. Other companies relocate manufacturing to such countries as China, India, and Mexico, where manufacturing costs are lower. There are advantages to both plans for manufacturers.

Imagine you are a manufacturer looking for a location for your factory. Is it better for you to locate your facility in your home country or in another country? Research the issue, taking note of facts that support one manufacturing location over the other. Organize the most convincing evidence (including statistics and quotations from experts) into a set of talking points and a brief speech. Hold a debate about the issue.

Where to learn more

WEBSITES

"Guide." American Parliamentary Debate Association. http://www.apdaweb. org/guide/rules (accessed August 27, 2015).

"Roberts Rules of Order Online." Rules Online. http://www.rulesonline.com/ rror-07.htm (accessed August 27, 2015).

"Rules of Debate." Nanyang Technical University. http://homepage.ntu.edu. tw/~karchung/debate1.htm (accessed August 27, 2015).

Activity 3: Science and sport

Related entries:

- ATV
- billiard ball
- football helmet
- jet ski
- paintball
- skateboard and longboard
- soccer ball
- sports drink
- tennis racket
- high-tech swimsuit

In the early twenty-first century, technology is an important part of sports. Professional and recreational athletes rely on technology for training, advances in equipment that increase performance, and innovations that improve safety during play. Some advances, such as helmet technology that protects football players from traumatic head injuries, are considered major improvements for the sport. Other technologies, however, such as high-tech swimsuits, are controversial because they are believed to give an unfair advantage to competitors.

Choose a sport that you enjoy playing or watching. Research the equipment used to train for and participate in the sport. Choose one technological innovation that you believe has had an important impact on the sport. Write a short paper in which you explain what the innovation is, how it came about, and how it has changed the sport. Finally, evaluate the change. Is it good or bad for the sport? Explain why, supporting your claim with evidence from your research.

Illustrate your paper with information in a chart or graph. Your illustration might show sales over time, for example; world or other records in the sport; or performance with and without the innovation.

Activity 4: Manufacturing careers interview

Relates to all entries.

The manufacturing industry offers many different career opportunities. Some of the manufacturing roles discussed in entries include assembly line worker, microbiologist, compounder, prosthetist, and research chemist. Choose one of these or another manufacturing career. The websites on the next page can help guide your search.

Find out what someone in your chosen professional does. What kind of education is required? What role does he or she play in the manufacturing process? Is he or she involved in a single stage of manufacturing or throughout the entire process? Do people who choose this career all work in the manufacturing of the same or similar products, or do they work on many different kinds of products?

Once you know the answers to these questions, find a partner. Step into the role of the professional you have chosen. Have your partner interview you about your career. Then interview your partner about his or her chosen career.

Where to learn more

WEBSITES

"Advanced Manufacturing Career List." Career ME. http://www.careerme.org/careers_list.php (accessed August 27, 2015).

"Manufacturing." O*NET OnLine. http://www.onetonline.org/find/career?c=13 (accessed August 27, 2015).

"Production and Manufacturing Careers, Jobs and Employment Information." Career Overview. http://www.careeroverview.com/production-careers.html (accessed August 27, 2015).

Activity 5: Understanding density

Related entries:

- billiard ball
- lava lamp
- memory foam
- roller coaster

Density is the mass of a substance in a given space. The greater the substance's density, the tighter its molecules are packed in the space. Density is calculated by dividing mass by volume. Understanding density will help you understand why some objects that look the same have different masses and why some objects that look very different have identical masses. You will understand this concept better if you experiment with it. The activities found on the websites below will get you started.

Where to learn more

WEBSITES

"Density, the Dynamic Duo: Mass & Volume." The Education Fund. http://www.educationfund.org/uploads/docs/Publications/Curriculum_Ideas_Packets/Density_Dynamic_Duo_of_Mass-and-Volume.pdf (accessed August 27, 2015).

"How Do You Calculate the Density of a Bowling Ball?" American Chemistry Council. http://plastics.americanchemistry.com/Education-Resources/Hands-on-Plastics-2/Activities/Day-5EXPLAIN-5-How-Do-You-Calculate-the-Density-of-a-Bowling-Ball-optional.html (accessed August 27, 2015).

"Liquid Density Experiments." Home Science Tools. http://www.hometrainingtools.com/a/liquid-density-project (accessed August 27, 2015).

"What Is Density?" Middle School Chemistry. http://www.middleschoolchemistry.com/lessonplans/chapter3/lesson1 (accessed August 27, 2015).

Activity 6: Polymer activities and experiments

Related entries:

- artificial limb
- artificial turf
- credit or debit card
- duct tape
- glitter
- high-tech swimsuit
- LED lightbulb
- memory foam
- mood ring
- skateboard and longboard
- sticky note

Polymers are substances whose molecular structure is made up of a large number of similar units bonded together. Many modern products are made with polymers. Polymers are useful because they are strong, usually lightweight, resistant to chemicals, and useful as insulators. They can be molded and shaped in many ways, and they can mimic more expensive natural materials such as marble, silk, and porcelain.

Polymers form when monomers (small molecules that bond easily with similar molecules) link together. They are classified according to how the monomers are attached to each other. Linear polymers are formed when monomers are joined end-to-end in a single chain. Branched polymers are formed when shorter chains branch off the central chain. Cross-linked polymers are formed when polymer chains bond together.

Different kinds of polymers are used to make different types of products. Linear polymers are used to make carpet fibers and food containers. Branched polymers are used to make products such as plastic milk jugs. Cross-linked polymers are used in manufacturing tires.

Hands-on activities, such as building a 3D polymer model, can help you understand the characteristics and structure of different kinds of polymers.

Where to learn more

WEBSITES

"Playing with Polymers." Michigan Reach Out! http://www.reachoutmichigan.org/funexperiments/agesubject/lessons/polymer.html (accessed August 27, 2015).

"Polymer Modeling Activity." MicroWorlds. http://www2.lbl.gov/MicroWorlds/Kevlar/KevClue1Act1.html (accessed August 27, 2015).

"What Is a Polymer?" Polymer Ambassadors. http://www.polymerambassadors.org/Whatispolymer.pdf (accessed August 27, 2015).

Activity 7: Display of a young inventor and entrepreneur

Relates to all entries.

Some of the entries in these volumes include information about young people who have invented products or started successful businesses. Using the Internet, the library, or community resources, find a young inventor or entrepreneur who inspires you. You might choose someone with whom you share an interest, someone from the area in which you live, or someone whose success you admire. Use reliable resources such as newspaper articles or reference resources in your school library to learn everything you can about the young person you have chosen. If possible, contact your subject for an e-mail or phone interview.

Create a poster or trifold table display to share what you have learned with your classmates. You might include a photo or drawing of the inventor or entrepreneur, information about his or her invention or business, a statement in his or her own words, or anything else that might help your audience understand more about the inventor or entrepreneur.

Activity 8: Understanding patents

Relates to all entries.

A patent is an official document that gives an individual or a company exclusive rights over the use of an invention. Patents include a detailed description of the invention, along with diagrams. Because of the complexity of many inventions, patents can be a challenge to read.

Choose one product that you would like to study. Use a resource such as Google Patents to search for a patent for an invention you already know about, or browse patents to find one that interests you. Study the patent, including the invention description and any diagrams that have been included. Look up any difficult words. Pay attention to how the parts work together. Test your understanding by explaining the invention to a partner or to your class.

Where to learn more

WEBSITES

Google Patents. https://patents.google.com (accessed August 27, 2015).

"Search for Patents." United States Patent and Trademark Office. http://www.uspto.gov/patents-application-process/search-patents (accessed August 27, 2015).

Activity 9: Home or classroom manufacturing survey

Relates to all entries.

The products we use every day are made in factories throughout the world. Look around your home or classroom for objects that have labels telling where they were made. Record each product and its country of origin. See how many different countries you can find.

Once you have finished collecting data, create a bar graph to display your results. Create a row for each country on your list. Divide the row into squares of equal size. Shade one square for each product manufactured in that country. Analyze the results. Which country made the most products? Were some kinds of products more likely to be manufactured in a particular country? Were there any countries missing from the list that you expected to see on it? Were there any countries on the list that surprised you? Discuss what you learned.

Activity 10: Assembly line activity

Relates to all entries.

Many products are manufactured on assembly lines. Assembly lines were first introduced by Henry Ford in 1913. Ford believed that he could decrease the amount of time needed to build a car if each worker became an expert in carrying out a single step of the process and if the product moved between workers on a conveyor belt so that workers could stay in one place. He was right. With the introduction of the assembly line, Ford was able to make cars that once took more than twelve hours to assemble in only two and a half hours.

The assembly line remains an important part of manufacturing more than a hundred years later.

Where to learn more

BOOKS

Mullenbach, Cheryl. *The Industrial Revolution for Kids: The People and Technology That Changed the World.* Chicago: Chicago Review Press, 2014.

WEBSITES

"Experiencing the Assembly Line." TCI. http://info.teachtci.com/forum/EE_1step.aspx (accessed August 27, 2015).

Roberts, Larry. "Assembly Line Activities Introduce Mass Production." techdirections. http://www.techdirections.com/assembly_line.pdf (accessed August 27, 2015).

Index

Italic type indicates volume; **boldface** type indicates main entries featured in UXL *How Everyday Products Are Made*; (ill.) indicates photographs and illustrations.

F

H 10/16